IMAGES
of America

BAY POINT

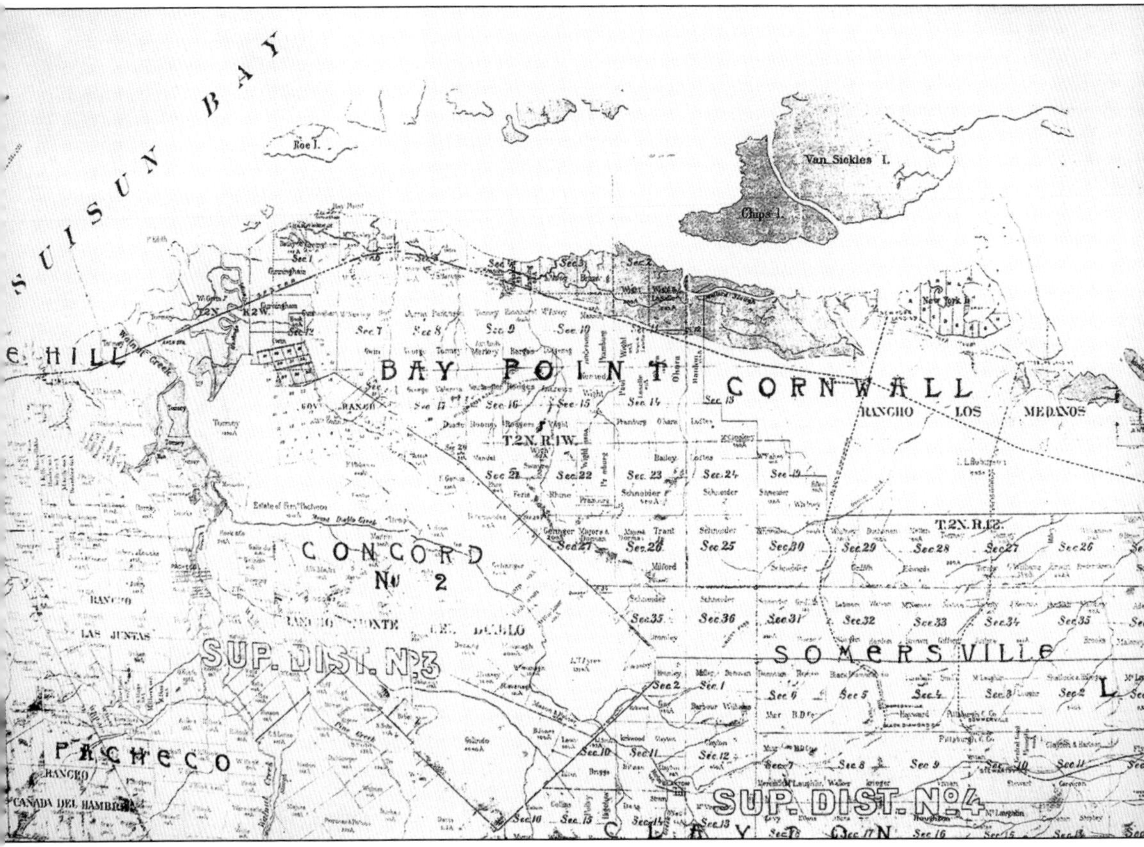

Suisun Bay. Bay Point takes its place among the communities of Northern Contra Costa County. Created as a school district in 1857, the community is shown situated between the old ranchos Monte del Diablo and Los Medanos.

IMAGES
of America

BAY POINT

Dean L. McLeod

ARCADIA
PUBLISHING

ISBN 978-0-7385-2907-3

Published by Arcadia Publishing
Charleston, South Carolina

Printed in the United States of America

Library of Congress Catalog Card Number: 2004105264

For all general information contact Arcadia Publishing at:
Telephone 843-853-2070
Fax 843-853-0044
E-mail sales@arcadiapublishing.com
For customer service and orders:
Toll-Free 1-888-313-2665

Visit us on the Internet at www.arcadiapublishing.com

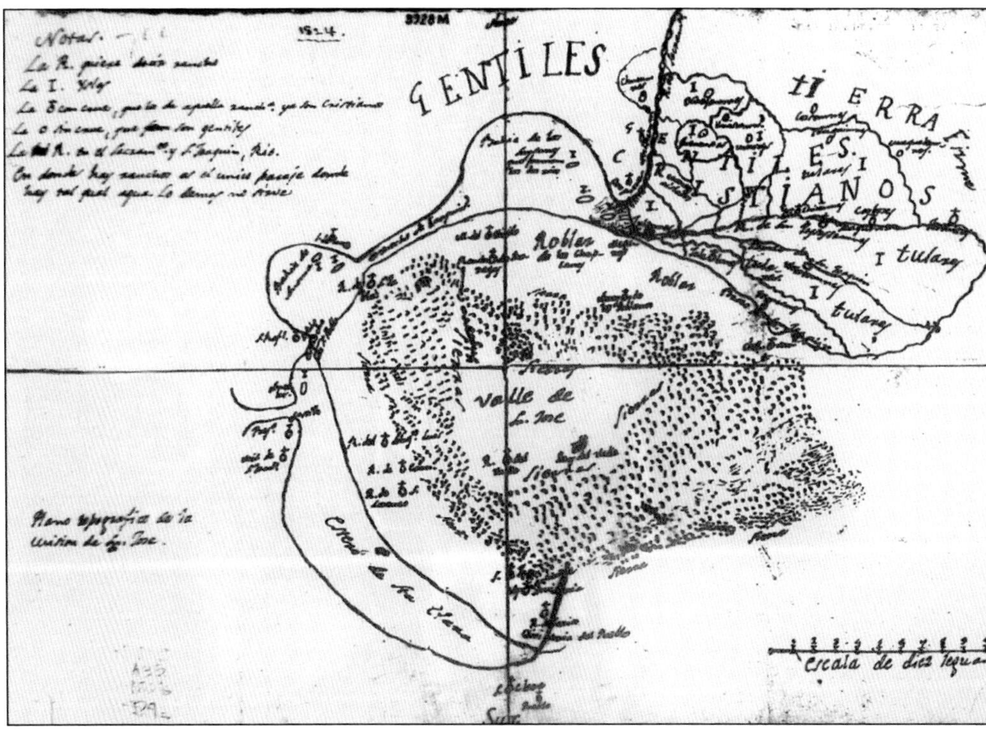

SPANISH BOUNDARIES. Father Narcisso Duran prepared this 1824 map depicting the Bay Area's Mission San Jose domain, including mission outposts and native village sites from the mission on the south to remote Indian villages on the Sacramento River. The peak of Mount Diablo is in the center of the map. Note "Robles de los Chupcanes" between the mountain and the bulging bay of Suisun. Just west are the two cross symbols, representing the Christianized Chupcan villages of Diablo Valley. Also visible are islands fronting on modern Bay Point. (Bancroft Library.)

CONTENTS

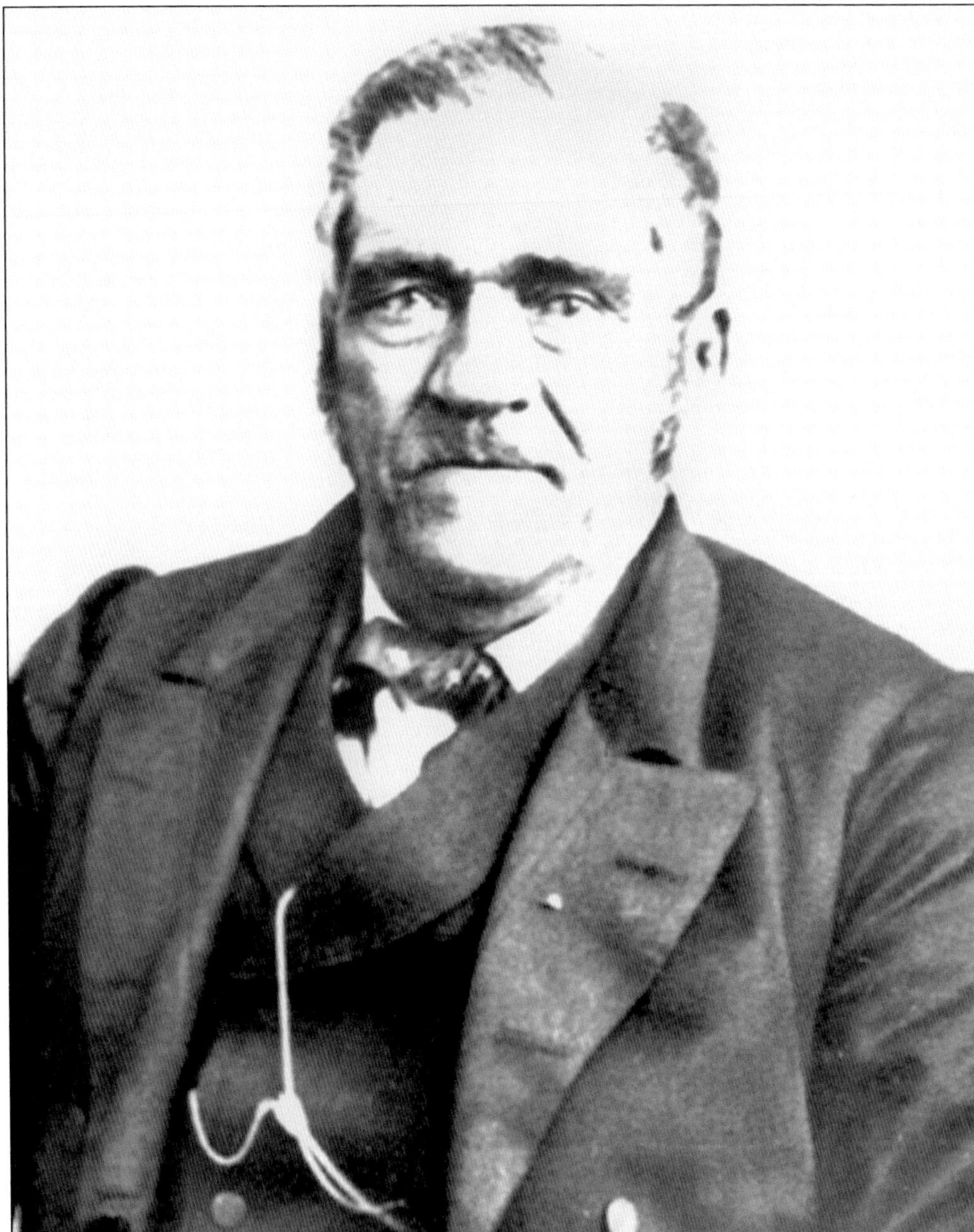

Salvio Pacheco. Grandson of the first Spanish settlers in Northern California, Salvio Pacheco's Rancho Monte del Diablo became the towns of Concord and Pacheco, and formed the 19th-century boundary to the west of the Bay Point School District. His cattle roamed freely through the entire valley. Pachecoville was the commercial center of the county for the first 20 years after statehood. Trade between farmers and ranchers in Bay Point School District and the village of Pacheco was constant.

Introduction

In August of 1993, an unincorporated community in Northern California called West Pittsburg decided to change its name to Bay Point. What's in a name? This book takes a good look at the land, its people, and its "separate communities." With boundaries that fluctuated over time and the various "communities" that came and went, why not consider the whole unincorporated area part of a unified history? Although not known to many, this concept was a reality before any of us were here. And it may provide a key to the future of Bay Point.

Modern Bay Point is a diverse community of 23,000 persons situated between Concord and Pittsburg on the north side of Highway 4. It is composed of older neighborhoods built between the 1930s and 1950s, and a large crop of newer subdivisions built in the 1980s and 1990s. There is some heavy industry. There is a dearth of retail establishments. It has a lengthy and somewhat convoluted history.

Perceptions of Bay Point have changed several times throughout the past 150 years. The election to retake the historic name resulted in some confusion about those boundaries. After the Civil War, ranchers who settled six miles east of Martinez knew the area as the Bay Point School District. It was the only school district between Pacheco and Pittsburg from 1857 until 1910. It had the only railroad station between Avon and Cornwall from the late 1870s until about 1900. It was made up almost entirely of ranches and farms throughout the 19th century.

In 1898, Township 16, or Bay Point Township, was created and included what became the settlements of Port Chicago, Clyde, Ohmer, Nichols, and Shore Acres, east to Willow Pass Road and Port Chicago Highway.

From 1908 to 1931, the unincorporated town of Bay Point, founded by the Charles A. Smith Lumber Company, was built in Section Six, immediately north of what is now Clyde. What became known as West Pittsburg from the 1960s, had, from after the Civil War until 1931, been closely associated with Bay Point. The modern boundaries are only a portion of the old Bay Point School District, created in 1857.

Geographic and institutional instability is fundamental to the long history of this place. With the comings and goings over a long period of time, there has been no attempt to maintain the common memory of the land. This book is intended to communicate in words and pictures what that largely forgotten common heritage is. The narrative begins in the gold rush and is about 19th-century ranchers and farmers. Bracketed by shipping, railroads, and wars, it is about natives and the generation after generation of newcomers who followed.

To the Chupcan Indians who hunted and fished here, the Spanish missionaries didn't belong. In the 1820s these missionaries considered the Mexican Rancheros to be rebels. In the 1850s refugees from the gold rush were the newcomers who were not particularly welcomed by the Mexicans of nearby Ranchos Los Medanos and Monte del Diablo. Fifty years later, the American, Irish, and Portuguese ranchers and farmers felt strongly proprietary when large industries, then subdividers, began to carve up their way of life. Not all the old-timers welcomed settlers moving into the early housing tracts. The process repeated when the last of the hillside ranches were covered with new subdivisions. The cycle continues today.

The Bay Point name is a banner reminding us of victories, tragedies, achievements, and lives associated with the area through the past 150 years. The fundamental reality of our heritage is its geography. The shape and substance of the land has determined how and when it was settled and used. Bay Point has always been identified by the spur of hills that run from Mount Diablo to Suisun Bay. The hills leading to the bay form a boundary, a barrier between what we know as east and central Contra Costa County. The idea that this is the gateway to east Contra Costa County is based in the reality of the Willow Pass through those hills.

The second geographic reality has to do with soil. The clay hills have never been supportive of trees, and the waterfront and adjacent land has always been tule bog. Only a small portion of the in-between land was prime for farming. Bay Point School District was bounded by Rancho Monte del Diablo (Concord) on the west and Rancho Los Medanos (Pittsburg) on the east. It has always been "a place between."

But some of the land made good ranches. From about 1853 until 1908, the area was nothing but ranches and farms. The history of those families who were the pioneers of this area has not been published. This is part of the heritage of Bay Point that needs to be restored to the community.

During the last quarter of the 19th century, the railroads came through Bay Point. Again, geography was the determining factor. The best way for the railroad to get to San Francisco was along the southern shore of Suisun Bay. In 1878, the San Pablo and Tulare Railroad linked Tracy with Martinez, and connected with the Northern Railroad to Oakland. The Bay Point rail station was built that year. The railroad made the town of Bay Point possible. It provided the impetus to the heavy industry on which the town of Bay Point was based. Where before the whole area was made up of ranches, now there was a growing, prospering village in one corner of the township.

As the 20th century dawned, geography again played a central role in local development. The very first business enterprise was Hastings Landing. From the relatively deep-water landing at Hastings Slough grew shipping facilities that, along with the railroad access, made Bay Point a regional distribution center. From 1910 until 1931, the town of Bay Point was the focal point of the township. During that period one of the largest lumber mills on the West Coast prospered there, as well as a substantial shipyard. Several smelters operated in the community during the first quarter of this century. General Chemical Company, one of the largest industries still operating in our community, started in 1910.

The ranchers outside of the town of Bay Point continued producing food, which they sold from San Francisco to Sacramento. The newcomers to the community worked in the blue-collar mills and factories of the town.

The business consolidations brought on by the Great Depression began the slow strangulation of the town of Bay Point. Seeing industry disappear, town leaders conceived a broad plan of development to save the town from dying. In what was essentially a public relations effort, the plan was to change the name from Bay Point to Port Chicago in an appeal to attract more industry. Bay Point ceased to exist in 1931. But the ranchers were still south of town. The Port Chicago that remained still had a few good years left in her, but the power that fueled her wartime recovery was later the cause of her death. That power was the U.S. Navy.

The Navy has a long history in Bay Point. From 1846, U.S. government scouts had appreciated the natural advantages at Bay Point. Some say that cattle to feed the Civil War army at Benicia Barracks were grazed at Government Ranch, which was on the western edge of the Bay Point hills. During World War I, the federal government contracted with Concord businessmen to build ships at Bay Point. Clyde was created with federal dollars to house the shipyard workers. World War II created boom times in Port Chicago. The Port Chicago Disaster of 1944 made this place nationally famous, and the shockwaves are still being felt.

The town of Bay Point is such a strategic place that it has played a key role in national defense since World War II. In fact, it became so important to the Navy that they evicted the inhabitants lock, stock, and barrel in 1968 and obliterated the town. The people scattered throughout Contra Costa County. This is another part of community heritage that all newcomers to Bay Point should know and all old-timers remember.

After World War II, there was a building boom in Contra Costa County and all over the country. Subdivisions gradually ate up many of the ranches and displaced the ranchers of the community. The earliest subdivisions were built in the flatlands. Enos Tract, Shore Acres, and other developments were filled with newcomers from other parts of the county, other states, and even other countries.

The Willow Pass corridor was made up of a few heavy industries, a fair number of churches, but very few retail businesses. The Ambrose Park and Recreation District was formed after the war and was the center of community activities in what became known as West Pittsburg. As they had done before the town of Bay Point existed, people went back to meeting their commercial needs either in Concord or Pittsburg. The effect was to create the perception and, to a certain extent, the reality that West Pittsburg was an appendage of Pittsburg.

During the 80s, a new era of home development began. Several thousands homes were built near, and then in, the hills east of Willow Pass. Most of these people worked in Central Contra Costa, Alameda, or even San Francisco. To these people, the Willow Pass barrier provided a way to have a nice home at less cost than in Central County. Mostly double-income families, they were not much different than the earlier migrants to Bay Point, Port Chicago, or West Pittsburg. More worked in white-collar jobs, but the main difference was that they were new, and they lacked roots in the community.

In typical bedroom community fashion, few became involved in events outside the walls of their houses, let alone in the very small crime area or struggling older parts of West Pittsburg. Some who attempted to participate were occasionally met with apathy or hostility.

The local war with crime was waged in the older flat lands, where the best farms and ranches had been built during the 19th century. All during the history of the area, until the last 40 years, the ranches and farms were peaceful and quiet, and the wild and woolly town of Bay Point/Port Chicago was where the angriest social problems festered.

Today, Bay Point uses the Ambrose Park facility as its community center. There is a growing sense of pride. The controversy surrounding the Bay Point name change increased involvement in community-wide issues. One third of registered voters got involved, which was the largest election turnout in some time. A subsequent groundswell of activity reflects the desire of many residents to change Bay Point for the better.

The outlook for the future is positive and the fundamentals are strong. Geography again will play a crucial role. The only developable real estate in Contra Costa County that combines hills and water views is in Bay Point. As the terminus of the BART system, substantial business and residential growth is projected. A widened Highway 4 facilitates the role of transportation that has been important to the community for 150 years. Perhaps now the community of 23,000 is ready for cityhood?

The heritage of Bay Point is change.

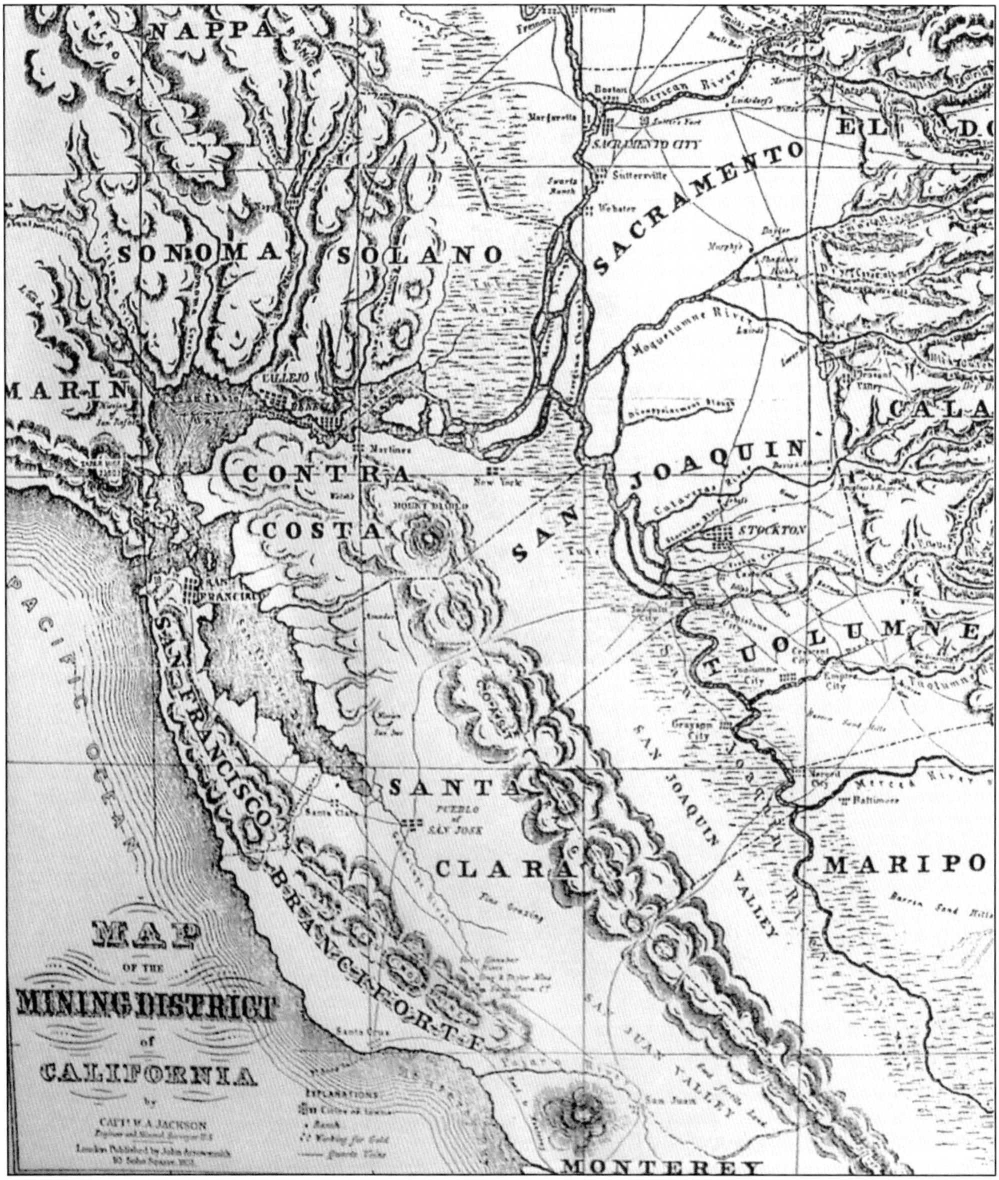

Map of the Mining District of California. This is the Bay Area as it was seen by those driven across seas and continents to try their luck in the California gold rush of 1849. The agricultural wealth of the new Contra Costa County attracted many once the seductive glitter of gold wore off. Productive land, especially suited to raising stock, made the Bay Point area appealing.

One

Bay Point Stirring

Bay Area Breadbasket

Cheap land was the major attraction in 1850. Like the rest of the West, homesteading of government land encouraged settlement. Most of the best farmland in Contra Costa County was part of the already spoken-for Mexican land grants. It was for those with greatest capital and strongest political levers to dismantle and displace the rancheros of Contra Costa County. But all of the land between Concord and Pittsburg was government owned, available to the first person who could settle and make improvements. By 1852, according to the first county history, "every available acre of Township Three was located on by squatters—not a quarter section (160-acre parcel) but had been taken possession of by those dispirited men from the mines."

The published histories of Contra Costa County make scant mention of the earliest squatters of Bay Point. A few of those who stayed on and became successful ranchers and farmers found a place in the history books. Those who attempted had hard realities to face. Part of that difficulty lie in the land. It was first measured and divided under the American system of township and range, and uniformly measured sections in the summer of 1851.

That July and August, Leander Ransom first surveyed and established the Mount Diablo Meridian and Base Lines. His group climbed to the highest peak of Mount Diablo, marking a point there from which all the surrounding township surveys would radiate. He then went due east nearly six miles, then north two and half miles, stair-stepped along the south shore of Suisun Bay through what became Bay Point, and then south through Diablo Valley. His notes describe not only the township and range boundaries, but also what the land was like. This township was defined as Township Two North, Range One West. In other words, it was two townships north of the center of Mount Diablo and one township west of that center point. Ransom then continued on to other parts of Contra Costa County.

The Ransom surveyors described in minute detail the hard soil, level plains, several ravines (including two deep ones), dry creek beds, several streams, watercourses, hollows, and coves. They measured four sloughs within the boundaries of the township.

Later surveyors summarized the terrain of the township. It had over eight miles of waterfront. Four sections were described as "hilly land," three sections were entirely swamp, three were "first rate soil," six were "second rate soil." Others were undefined.

Surveying continued in 1870. Reflecting 20 years of settlement, U.S. Surveyor William J. Lewis wrote that the character of the land was very hilly.

> The hills are not rugged or very abrupt, but are generally bold with curved outlines and are mostly fit for the plough; the soil is generally second rate, but produces a plentiful crop of wild oats, which over a good extent are cut for hay. For about a mile . . . south of the edge of the Salt Marsh the land is rich and under cultivation.
>
> 'Nearly the whole' of the overflowed lands on the north of the township have been reclaimed by the construction of ditches along north-south fence lines and across the river frontage."

The first permanent Anglo-American settlers in Township Two North, Range One West arrived sometime after 1850. Oliver Olmstead and his wife Mary built a home near the present-day junction of Willow Pass Road and Port Chicago Highway. Oliver was an inventor and mill owner, and in 1856 was a member of the board of supervisors of Contra Costa County. By 1853, Randoph H. Wight and his family appear on the county tax list. They farmed at the eastern part of the district, near the border of New York of the Pacific (Pittsburg). A year later, Addison H. Neely paid taxes for the first time on his horses, cattle, and hogs. His farm was in Section Six, where the town of Bay Point/Port Chicago would be built 55 years later.

Four brothers also settled in the area in 1854: Newton, Asa, Simeon, and Philo Woodruff. A fifth brother, David S., came to the area in 1858 to become the first schoolteacher in the area. David Woodruff served later as county superintendent of schools.

Samuel S. Bacon claimed land in the township from 1855–1860, and then later invested here in 1868. He and a partner "built a 50 by 100 foot warehouse" near the wharf at Seal Bluff, the future site of the Bay Point docks.

Other early settlers were Daniel and his wife Fannie Hickey Cunningham. Natives of Ireland, they married in Albany, New York, and first settled in Sonoma County in 1850. While there they bought a large herd of sheep and re-settled them on 640 acres of what was to become the town of Bay Point/Port Chicago. They later bought the homestead and preemption rights from Henry H. Smith. The Cunninghams became one of the most prominent local families in Bay Point in the late 19th century.

The Bay Point School, begun in 1857, received a new teacher in 1867. Sarah E. Huntington came from New England after the Civil War and "attended the Academy in Benicia and taught at Bay Point from 1867 to 1870." She married one of the Bay Point school trustees, Charles N. Wight, the brother of Randolph. Their son, Ralph H. Wight, went to Bay Point School and, after advanced education, became city attorney in Martinez in 1935.

The settlers of the Bay Point School District received a major shock in 1862. Congress passed the Pacific Railroad Act, granting Union Pacific and Central Pacific Railroads alternate, odd number sections of land for 10 miles on each side of the road. The entire township was removed from the public domain. The unconfirmed claim of every settler's ranch or farm became subject to the needs of the transcontinental railroad. Some settlers gave up and moved away.

The population of the area was still quite small by 1870. Resident families were those of James McClosky, John Loftes, Henry O'Hara, Albert Trask, Charles Pramberg, James Kennerly, William Burress, Loomer Curtis, Lucy Bird, Smith Sayles, Daniel Cunningham, James Sullivan, Charles Murray, Henry Smith, John Neely, Putnam Hays, Sarah Meddel, Obed Ayer, and of course, the Wights.

Bay Point was 1 of 33 school districts in Contra Costa County in 1871. Florence Ashley became the new teacher at Bay Point School when Sarah Huntington got married. By 1873, there were 49 property holders in Bay Point School District. Most went to either Concord or Black Diamond (Pittsburg) to get their mail since there was no closer post office.

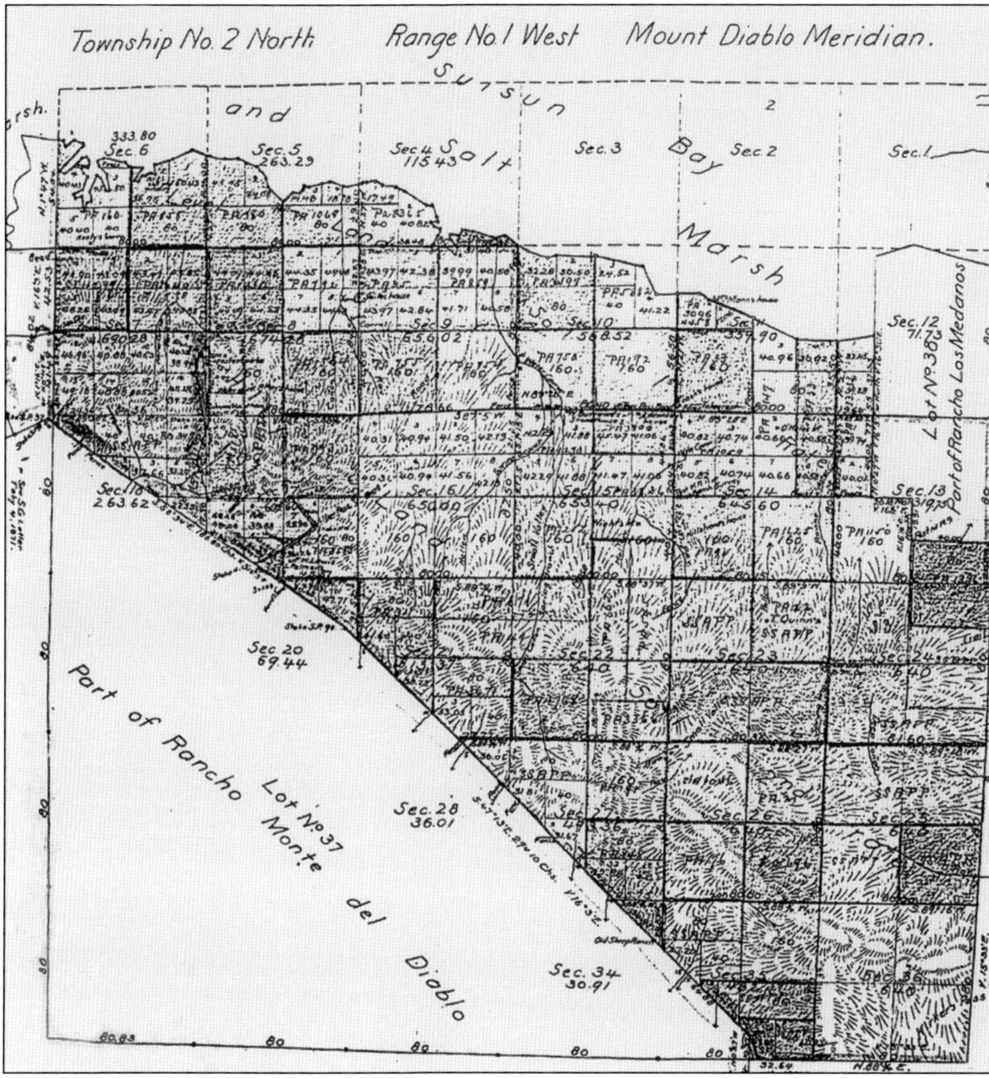

Bay Point School District, 1864–1910. The land was surveyed in 1851, 1860, and later using the national grid system of townships, ranges, and sections. Bay Point was officially Township Two North, Range One West, which describes its geographic relationship to Mount Diablo, and where 14 families settled by 1860. By 1870, a second wave of settlers claimed land and moved in. A third wave settled in by the 1880s and the agricultural population expanded again. There were many schoolchildren in the district.

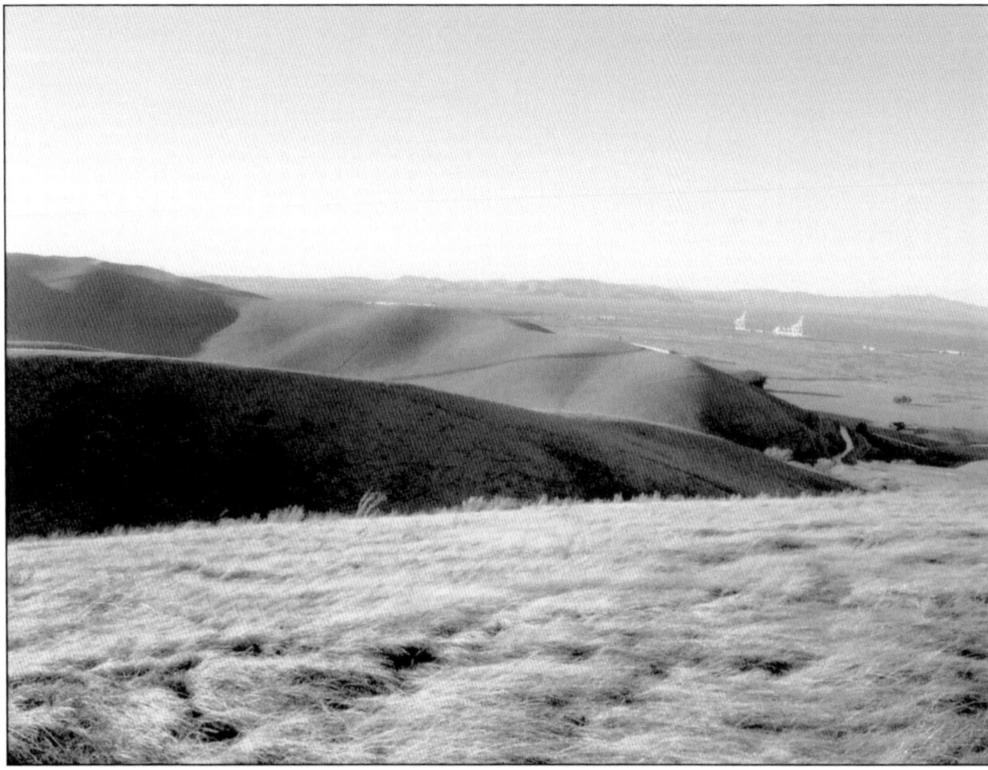

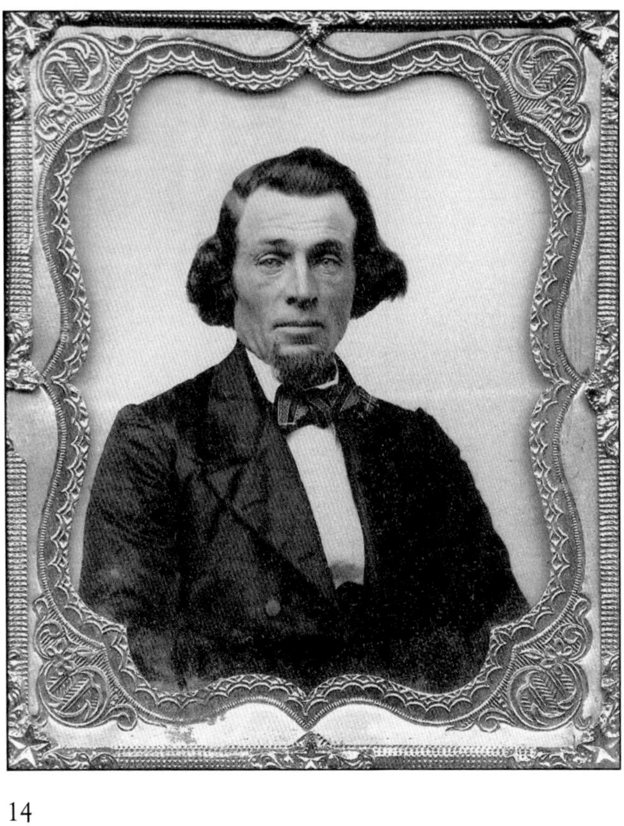

A VIEW OF THE LAND. The Bay Point district was composed of largely treeless hills, agricultural flatlands, and eight miles of swampland bordering Suisun Bay. The land is only partially used today.

OLIVER OLMSTEAD, ANGLO-AMERICAN SETTLER. One of the first Yankee families, Oliver and Mary Olmstead and their children built a home on one of the most strategic spots in the district. They located at the confluence of three streams near the present-day intersections of Willow Pass Road and Port Chicago Highway. Oliver, an inventor and early county supervisor, surveyed the first county road from Pacheco to Antioch. It became State Highway 4.

Samuel S. Bacon. Another New Englander with a commercial bent, Bacon arrived early and claimed Seal Bluff (part of the disputed lands either owned by Pacheco or a couple of majors from the Benicia Army installation, Loring, and Allen). Outranked, he moved over to Pachecoville, where he set up a store in 1860. After disastrous floods, he moved his home and business to Concord. He was a leading merchant there, but continued his interest in Seal Bluff. Eventually, with a partner, he built a dock and warehouse there. The site was ground zero for much of the district's explosive history for 100 years.

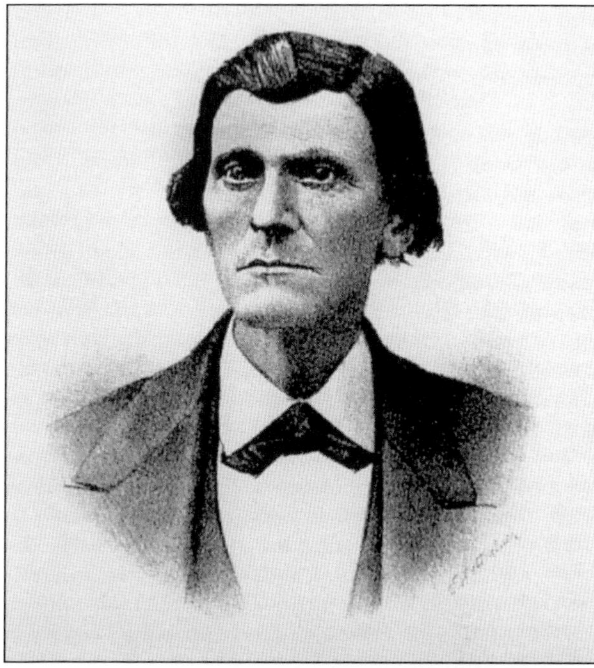

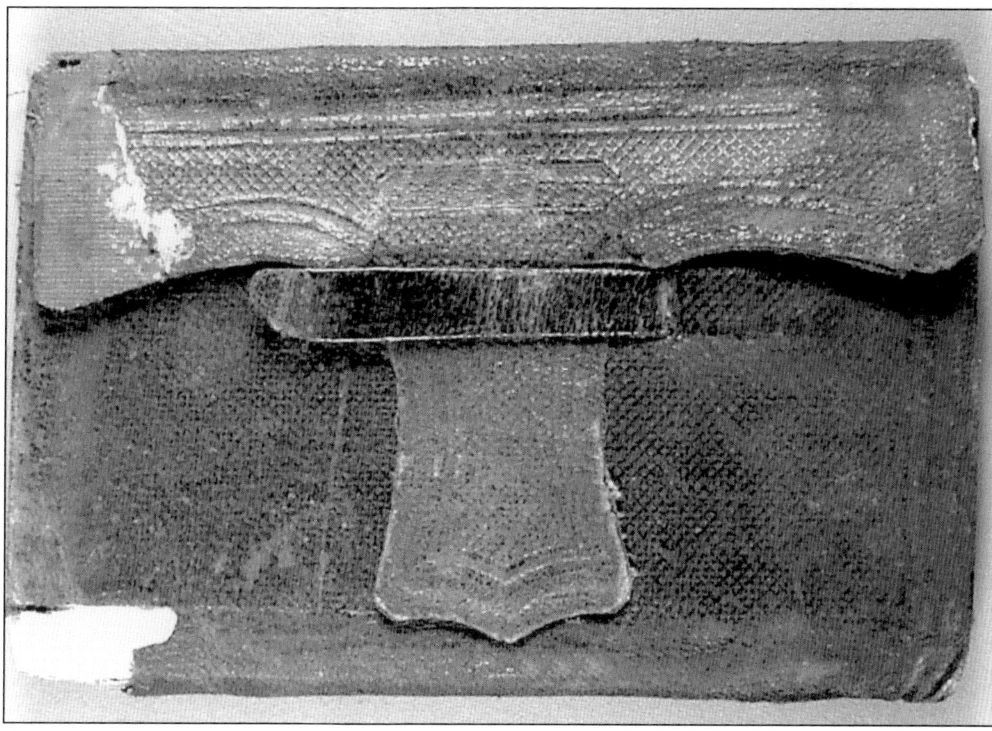

Farm Journal of Randolph Wight. The earliest permanent settlers on the eastern side of the Bay Point School District were New Yorkers Randolph and Orpha Wight and Randolph's brother, Charles. They settled at Kirker Creek where their lands straddled both sides of the entrance to Mallard Slough. Some 29 volumes of his unpublished farm journals describe in tantalizing detail the life of the Wights and their neighbors during nearly half a century.

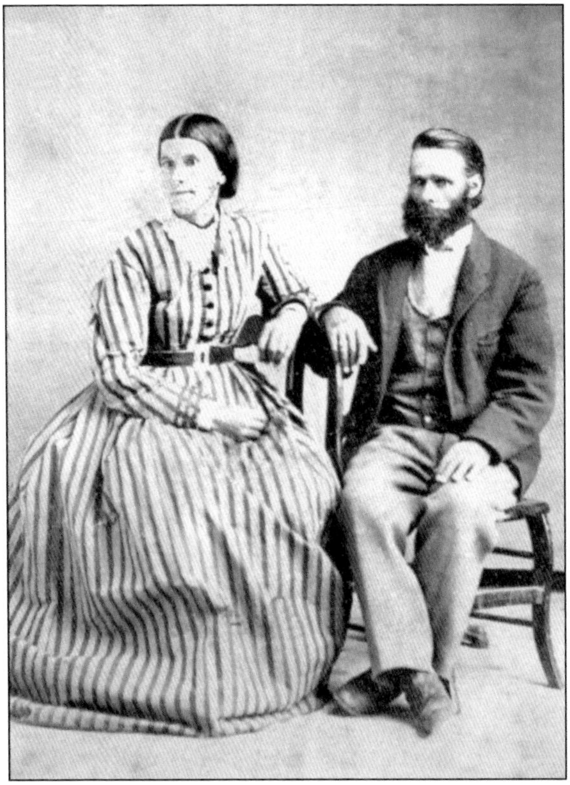

James and Elizabeth Kennerly. British born, the couple was married in 1862, settled for several years in Australia, then established a ranch in the district in 1867. They raised horses, poultry, and hogs. James was also a blacksmith.

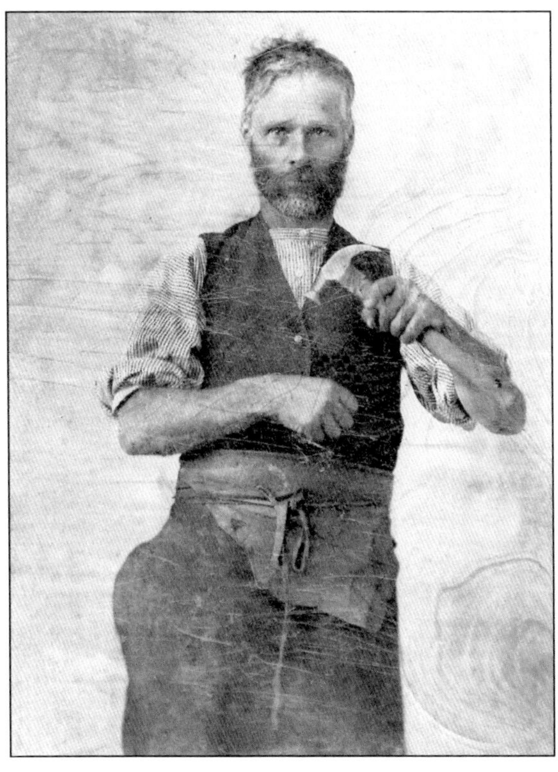

James Kennerly, Blacksmith. Perhaps of Irish birth and British military beginnings, Kennerly worked hard and prospered in Sections 10 and 15, now the "business district" of Bay Point. His closest neighbors were the families of Wilburn Burress, the Wights, Henry O'Hara, and Charles Pramberg.

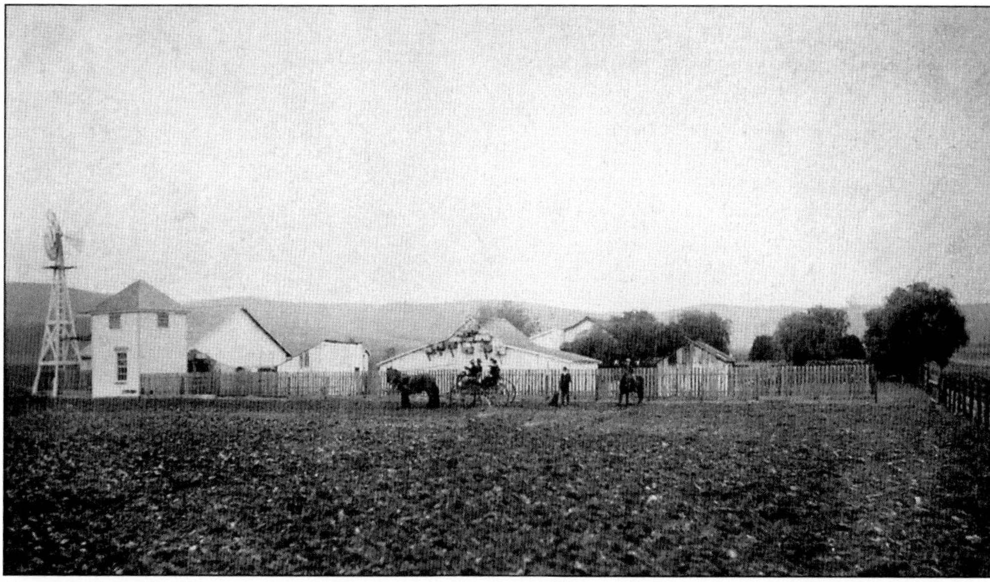

Kennerly Ranch on the "Concord Road." This well-kept and prosperous operation included the house, a large barn, and four outbuildings. Notice the treeless terrain in the background.

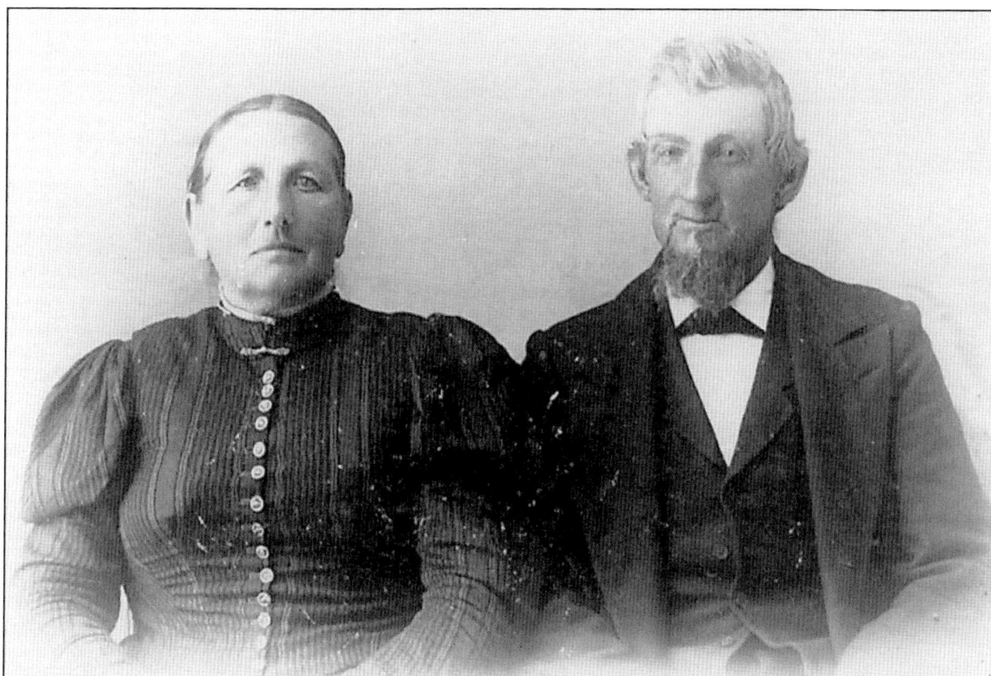

Charles and Ann Murray. Another pioneering Irish family in the Bay Point School District was that of Charles and Ann Hickey Murray. Residents of Section Eight from about 1868, their farm passed to the Tormeys after their deaths early in the 20th century. They had six children, some of whose descendants still live in the county.

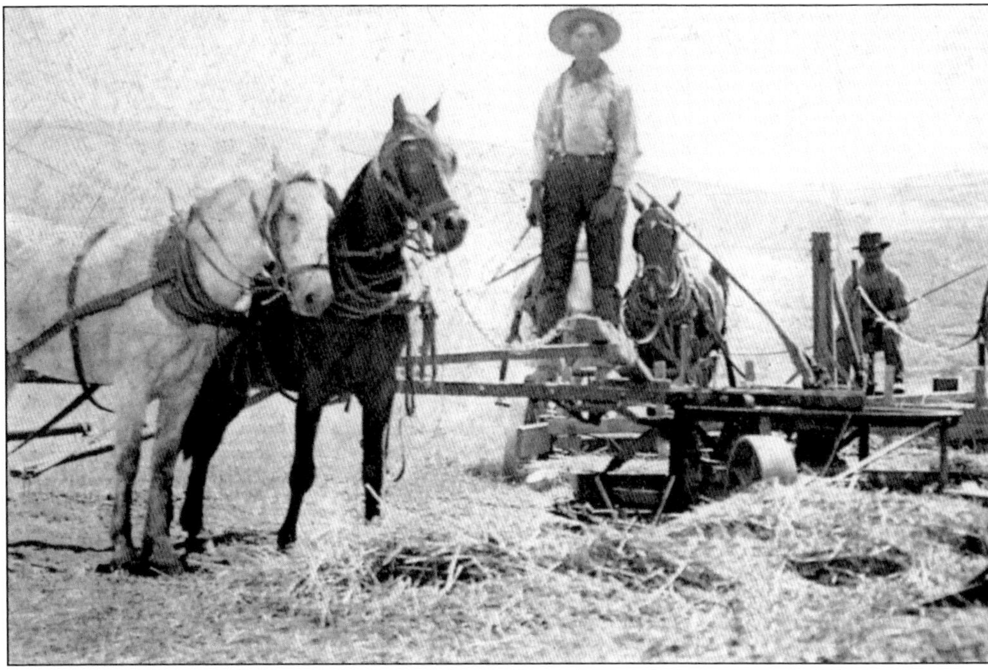

HARVESTING HAY. Charles and Randolph Wight, who settled in Section Three, first grew wheat in the district in 1852. The harvest rig and crew shown here in later years gives a sense of man, horse, and machine power used to bring in the crops.

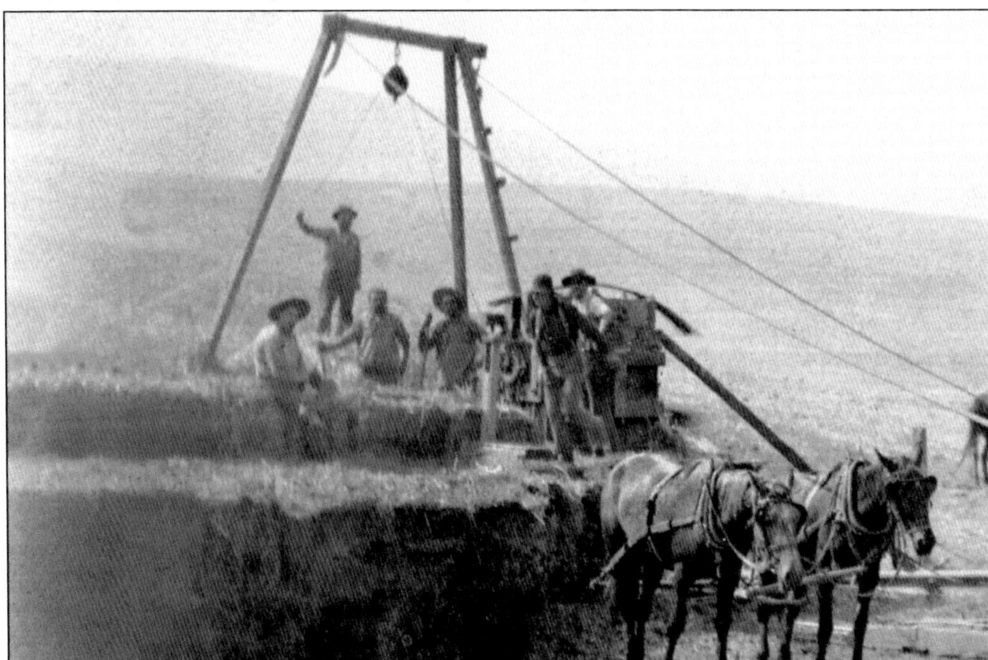

WINCHES, PULLEYS, AND MUSCLE POWER. Harvest time called for communal effort. Stacking hay, this six-man crew takes a rest. The horses look ready for a rest (and a drink under a shade tree), too.

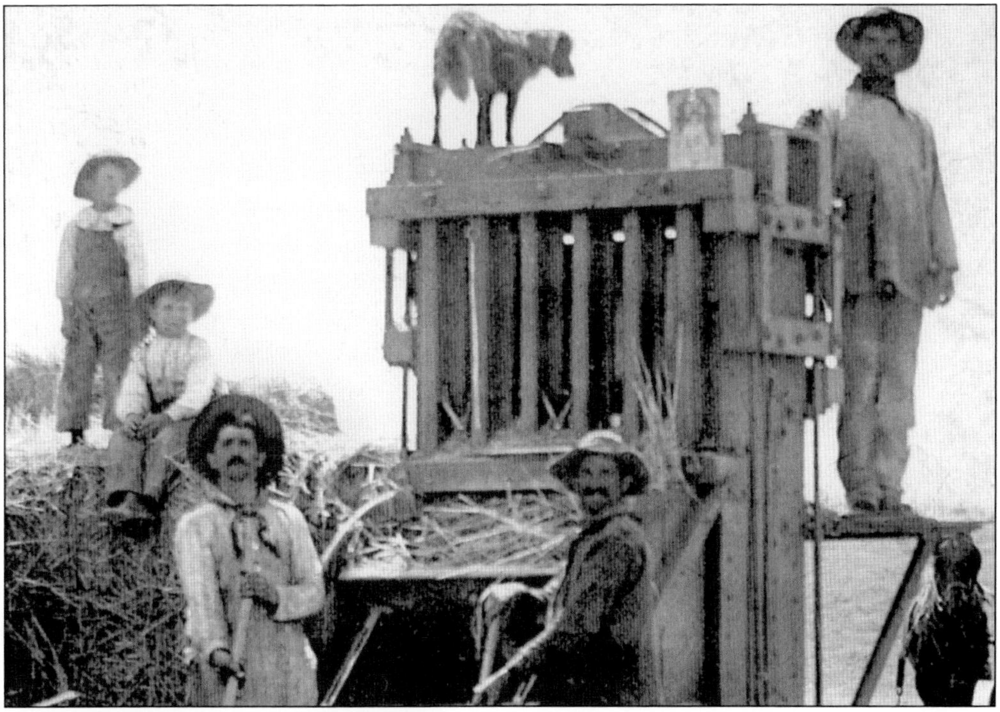

Making Bales. Boys, men, and dogs get in the picture for the traveling photographer. It was probably taken on the ranch of Frank Kennerly, son of James and Elizabeth, on his Bailey Road property.

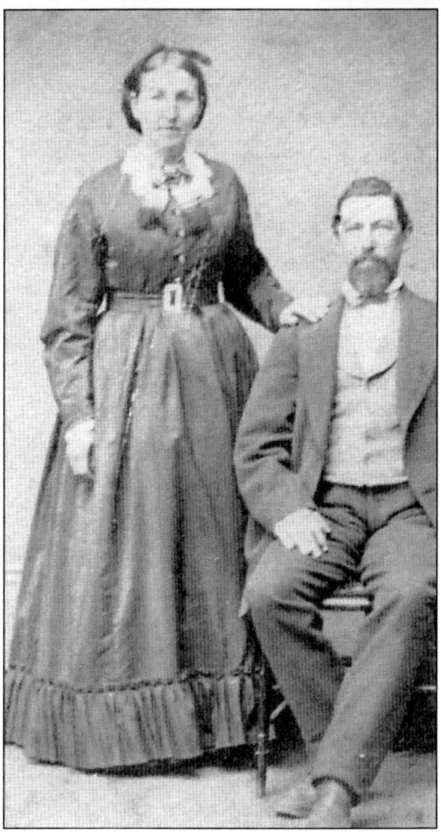

Daniel and Fanny (Hickey) Cunningham. Another of the Irish couples, Daniel's family settled first in Sonoma County, where he apparently acquired a herd of sheep, which he moved onto Section Five prior to 1859. He later raised horses and dairy cattle. The couple had eight children, some of whom remained in Bay Point for 100 years. He sold portions of his 1,200 acres of land to Smith Lumber Company, and it became the City of Bay Point in 1908.

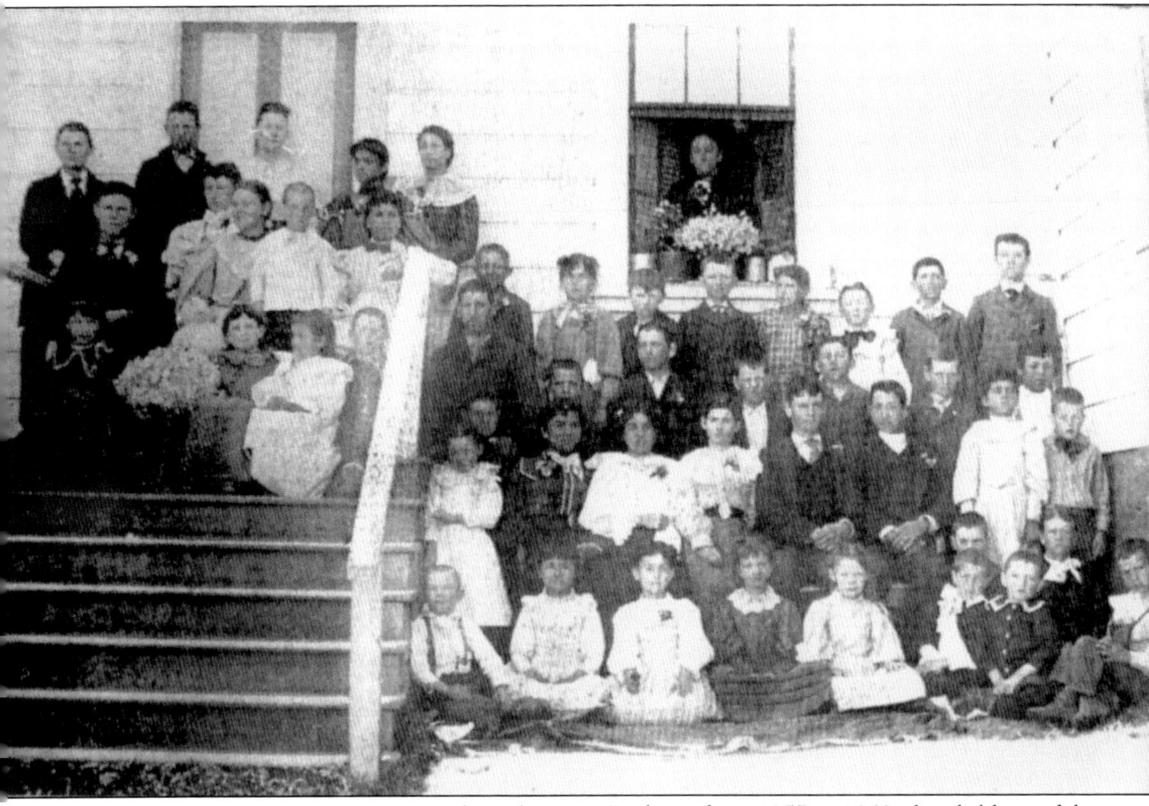

Bay Point School, 1897. Attending classes in Pacheco from 1857 to 1868, the children of the Bay Point District got a school closer to them in the fall of 1868. Built on what is now Pacifica Avenue, just west of Rio Vista Elementary School, ranchers and farmers from the Pittsburg border to the outskirts of Pacheco sent their children there. At the time of this picture, there were 48 students from 17 families attending. Teachers included Etta E. Andrews and Cecelia M. Henry. Children included Weaver Bailey, Willie Wildes, Minnie Roque, Hughline (?) Grennan, Ida Ludgering, Manuel Roque, Willie Markey, Ethel Wildes, Frances Wildes, Johnnie Hanlon, Marie Roque, Andrew Pramberg, Annie Enes, Lennie (?) Martin, Frances (?) Ludricks, Willie Hanlon, Eva Pramberg, Louie Rief (?), Ella Markey, Emma Ludricks, Minnie Wilds, Bert Cunningham, Ralph Wight, Aquila Bailey, Frank Ludricks, Teresa Enes, Marie Simas, Frances Cunningham, Alice Pramberg, Jamie Ludgering, Willie Tormey, Henry Pramberg, Albert Ludgering, Frank Enes, Manuel Enes, Ynes Ludgering, Fritz Ludgering, Ellie Wildes, Della Markey, Angie Enes, Lily Markey, Charlie Roque, George Ludricks, Edmond Tormey, Thomas Bailey, Frank Roque, Mary Silva, Johnnie Shinnott (?), Mae Martin, Agnes Bailey.

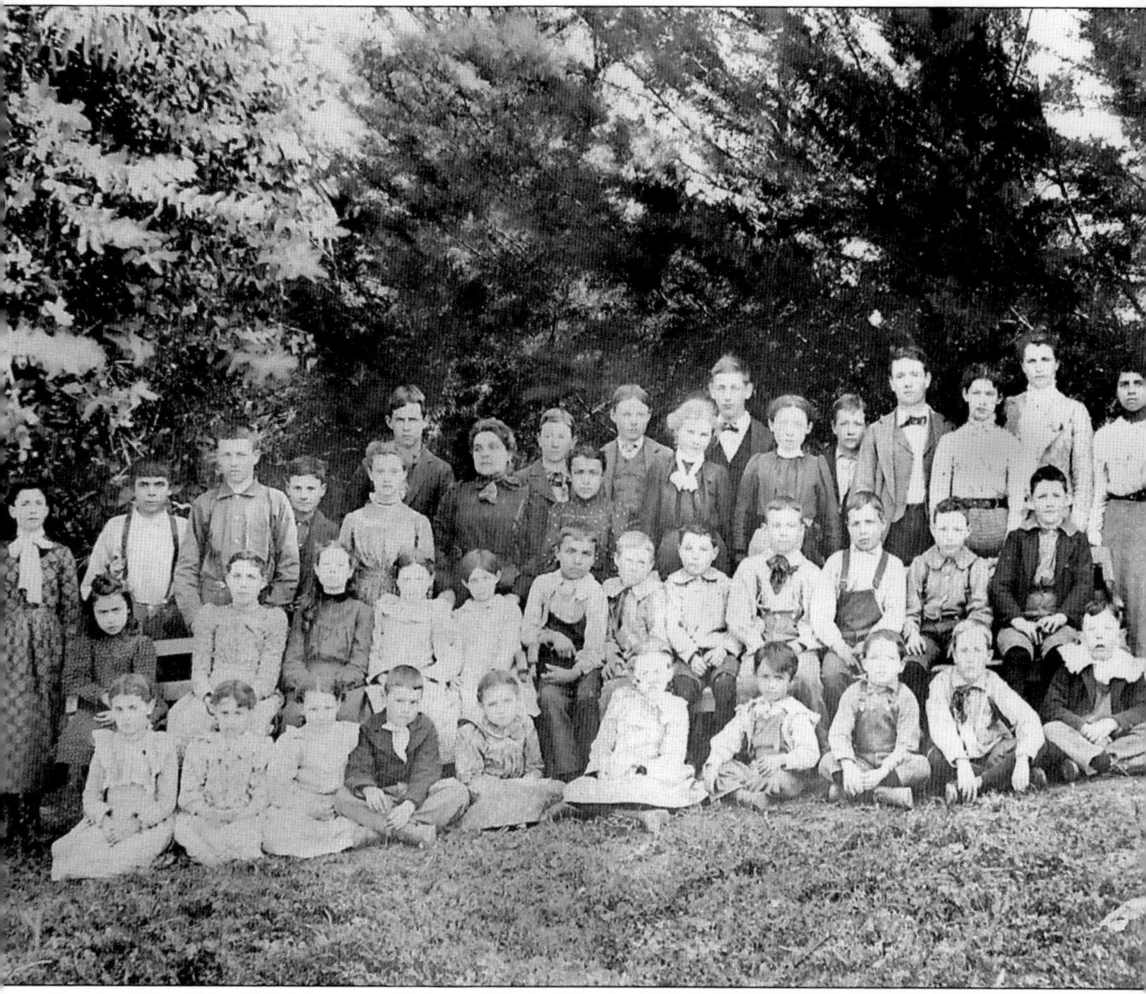

SCHOOL PICTURE, 1900. Principal Mattie Wight (upper right, second figure) and her 38 students pose in the schoolyard near the future site of Rio Vista School. They were visited that day by Dr. L.L. Martin, of Concord (fourth from right, upper row). Other adults were teacher Louise Williams Cunnningham (seventh from left, upper), and Ralph Wight (seventh from right, upper row). Some of the families represented in the photo are Wilds, Enes, Bailey, Pramberg, Grennan, Cunningham, Wight, Martin, Ludricks, Tormey, Sellers, and Markey.

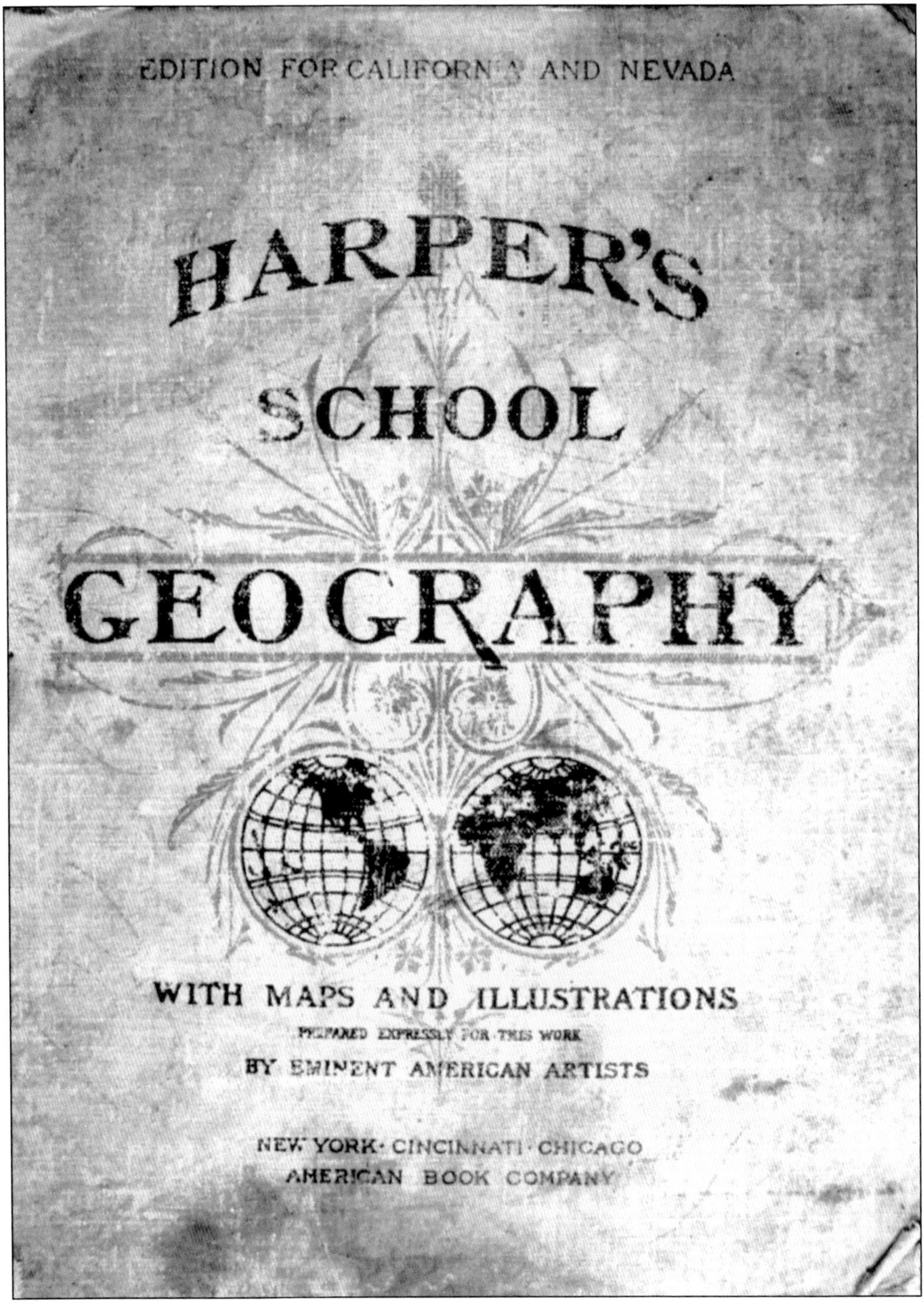

SCHOOL DAYS, 1894. This is the cover of *Harper's School Geography*. The flyleaf reads, "Hattie S. Kennerly, Bay Point, California." This late–19th-century elementary text would prove challenging to high school graduates today. (Courtesy Bay Point Historical Society.)

Two

Linked to the World
Transformed by Industry

In the late 1890s, further railroad lines were laid through the township. The Santa Fe and the Southern Pacific follow the northern coastline of Contra Costa around the point. The Santa Fe and Southern Pacific had stations at Bay Point by the turn of the century. Edson Hazen was a railroad agent in 1898, probably for the Southern Pacific. A native of Vermont, he first registered to vote at Walnut Creek in 1896. J.W. Hays was the first agent for the Santa Fe Railroad at Bay Point, arriving in 1900. There was also a railroad flag stop at McAvoy Landing.

Copper King Mines Ltd. built a smelter at Bay Point in 1898. This was the first major industrial undertaking in Bay Point, and the first to fail. It has an interesting history. Frank L. Gardiner was primarily responsible for putting together the capital that resulted in its construction. His profligate lifestyle was blamed for its demise, but a recession recognized in 1903 may have also contributed.

Gardiner's story is summarized in the June 6, 1903 edition of the *Contra Costa Gazette*. As a "poor assayer in San Francisco" in 1888, Gardiner, who had a wife and several children, became enamored with an actress playing at the Bush Street Theater. Carrie Swain, who was performing in *Cad, the Tom Boy*, "left San Francisco for Australia with Mr. Gardiner." The two were apparently financially successful there and settled in very expensive accommodations in Paris.

Prior to 1898, Gardiner spent $25,000 of Carrie's money to put together a large consortium of British investors, notably headed by famous shipbuilder and member of Parliament, Sir Christopher Furness. Crocker-Woolworth Bank in San Francisco provided local financing for the deal.

According to local historian George Emanuels, ore came from a mine 28 miles east of Fresno. Known as Pacific Coast Smelting Works, they processed gold, silver, and copper ore. Petroleum driven, the generator and smelter at Bay Point processed over 200 tons of ore per day.

Gardiner's friend, W.H. Daily, who started out as a drug store clerk, became manager of the smelter at Bay Point. According to the *Contra Costa Gazette*, Daily lived an extravagant life at the Palace Hotel in San Francisco the entire four years managing the smelter.

Gardiner apparently lived in splendor in Paris during the construction and running of the smelter. He became preoccupied with Mademoiselle Tourette, "a beautiful but poor French girl" that his second wife had befriended and made a member of the household. Carrie Swain Gardiner eventually obtained a divorce and a $500,000 settlement, while he received the pretty French girl and the bankruptcy of Copper King in 1903.

In 1898, the number of Contra Costa County's townships expanded. Among the new divisions was Township No. 16, which included 10 square miles, a constable, and a justice of the peace. Justin M. Goodall, a native of Vermont, was the first justice of the peace. The town constable was George Weidemann, a native of Nicaragua from a European family. The justice court conducted traffic, civil, preliminary felony trials, and marriages. Bay Point was part of Concord Voting Precinct No. One and was in Supervisory District One. The nearest post offices in 1898 were Concord, Martinez, and Cornwall.

A few of the laborers losing their jobs when the smelter closed in 1903 were A. Perriera, E. Blowers, J. Cornelius, R.S. Dulin, W.H. White, Anna Blowers, George Bubish, F. Furtado, E.B. Price, and D. Davis. Although the smelter provided work for many newcomers, the main population of Bay Point continued to work at agriculture and the transportation of agricultural goods.

The prime land of the Copper King Smelter, served by deep-water portage and the transcontinental railroad, would soon become commercially viable again.

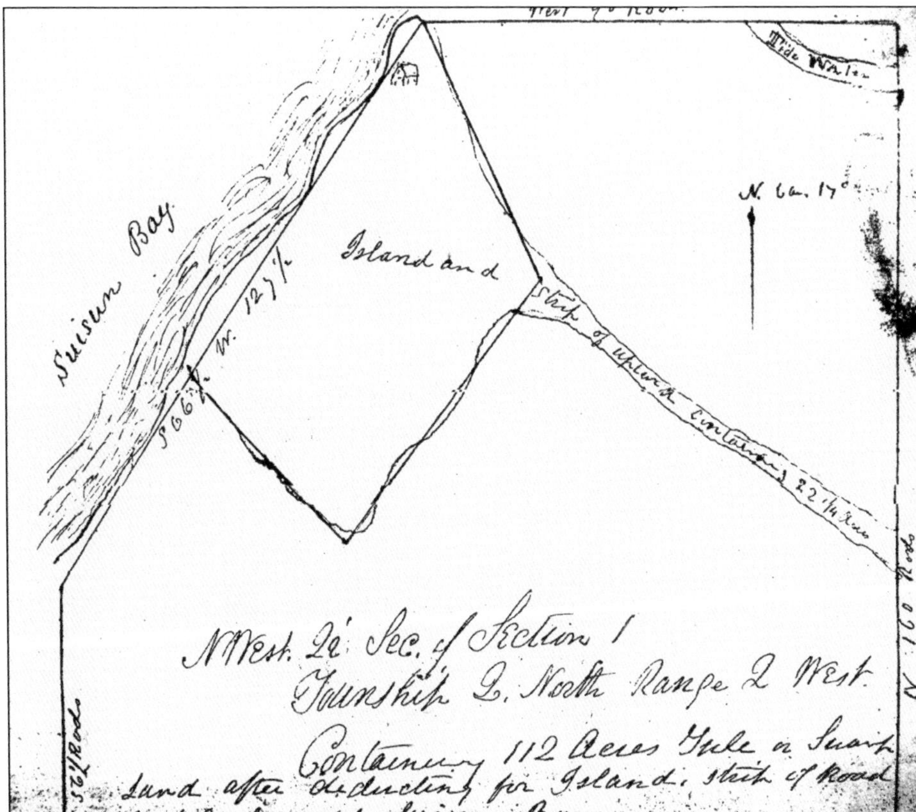

Seal Bluff, Site of Major Action, 1850. This small rise of dry land in the Suisun wetland, near the Seal Islands, was a ship anchorage in 1810, held a grain warehouse in 1876, was the site of Copper King Smelter at the turn of the century, housed the main offices of the Smith Lumber company for over 20 years, and was the site of the Port Chicago Explosion of 1944. Today, the ground is the site of a U.S. Navy toxic dump, which is unsafe for humans, the bay, and wetlands wildlife.

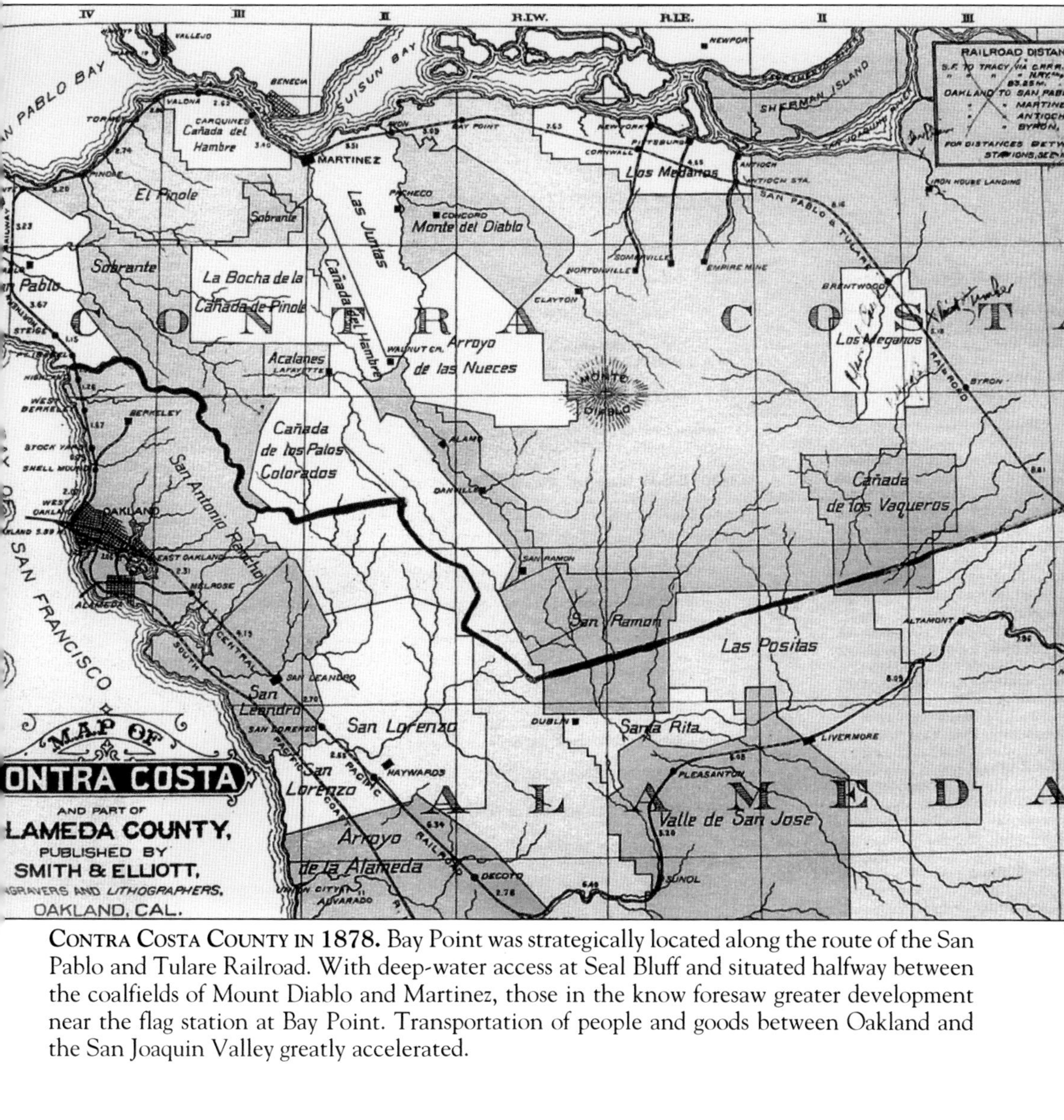

CONTRA COSTA COUNTY IN 1878. Bay Point was strategically located along the route of the San Pablo and Tulare Railroad. With deep-water access at Seal Bluff and situated halfway between the coalfields of Mount Diablo and Martinez, those in the know foresaw greater development near the flag station at Bay Point. Transportation of people and goods between Oakland and the San Joaquin Valley greatly accelerated.

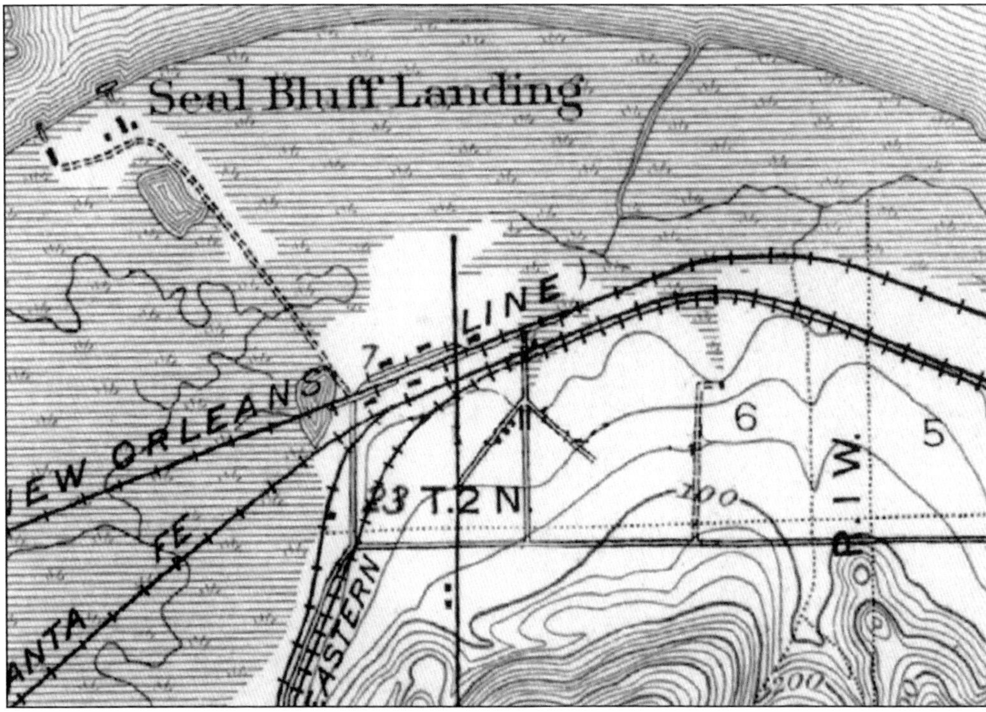

Nascent village of Bay Point. This portion of the USGS map shows essential rail and water transportation in the first part of the 20th century. Two transcontinental railroads and the Oakland, Antioch, and Eastern electric railroads were forced by the thrusting Bay Point hills to skirt Suisun Bay through what became the town. The deep water at the landing became a major West Coast shipping point.

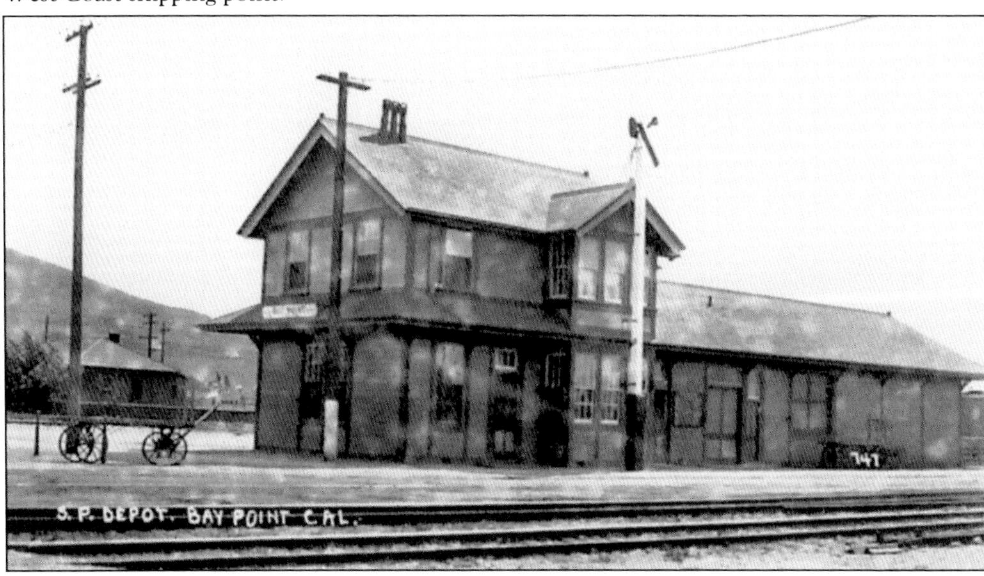

Southern Pacific Train Station. The San Pablo and Tulare Railroad, incorporated in Martinez in 1871, extended from Martinez through Contra Costa County to Tracy by 1878. The Bay Point flag station was established that year. The SP and TRR merged with the Southern Pacific Railroad in 1888.

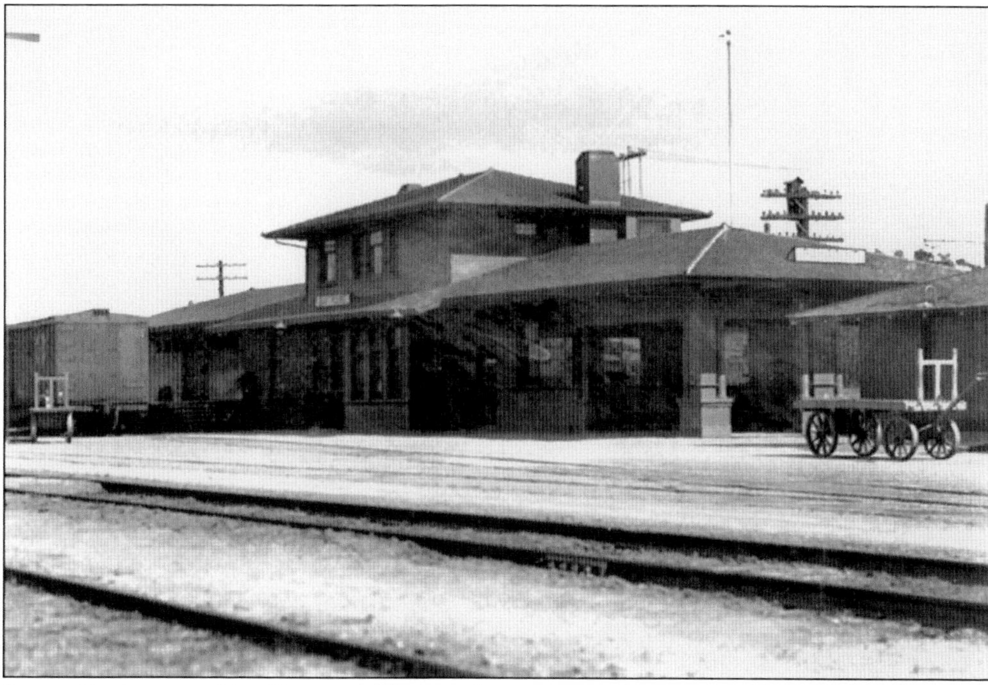

SANTA FE STATION, BAY POINT. Adding to the strategic importance of the town of Bay Point, a second transcontinental line ran along the edge of the village. These transportation facilities paved the way for 20th-century industrial growth.

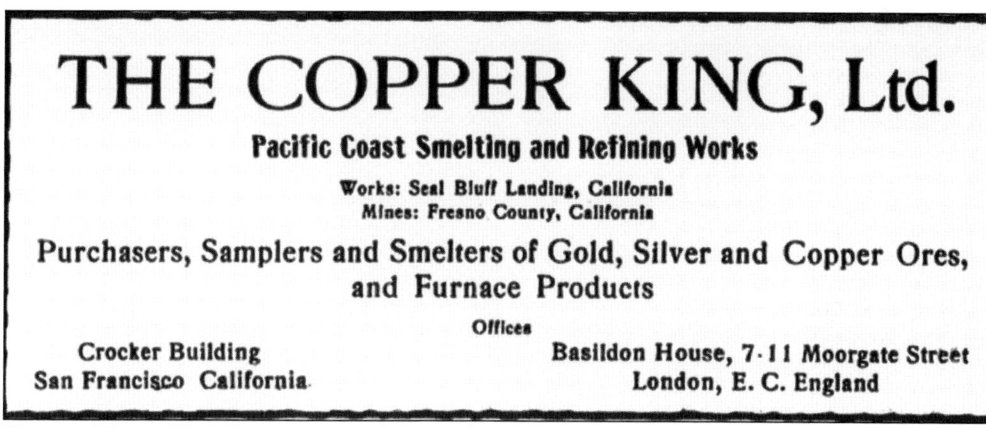

COPPER KING. The European need for industrial materials, constant throughout the 19th century, led multinational conglomerates to establish themselves in California. The Pacific Coast Smelting Works, a division of Copper King, Ltd. in London, acquired a copper mine near Fresno and built a large smelter at Seal Bluff Landing. With mostly English and French capital, their West Coast headquarters were in San Francisco.

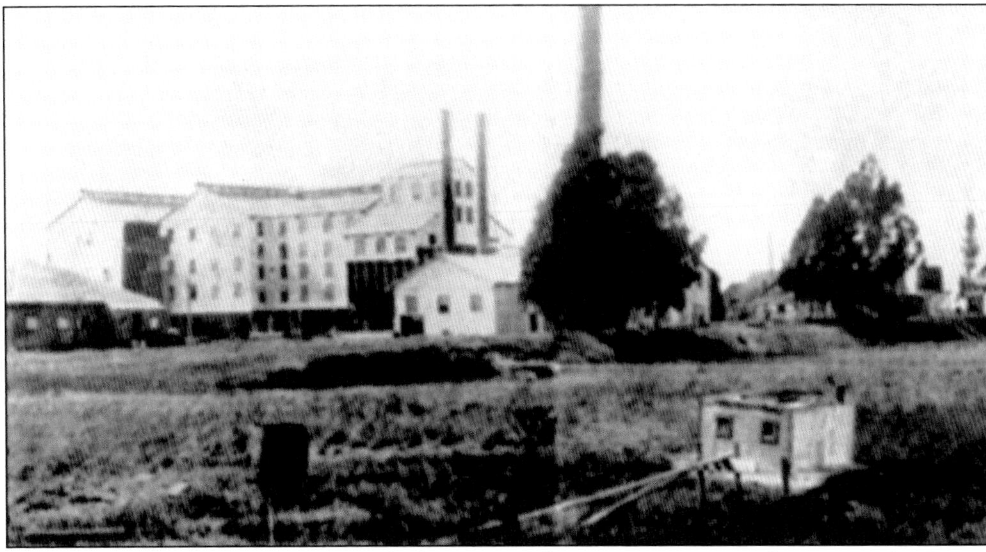

Copper King Smelter, 1901. Described as "one of the most important industries on the Coast," the smelter was the first large industrial site at Bay Point. It was built on Seal Bluff, the same ground previously claimed by William Jones, then later Samuel Bacon. A lumber company eventually took over the site, followed then by the U.S. Navy.

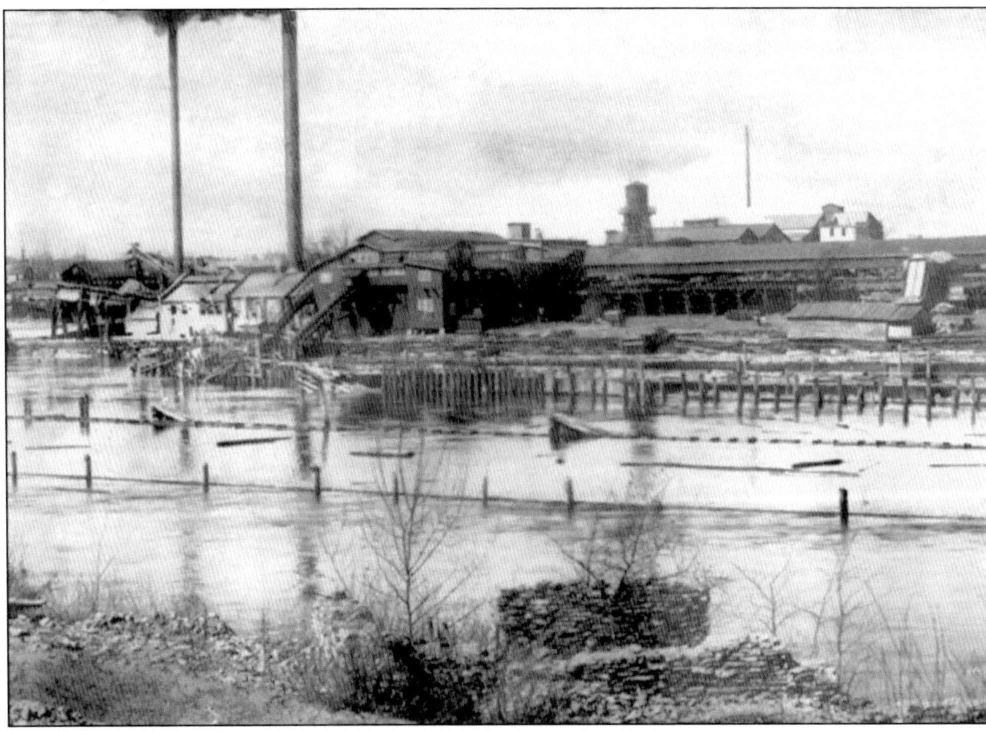

Another View, Copper King, 1901–1902. Built at a cost of $1,375,000, the smelter promised to transform the agrarian Bay Point School District. By 1902, the oil-powered plant was processing 200 tons of ore per day. Personal problems of the managers and a financial panic in 1902–1903, brought about a swift bankruptcy, throwing many local men out of work. Notice the adobe ruins in the foreground.

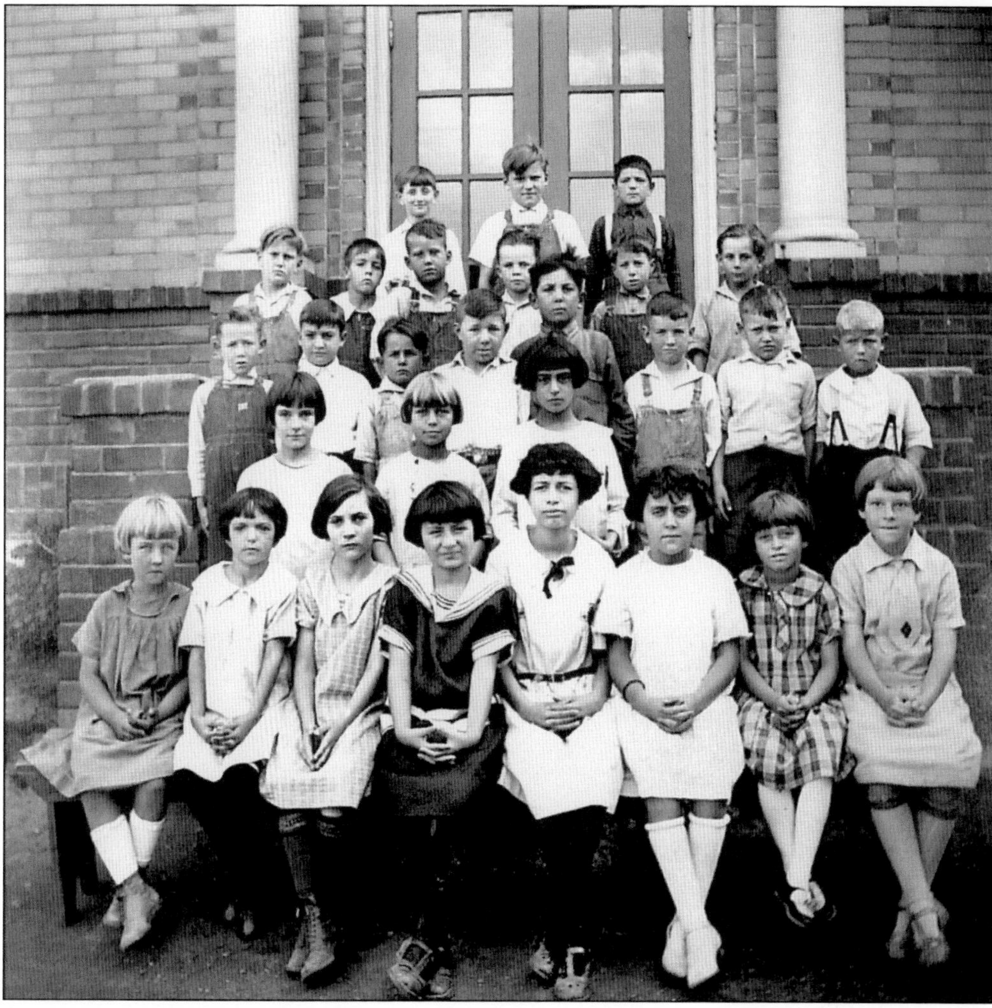

CUNNINGHAM SCHOOL AT BAY POINT, 1911. Before industry and railroads, the school district defined the community. From 1857, the ranchers and farmers between Pacheco and Pittsburg had their own school. Initially, it was located in Pacheco. By 1868, it was located near the site of Rio Vista Elementary. This early photo, taken at the new school in the booming town, shows the girls in their best dresses and the boys in their best overalls.

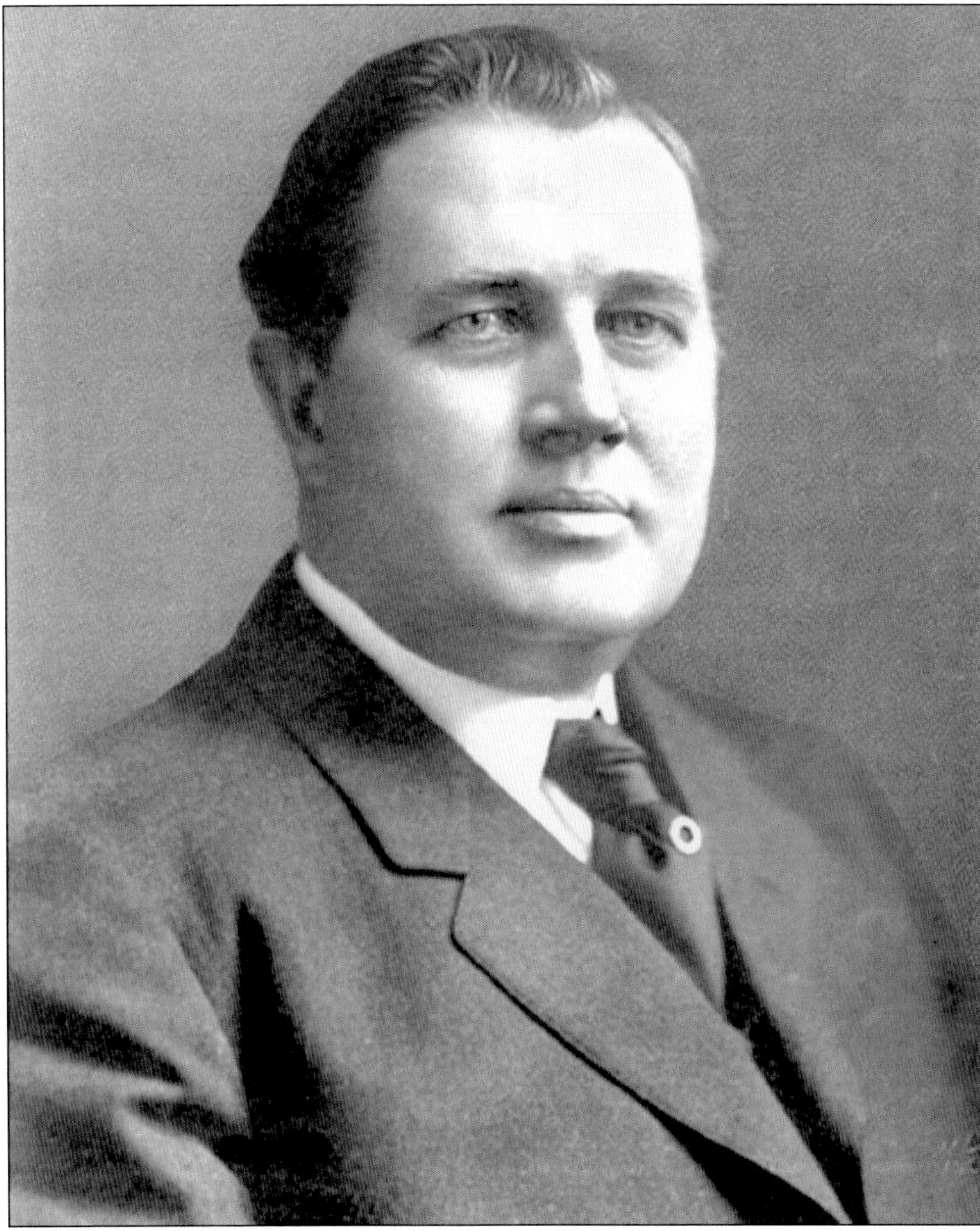

Charles Axel Smith, 1911. The founder and builder of the Smith Lumber Company, C.A. Smith was born in 1852 in Osergotland, Sweden. He was a protege of John S. Pillsbury, a 19th-century industrialist and governor of Minnesota. Pillsbury financed Smith's early timbering business in the 1870s and 1880s, and was a partner when C.A. Smith and Company formed in 1884. By 1893, when the company was incorporated, it built the largest, most expensive, most complete mill ever constructed in Minneapolis. Smith was a member of the Board of Governors of the National Lumber Manufacturer's Association and was director of the Mississippi Valley Lumberman's Association. He served as a delegate to the 1900 presidential convention for the nomination of McKinley and Roosevelt. He built the company town of Bay Point, starting in 1908.

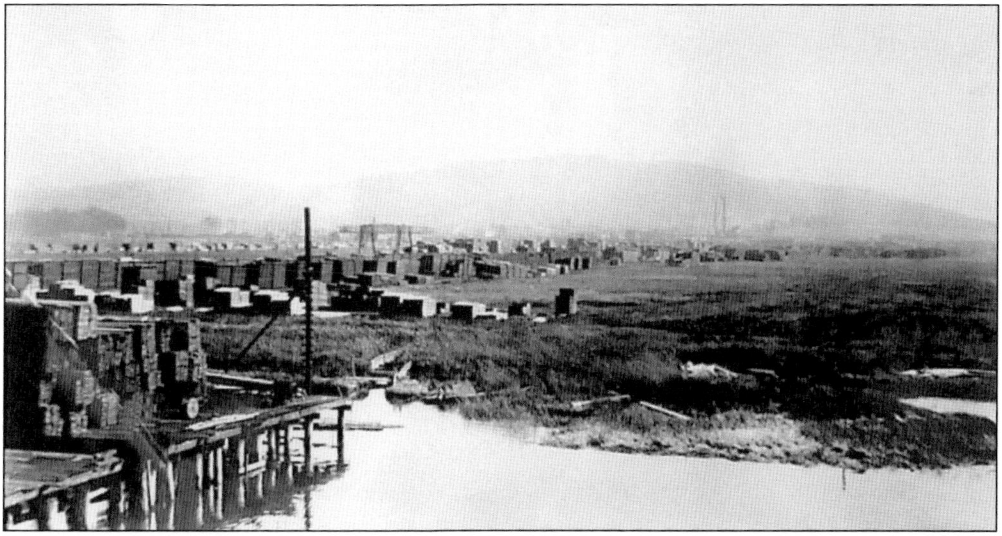

FIELDS OF DRYING LUMBER, LOOKING SOUTHWEST, 1915. The Smith Lumber Company took advantage of the flats along the waterfront to dry acres of stacked lumber, before shipping it east and west via the adjacent railroad lines. The hills of Bay Point are barely visible in the background.

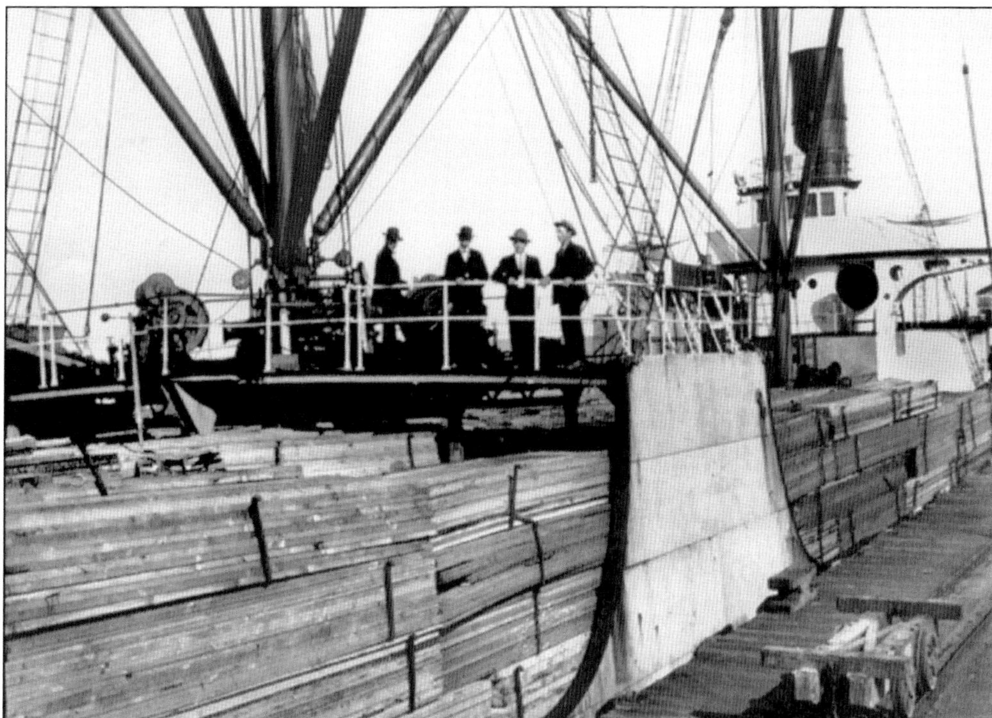

THE *NANN SMITH* UNLOADS, 1911. Named for one of Smith's daughters, this custom-built steamer transported cut lumber from the Smith holdings around Coos Bay, Oregon. Using winches and hoists, lumber was unloaded at a rate of 120,000 feet per hour. This required 12 men on the ship and 10 men on the wharf.

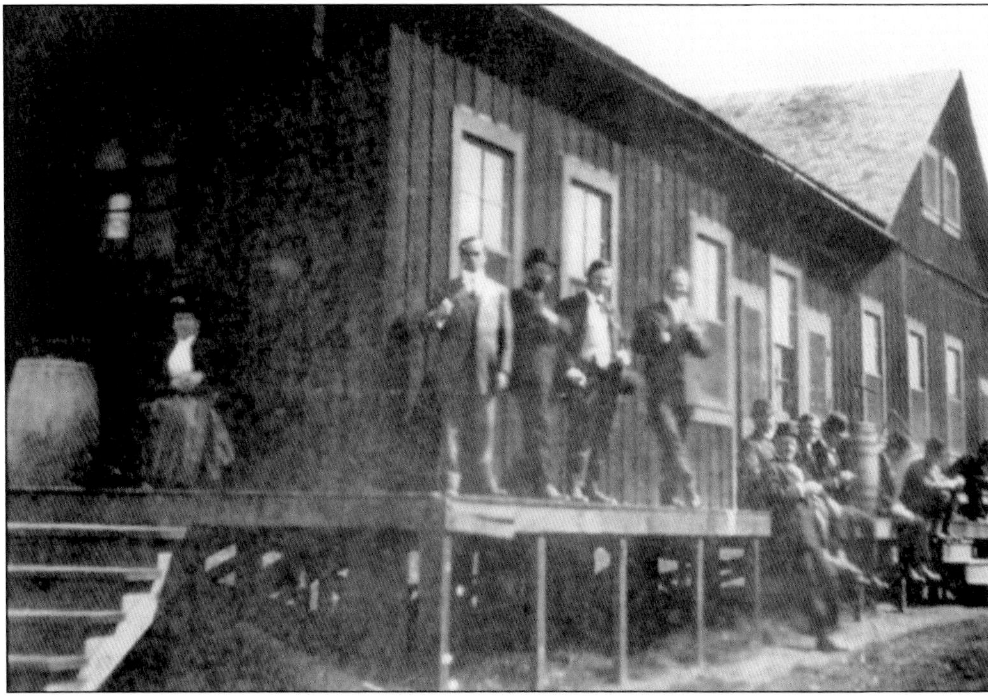

BOSSES AT REST. Striking casual poses, managers of the huge lumber facility mug for the camera. Some of the officers in 1911 were Arno Mereen, vice president and general superintendent; J.V. Smeaton, general manager; Louis B. Berglund, superintendent at Bay Point; C.B. Johnson, assistant superintendent; Joseph Johnson, chief engineer; D.C. Desmond, sales manager; and C.A. Hartman, manager, box department.

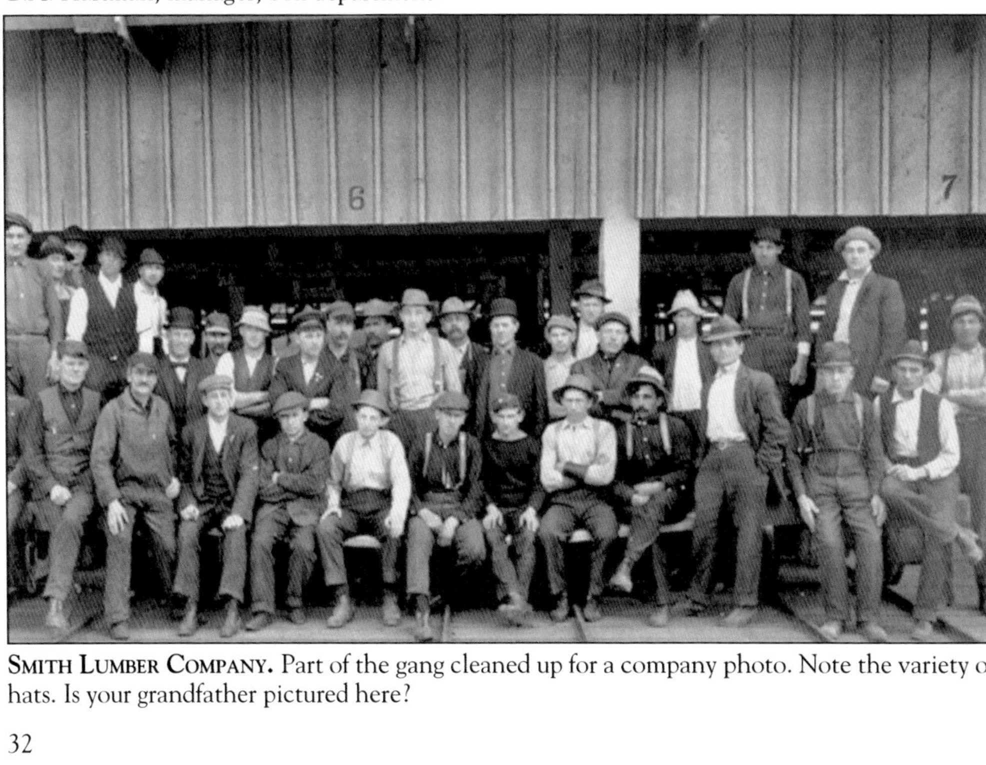

SMITH LUMBER COMPANY. Part of the gang cleaned up for a company photo. Note the variety of hats. Is your grandfather pictured here?

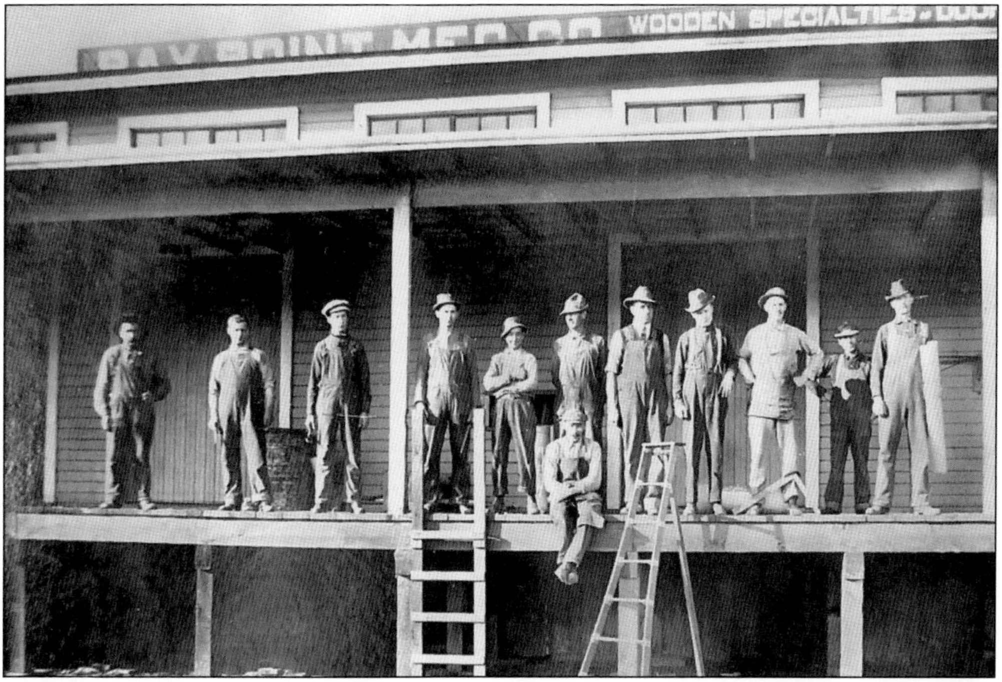

Bay Point Manufacturing—Wooden Specialties. Shown here are craftsmen in the door-manufacturing subsidiary of Smith Lumber. Note the prominently displayed "L" square. No smoking was allowed on the premises.

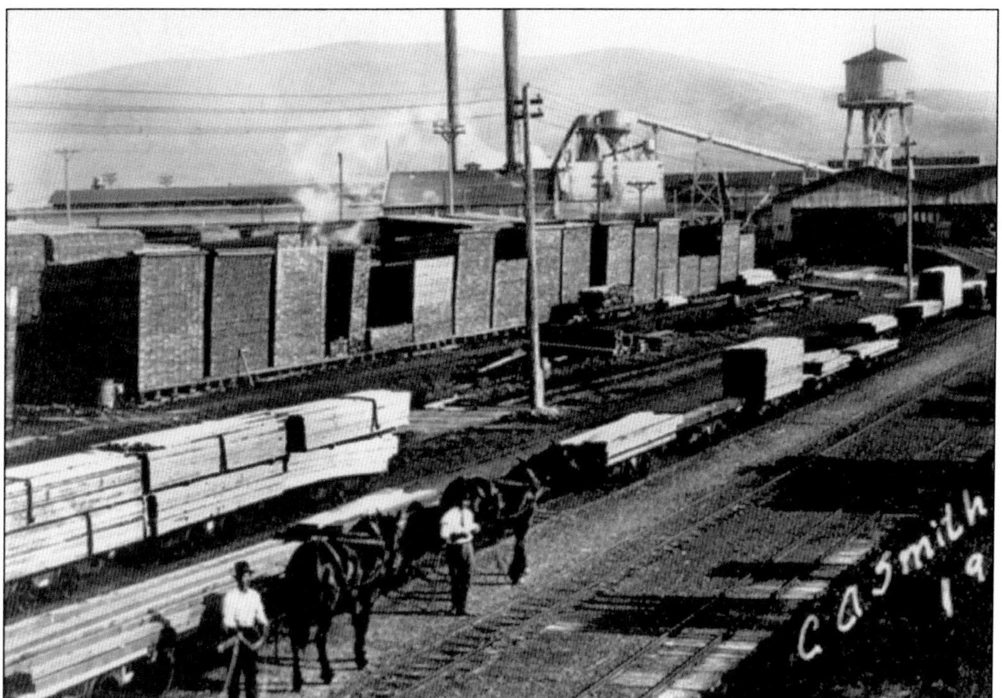

From Wharf to Track. Teamster-driven horses pulled the loaded lumber trucks along rails throughout the yard.

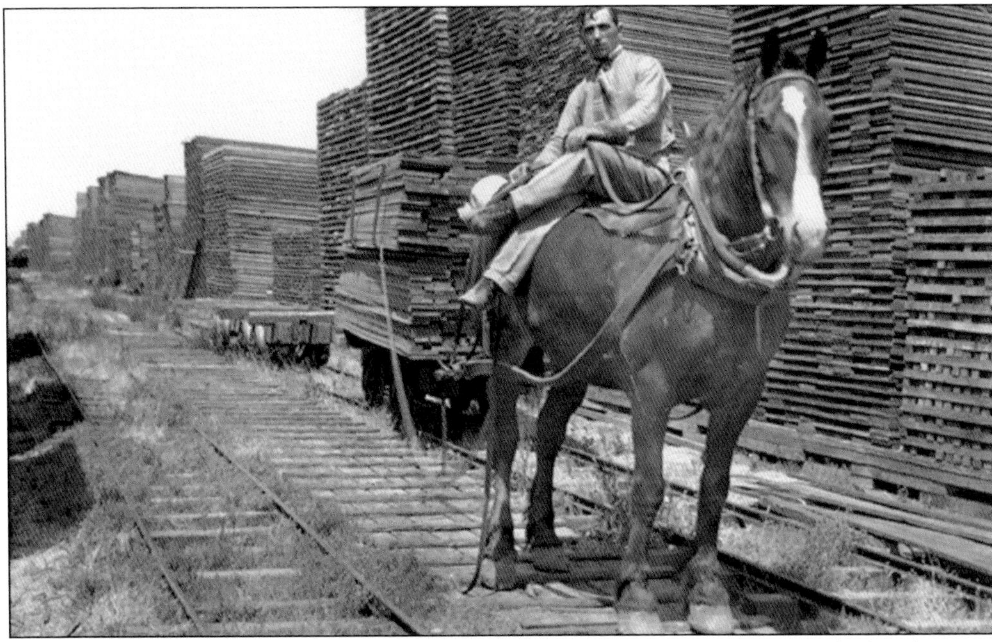

Dray Horse and Rider. Comfortable in his daily office, a teamster relaxes on the hindquarters of his one-horsepower trackster. The Smith Lumber Company owned 80,000 acres of timberland in Oregon, estimated to contain 4.5 billion board feet of saleable timber.

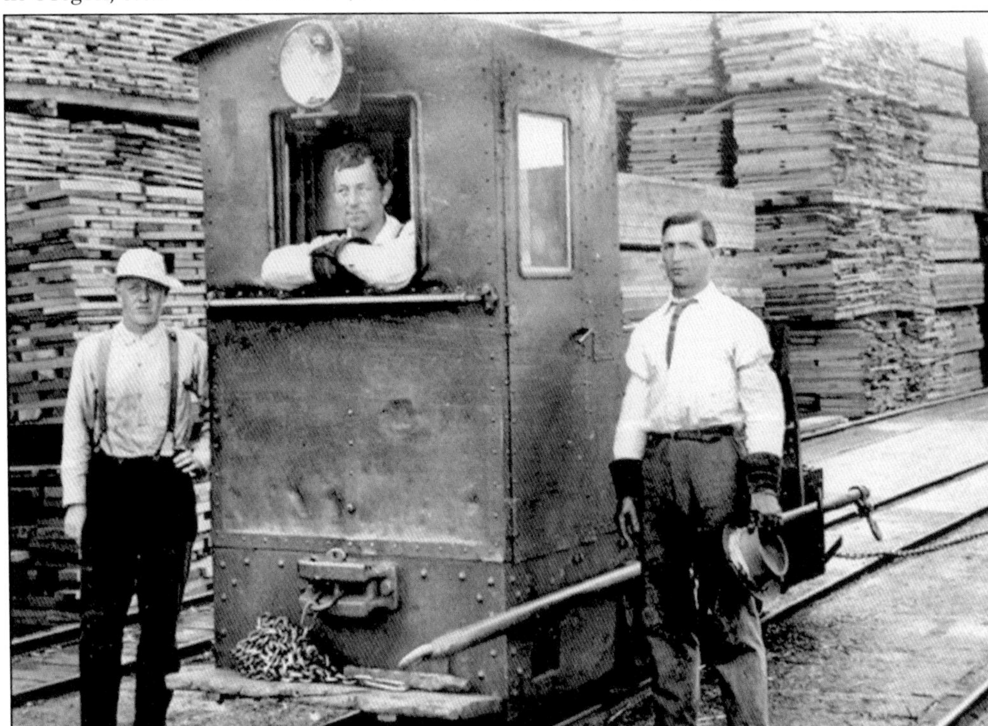

Electric-Powered Vehicle. A six-ton electric engine hauled loaded cars. It moved them between the stacking fields, the planing mill, the drying kilns, and the main rail cars.

Three

Designed by Nature, Developed by Man

The "City"

The first burst of modern growth in Bay Point occurred in 1907–1908. In the summer of 1907, C.A. Smith, owner of the C.A. Smith Lumber Company, which had lumber interests in Oregon and California, sought a site on which to build "a manufacturing and distributing plant." He sought "proximity to railroad lines for shipment of the forest product, deep water for his vessels that brought the raw product from the mills, and proper drying conditions for lumber." Several months later, he purchased 1,500 acres, including 1.5 miles of tidewater frontage.

In 1908, Smith filed a plat map at the County Recorder's office, creating The City of Bay Point. The village grew rapidly, and the new town took for itself the name of the much larger area that had been known as Bay Point School District. Instead of referring to all of the area between Concord and Pittsburg, the name now came to refer just to the town in one section.

Before Smith came along in 1907, the village of Bay Point consisted of "a post office, a grain warehouse, a ranch house, a saloon, and a general store." By 1911, the Odd Fellows Hall was built and there was a moving picture theater. A fire destroyed Smith's Lumber mill in 1913. The company reorganized two years later as the Coos Bay Lumber Company and rebuilt the mill. In 1916, the two-story California Hotel was built in Bay Point. By 1917, Bay Point had a population of about 1,000 people that included a grade school, several stores, streets, curbs, sidewalks, and a sewer system.

By 1918, there were Catholic, Lutheran, and Congregational churches. Four wells in the foothills south of town provided water. Outside the limits of the Bay Point town plat, the township was largely rural.

The Smith Lumber Company "had one of the largest finishing mills anywhere in the United States. Its annual payroll came to nearly $300,000." Spruce and pine were shipped weekly from Coos Bay, Oregon. Within a year of its construction, the mill employed about 190 men. It was the major employer in Bay Point until after the stock market crash of 1929. The demand for lumber ceased and the plant closed in 1932.

During 1909, the William H. Nichols syndicate, under the auspices of General Chemical Company in New York, built a chemical manufacturing plant southeast of "the City of Bay Point." By 1910, the plant projected to employ 300 men, which still operates today on Port Chicago Highway and Nichols Road as the "Bay Point Works" of General Chemical Company. Also in 1909, The Morton Brass Foundry was also operating in Bay Point. The company, a branch of T.W. Garrett and Company, built a 40-room hotel to accommodate its 60 employees.

As was common in the early decades of the 20th century, Nichols provided housing for his workers. The subdivision of Nichols became a "community." The sudden growth brought a call for another school district, and the children, who had just three years earlier begun attending the new school in the town of Bay Point, got their own school just across the road from the chemical plant. Those who grew up in Nichols remember well their experiences at the Nichols School.

After World War II ended, the close proximity of the Nichols School to the dangers of the chemical plant led to the school's closure. The children again were sent to Bay Point School. In 1957, the schoolhouse was sold to a church group in Port Chicago, who moved it into town. By 1965, the company sent out notices that all residents of Nichols should vacate their houses. The handful of families who remained moved out and their homes were torn down in 1968.

Land speculation by capitalists has deep roots in the history of Bay Point, and Clyde was a major focal point. Legislation promoting the transcontinental railroad was being introduced in the United States Senate in the early months of 1849. Ohio senators Benton and Atchison of Missouri, and Douglas and Breese of Illinois sought a central route to the Pacific, terminating in the vicinity of the gold region. "It was believed that whichever group succeeded in promoting enough improvement on the transcontinental route that ran through its locality would make its city the 'future great city of the world.' "

The first claimants of Clyde were Majs. Charles Loring and Robert Allen at Benicia Arsenal. They called it Government Ranch. One year they grazed Army mules there. Essentially speculators, they hoped to build a port that they could sell to the Navy, and also hoped the coming railroad would go through their property.

It seems obvious that government insiders at Benicia had a pretty clear picture where the railroad was headed. Judge Serranus Hastings of Benicia certainly must have known. When government surveyors first visited Benicia, Hastings, the former chief justice of the California Supreme Court, entertained them.

Allen and Lorings' problem was one of timing. The arrival of the railroad at Government Ranch didn't occur until 1877, about 25 years too late for them to make a fast dollar. Serranus Hastings, the second owner, also failed to profit from any possible inside information on the railroad for the same reason Of course, this was only one of his many land investments.

Government Ranch was eventually sold off in large parcels, the largest for a subdivision in 1884 by William M. Gwin Jr., the son of the governor. Little success followed this subdivision, as there were few takers of the land. By 1892, former governor Leland Stanford (a major railroad stockholder) owned tracts A and B of the eastern half of Government Ranch. At the same time, former county supervisor Patrick Tormey of Rodeo owned the western half of the ranch.

Ranching could hardly have been Stanford's purpose, as the planning for additional rail lines through Bay Point was underway. In 1892, Stanford owned 2,864 acres in the district, valued at $65,364. In 1897, Stanford's properties were put on the real estate market again. Surprisingly, he was just in time for the transcontinental railroad.

By 1907, Frank Foskett and Robert Elsworthy, Concord butchers and land speculators, purchased 1,300 acres of the eastern half of Government Ranch from C.A. Hooper. They later bought the Willow Pass-Concord section of Government Ranch. Three years later they sold seven ranches, including Government Ranch, to R.N. Burgess of San Francisco.

A year later, Burgess opened the Government Ranch subdivision, adjacent to Bay Point, for public sale. Again, sales of the land were sluggish until international events transformed the local economy. On April 6, 1917, the United States entered World War I. That year, Burgess obtained a government contract (probably from the U.S. Shipping Board) and the financing to build the Pacific Coast Shipbuilding Company, and 400 jobs were created almost overnight.

With the jobs came the need for housing. The town of Bay Point, adjacent to the shipyard, was crying for new housing—but Burgess had other ideas. He didn't own property within the town of Bay Point. He did, however, have his previously subdivided Government Ranch, which he had been trying to sell for seven years.

The local newspaper protested loudly at Burgess's success in receiving federal money from the U.S. Bureau of Federal Housing to subsidize the construction of Clyde. The principal objection was that the housing could have been built within the town limits of Bay Point, within walking distance of Pacific Coast Shipbuilding docks, rather than several miles away. Bay Point, Concord, and Martinez belatedly and unsuccessfully lobbied for the federal largess. The neighborhood of Clyde, no doubt named after the Clyde Shipping Works near Glasgow, Scotland, was thus born of one man's shrewd ability to tap into federal grant programs.

The Clyde neighborhood continues today with a strong sense of community identity. Snuggled compactly between the Tesoro Oil Refinery, the defunct Naval Weapons Station, and Highway 4, residents have a distinct view of life in Contra Costa County.

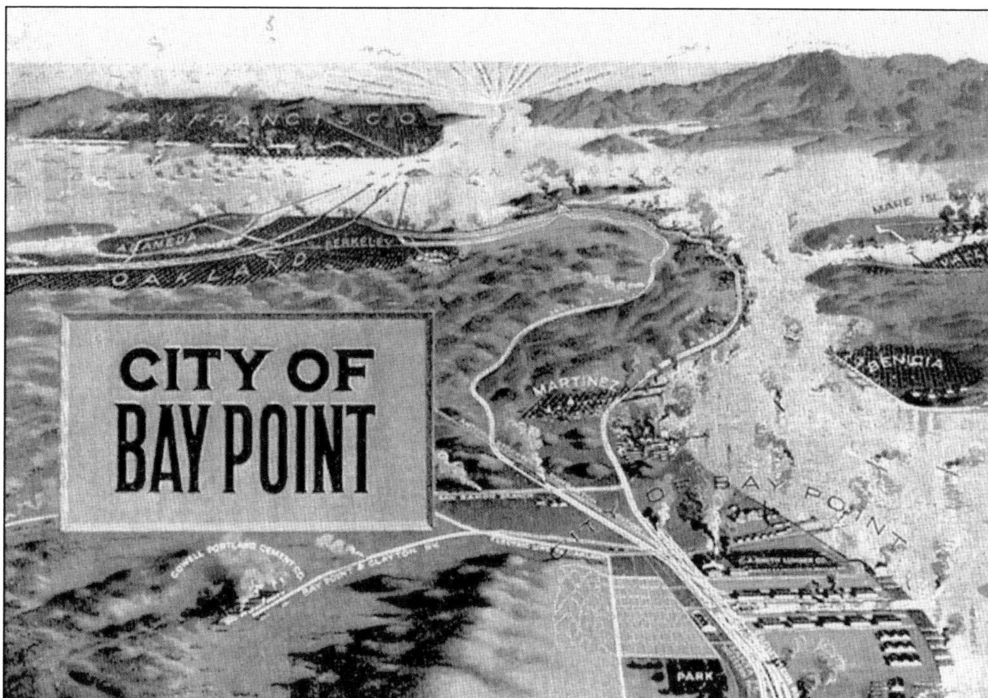

SMITH'S VISION OF THE CITY OF BAY POINT. This promotional piece, which appeared in *The American Lumberman* in 1911, illustrates all of the strategic advantages when locating industry in Bay Point. Had rail access to Coos Bay been available during this period, the manufacturing and distribution facility (and the town site) might never have been selected, according to company sources.

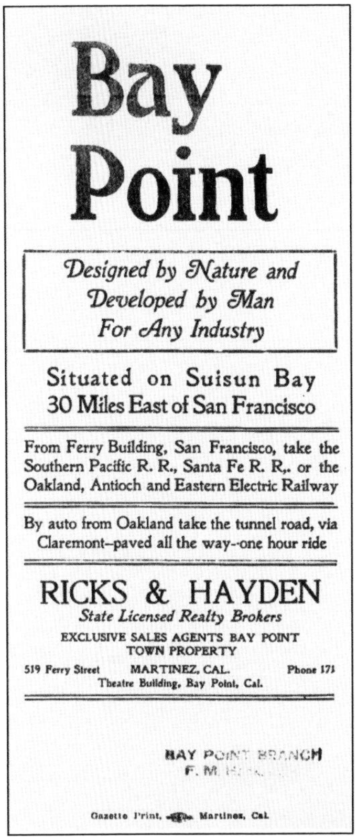

One-Hour Auto Drive from Oakland. Promotion of town lots in Bay Point was handled by exclusive contract with Martinez brokers, Ricks and Hayden. The role of natural geography was recognized, as well as the industriousness of men who defined early 20th-century Bay Point.

Shideler Residence. As one of the original promoters of the town of Bay Point, Mr. Shideler's prosperity was reflected in his gracious town home.

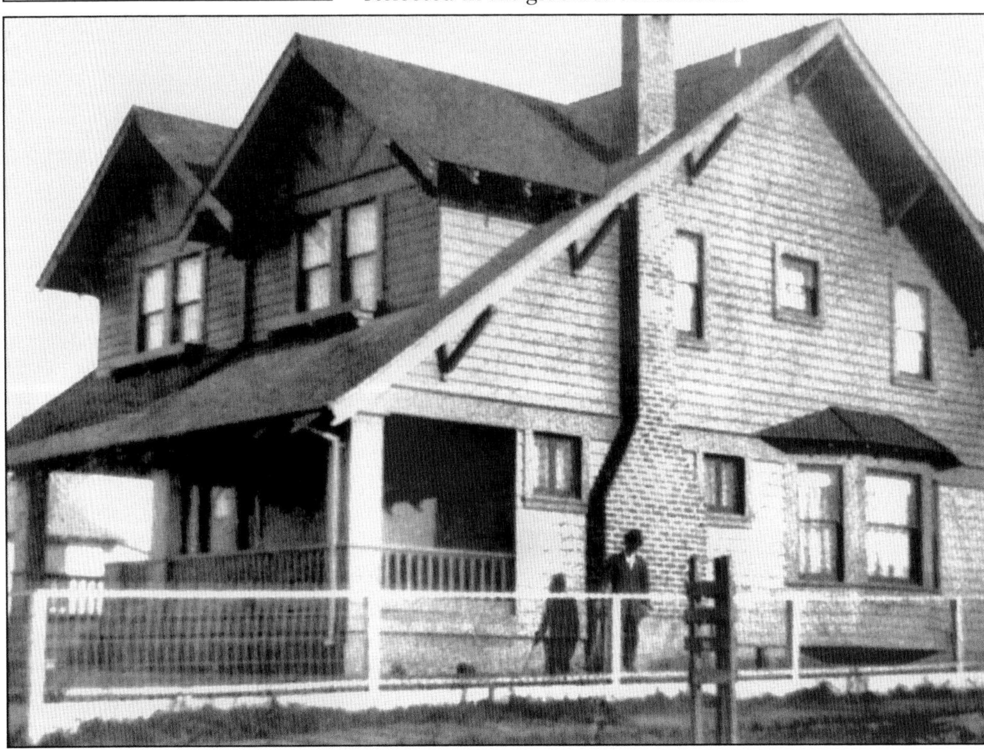

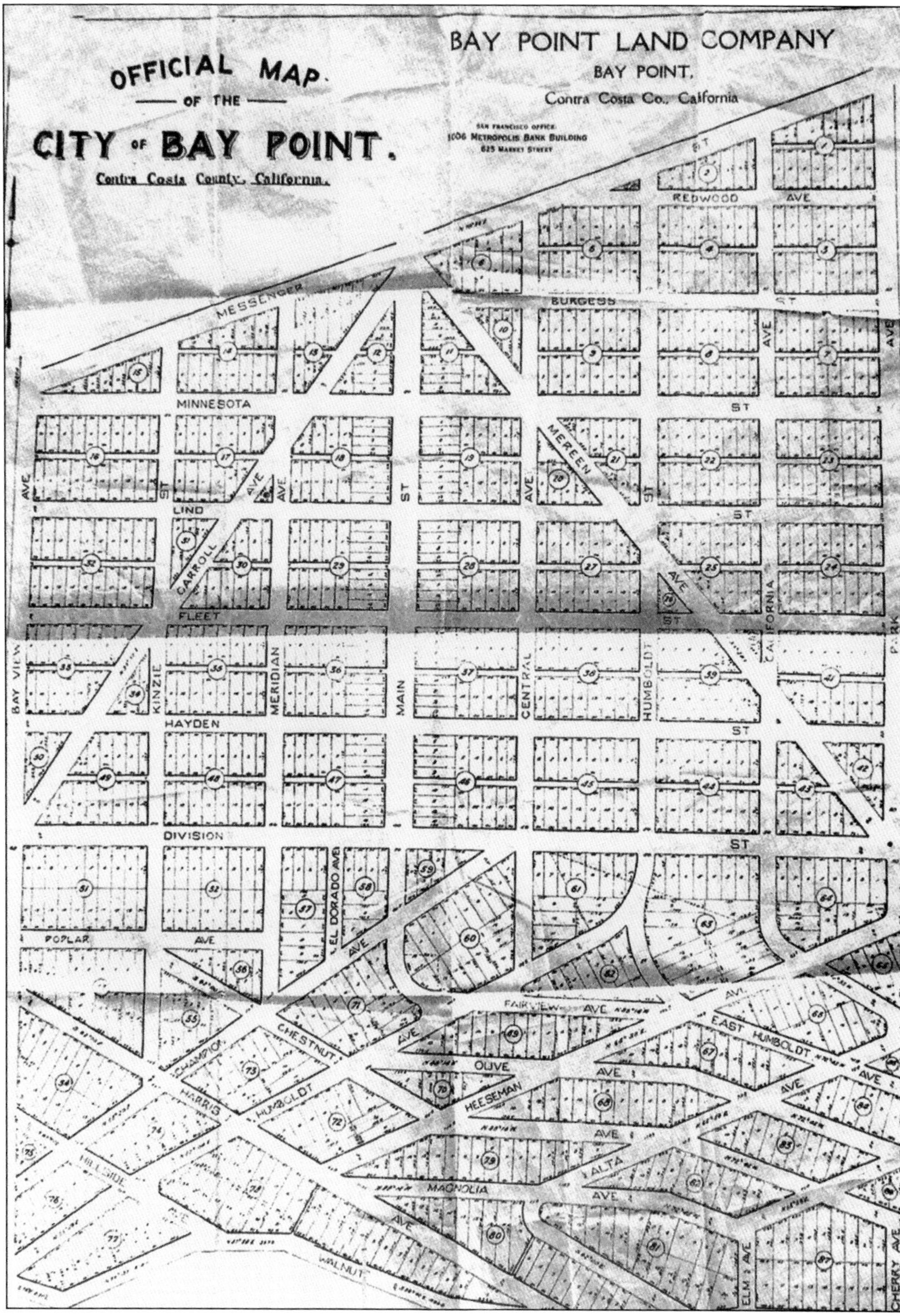

The "Bay Point Land Company." With a San Francisco office at 1006 Metropolis Bank Building on Market Street, the developers filed an official plat map at the Contra Costa County Recorder's Office in 1908.

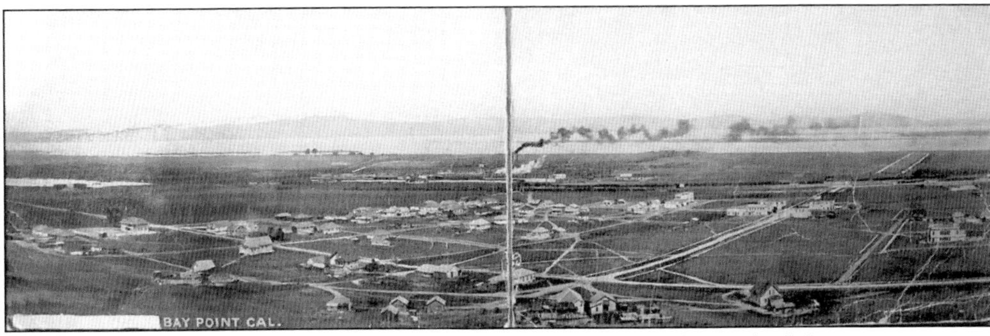

"Biggest Little City on the Pacific Coast." This postcard was doubtless sent to major manufacturers all over the country. Bay Point was "the only city on the Bay to have three big railroads, five pipelines of fuel oil, two high power electric lines and a half mile of deep water frontage." According to the promoters, it was "destined to be THE manufacturing city of the West.

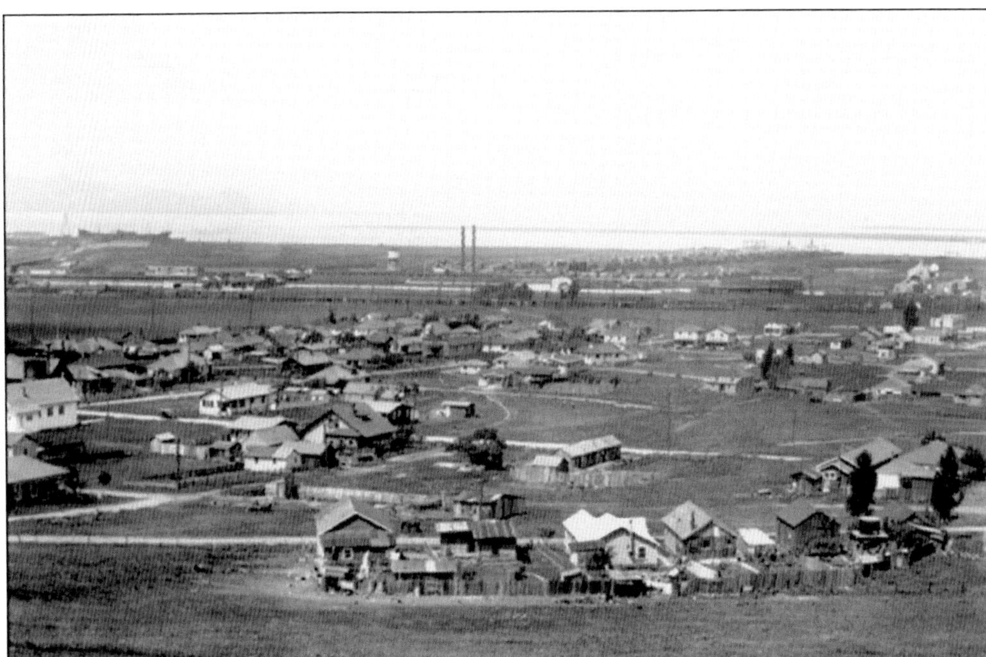

Bay Point in 1918. Although appearing ramshackle by today's standards, this view of the town reveals urbanization beyond most towns in Contra Costa County in the early 20th century.

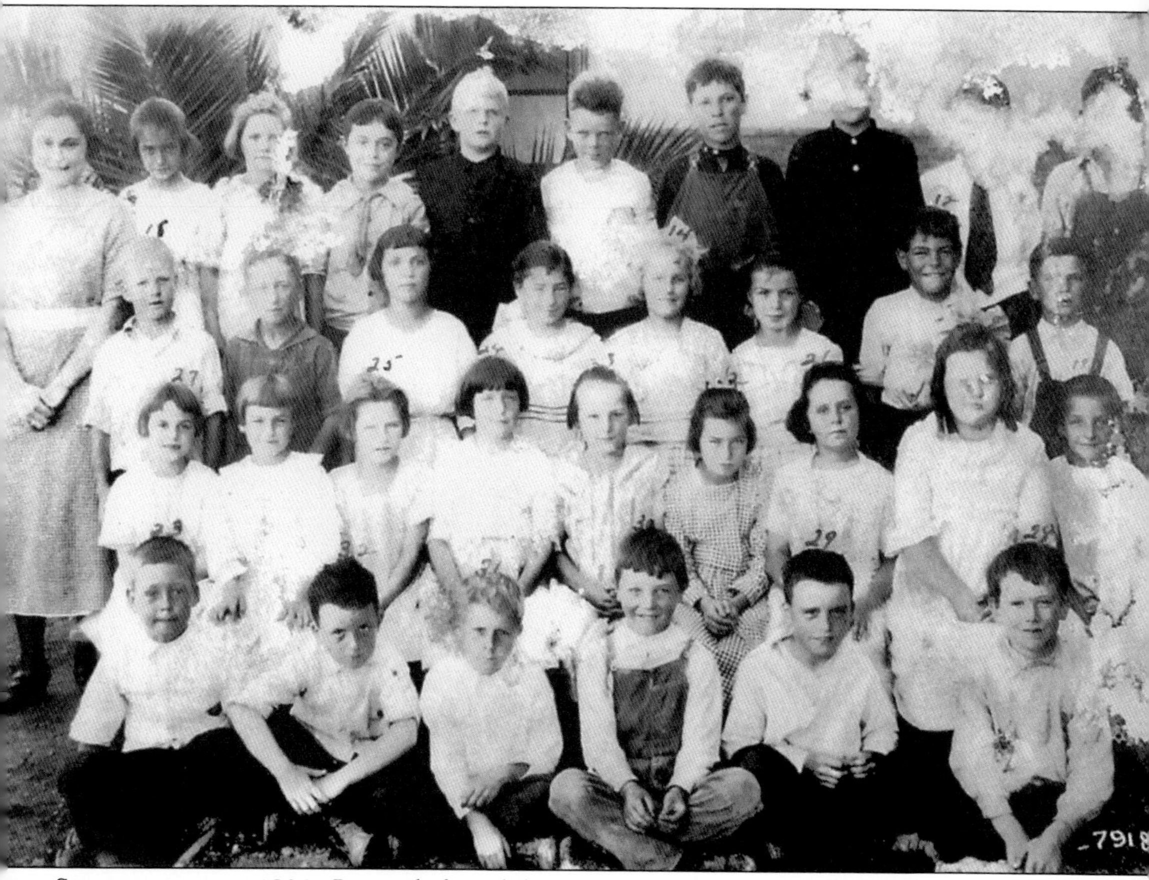

SCHOOLCHILDREN, 1920. Pictured, from left to right, are (front row) Elmer Johnson, Jack McEwen, Clarence Westlund, Joe Deberry, Paul McEwen, and Ernest Palubicki; (second row) Valora Eaton, Helen Christian, Lillian Powell, Bernita Conser, Genevieve Shideler, Josephine Rubidge, Lena Pacini, Mary Hartlett, and Thelma Morehouse; (third row) Lorel Robards, Leslie Johnson, Augusta Dellagnese, Marion Paganini, Tholine Johnson, Victoria Lombardi, Bruce Skaggs, and John Bellomo; and (fourth row) Charles Skaggs (damaged), Orville Bilyeu (damaged), Clarence Olsen (damaged), Richard Dellagnese, John Hines, Norman Olsen, John Silva, Frances Pate, Grace Noia, and Geraldine Kennerly (teacher).

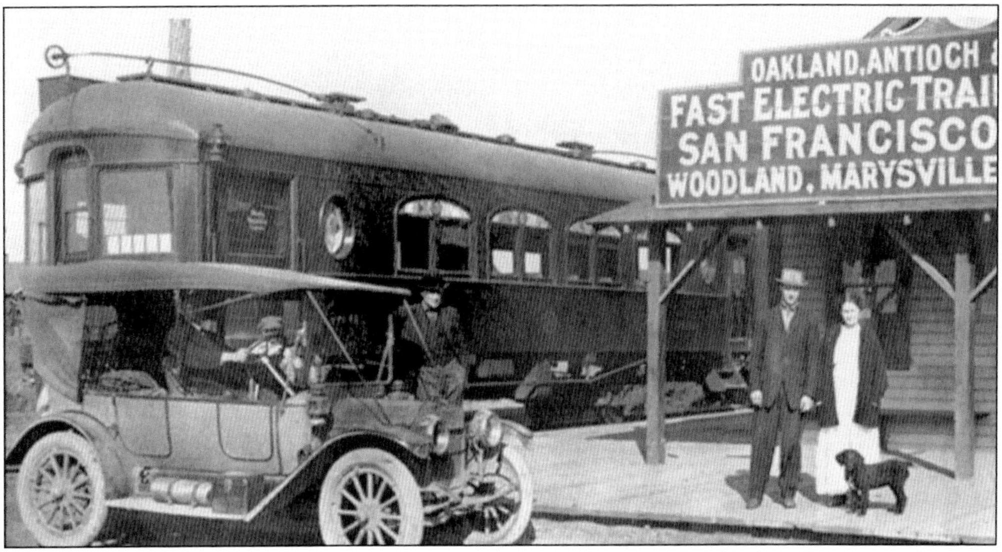

Bay Point Station, Oakland, Antioch, and Eastern Railway. The first E-BART of Contra Costa County, built nearly 100 years ago, provided progressive passenger transportation through Bay Point. Finished between Bay Point and Concord in 1911, this electric train eventually became the fast commuter between Sacramento and Oakland, with ferry connections to San Francisco. Popular for a generation, it provided 16 stops in Contra Costa County from Antioch to Danville and Diablo.

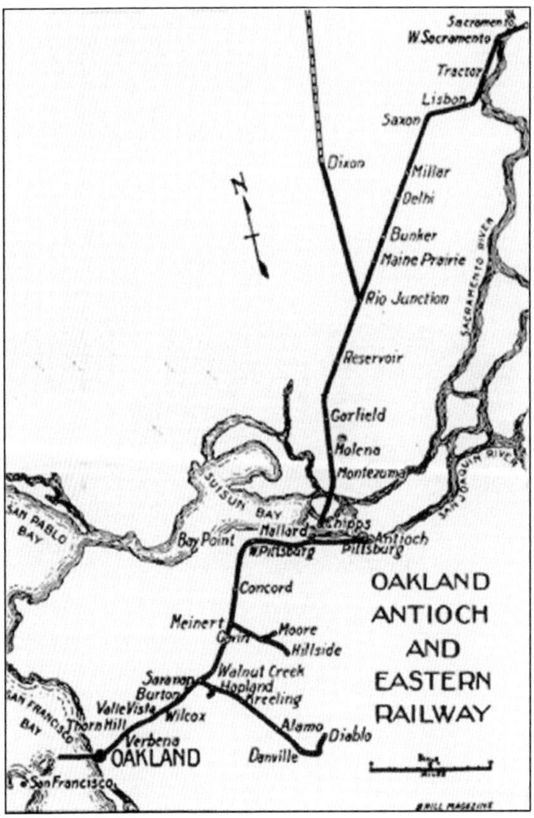

Oakland, Antioch, And Eastern Railway. At its height the Oakland, Antioch, and Eastern Railway provided efficient commuter transport from Sacramento to San Francisco. Many of the stations shown on the map no longer exist and are largely forgotten in Contra Costa County history.

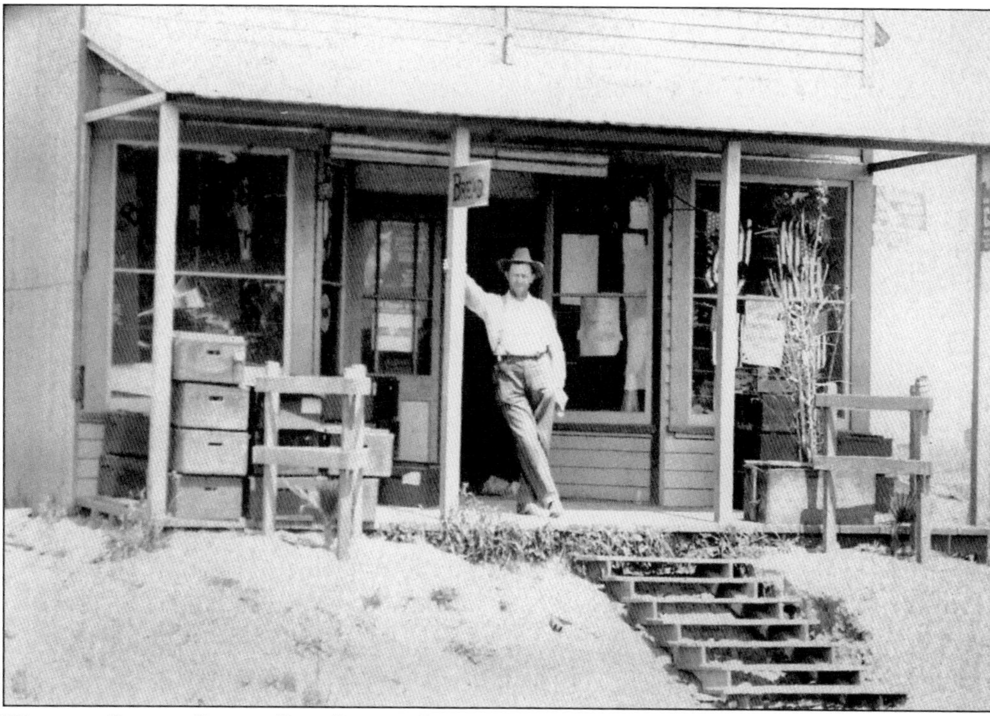

William South Store, Bay Point, Late 1910s or Early 1920s. Daniel Cunningham and his family settled on the town site of Bay Point in 1859. In the late 1800s, they opened a general store and saloon. In the early 20th century, they sold the store to William South, who remodeled the building by putting in larger windows and exchanging the saloon space for a barbershop.

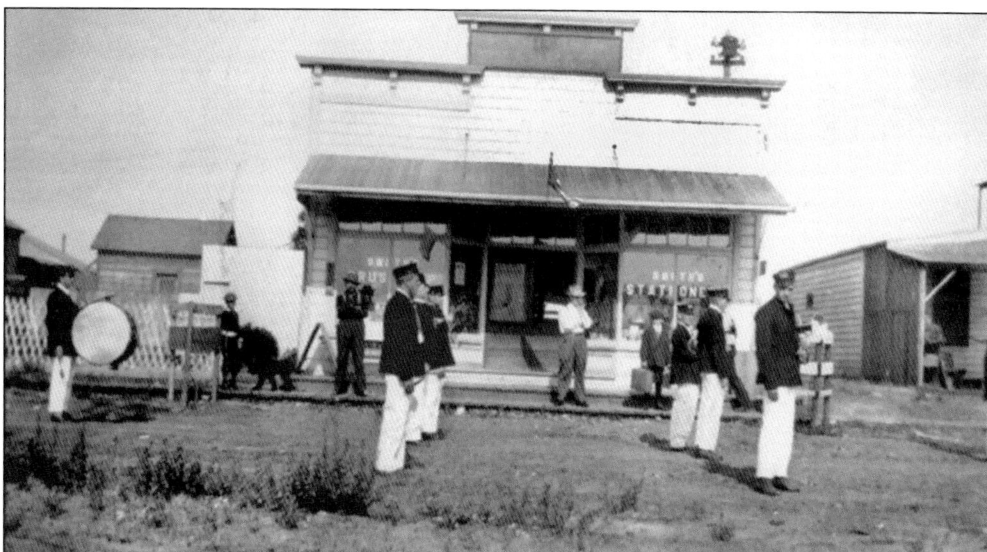

Marching through Town. Perhaps taken on the Fourth of July 1918, this photograph shows the local marching band parading past Doc. Smith's Drug and Stationery store. A boy, his dog, a workman, and businessman join a young traveler on his way to the train station, to watch the hoopla on the dirt road.

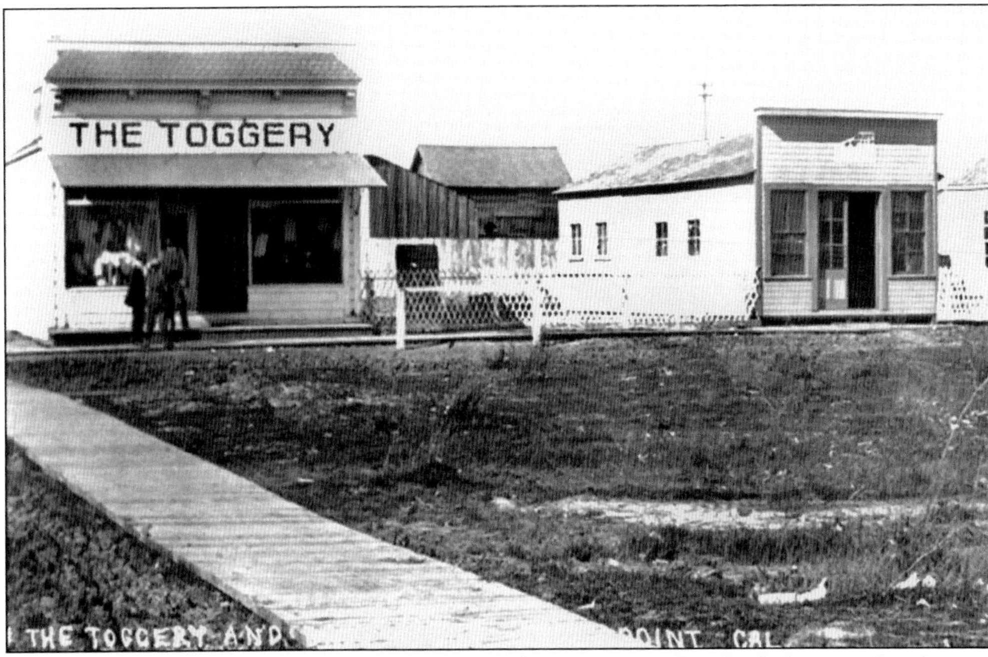

Toggery in Downtown Bay Point. Notice the amenities for the ladies, in the form of boardwalks, to keep their skirts clean.

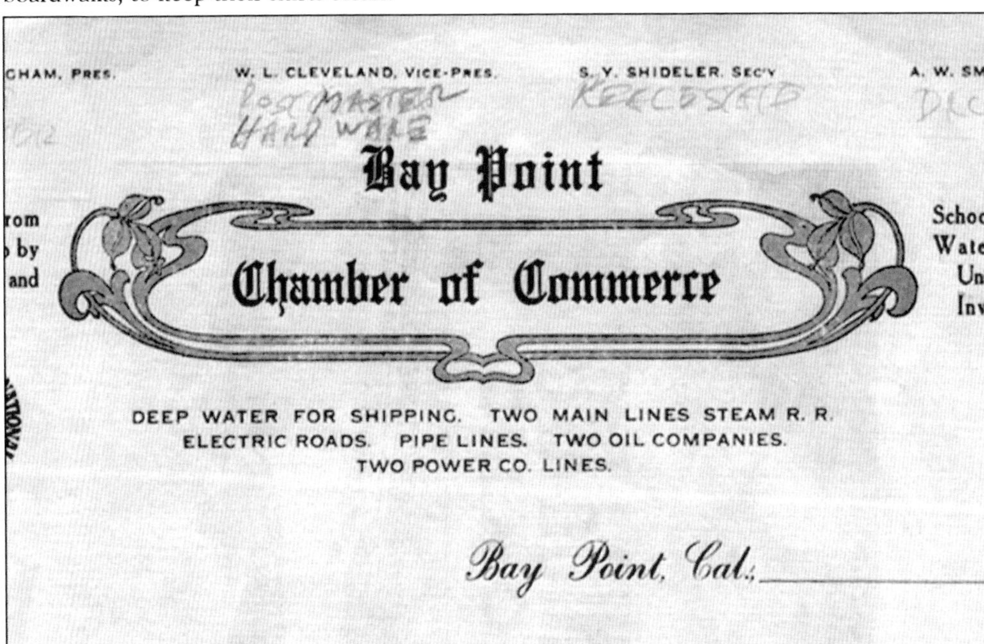

Bay Point Chamber of Commerce, c. 1915. Always looking for ways to commercially promote the town, the chamber provided business leadership to the community. Officers at the time were Cunningham, Cleveland, Shideler, and Smith. Ironically, in the latter years of its existence, the Chambers of Commerce of the surrounding towns betrayed the town of Bay Point/Port Chicago. Their cooperation was helpful to the U.S. Navy in its public relations battle to confiscate the town in 1968.

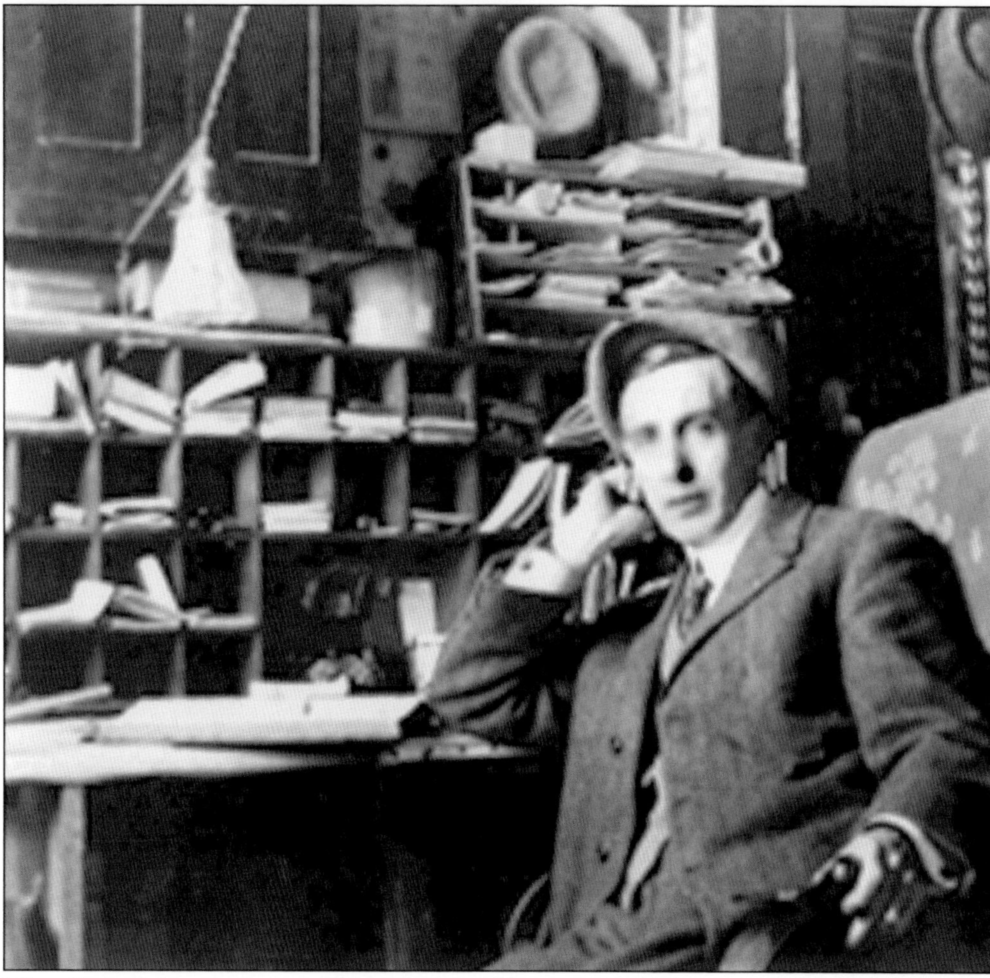

"DOC SMITH" PAUSES FROM HIS BOOKKEEPING. Shopkeeper Smith, using modern office systems, kept track of his suppliers, customers, and debtors. As the 1920s moved into the 1930s, his debtor ledger became more and more full.

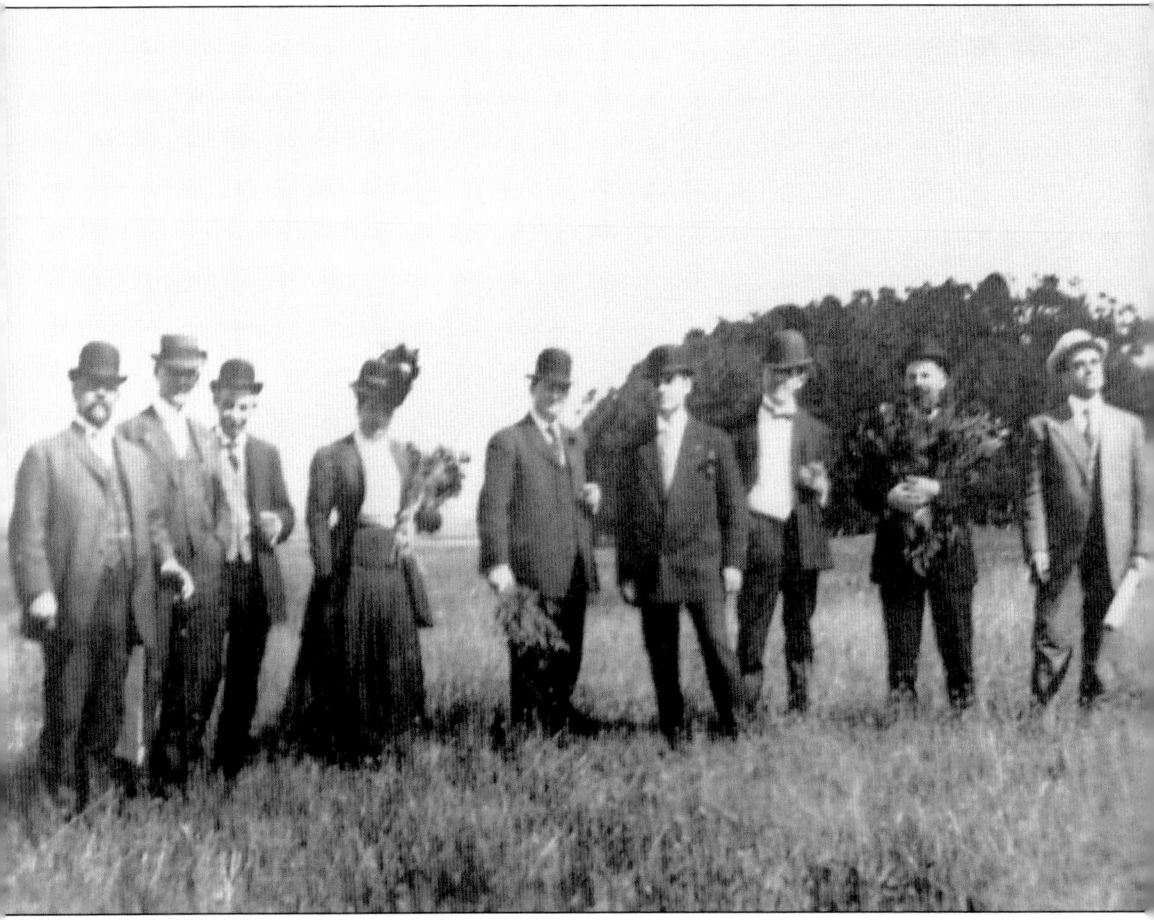

Founders and Promoters of Bay Point among the Wildflowers. C.A. Smith, his wife Nann, Henry Schideler, and other founders of Bay Point stand on the empty ground in 1908 that would become the town. It was a heady time, building a company town from scratch—a time of promised prosperity and growth.

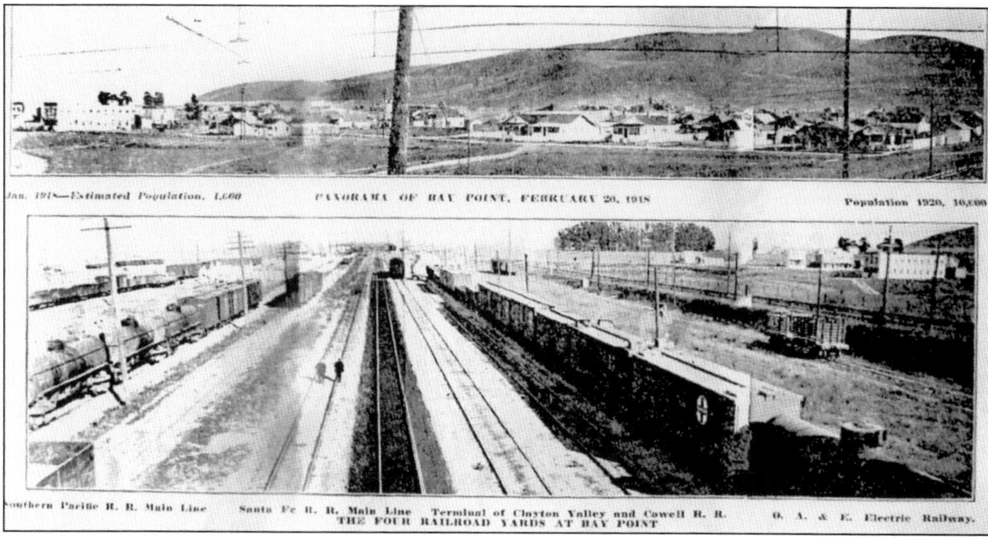

Town of Bay Point from the North, 1918. Poised for growth, the January 1918 population of 1,000 was projected to be 10,000 by 1920. The lower picture, touting the four railroad yards, was intended to attract shippers of all types of goods. The four were the Southern Pacific, the Santa Fe, the Clayton Valley and Cowell, and the Oakland, Antioch, and Eastern Railway. Competing with the cities of Richmond, Oakland, and San Francisco for rail business, those cities eventually gained the lion's share of the terminal business. County development interests began promoting the port to the U.S. Navy as early as 1917.

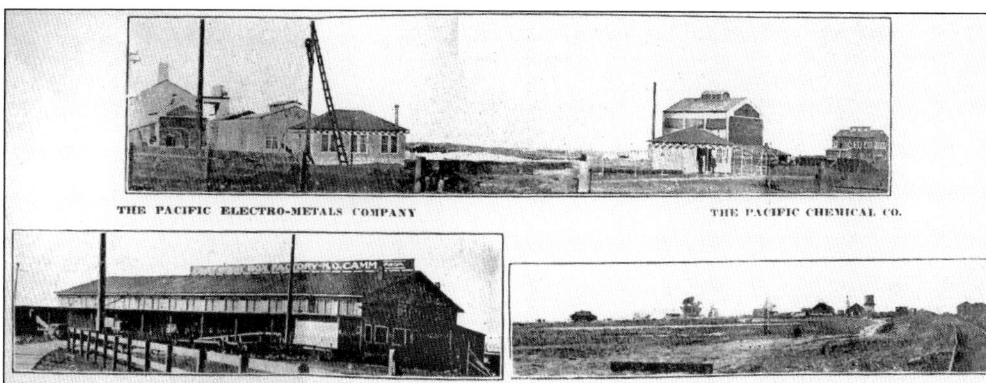

World War I Industrial Start-ups. By 1918, related industries had grown up around the Smith Lumber Company. They included the Pacific Electro Metals Company, Pacific Chemical Company, H.O. Camm's Box Factory, and the under construction Pacific Coast Shipbuilding docks.

BAY POINT NEEDS HOMES, HOTELS, APARTMENTS AND MANY LINES OF BUSINESS

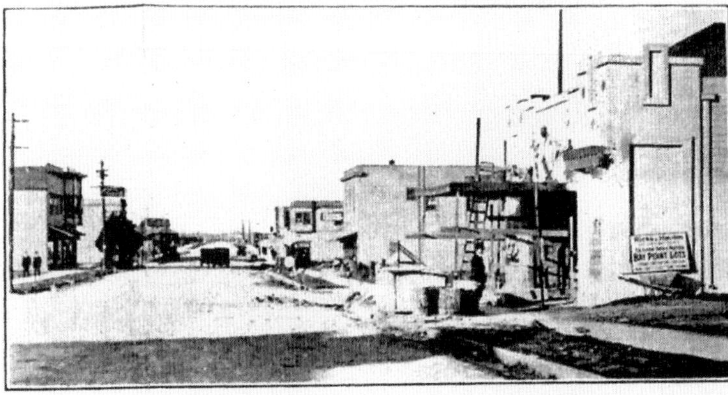

MAIN STREET BAY POINT, LOOKING NORTH
New "Liberty Star Theatre" in Foreground

BUY AND BUILD ON THIS STREET FOR PROFIT
We Finance Your Building
Lots Here Sell For $30 per Foot and Up

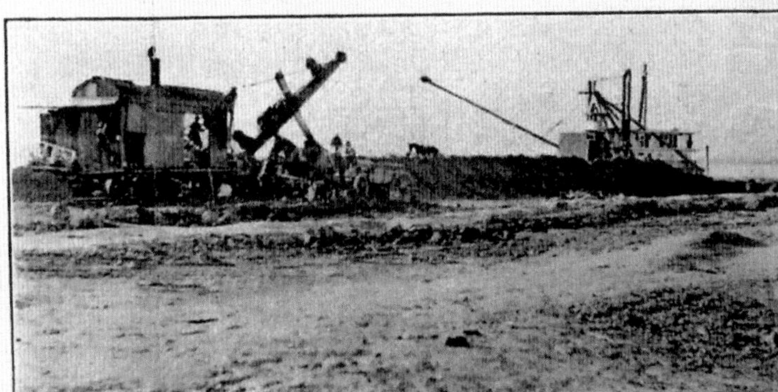

About 300 Men were at work on the construction of the Pacific Shipbuilding Company's Plant, in March, 1918.

It is expected to have 2,000, or more, men at work before the end of 1918

GET IN ON THE GROUND FLOOR
GO UP IN THE ELEVATOR

BUILDING BOOM, 1918. Above, a view of Main Street shows the nearly completed Liberty Star Theatre, where the new moving pictures could be seen. Building lots sold for "$30 per foot and up." Below, heavy equipment prepares the ground on the filled swamp for the buildings of Pacific Coast Shipbuilding Company. This government-funded firm made a huge impact on the capital positions of its founders, though federal taxpayers and the local community ultimately gained little ground.

SOCIALIZING AFTER SUNDAY MEETING. Mrs. A.W. (Doc) Smith, on the right, greets a well-dressed denizen of the "city." Decked in a simple white dress, with matching white gloves and purse, Mrs. Smith admires the fancy feathered hat and ruffled blouse of her younger companion.

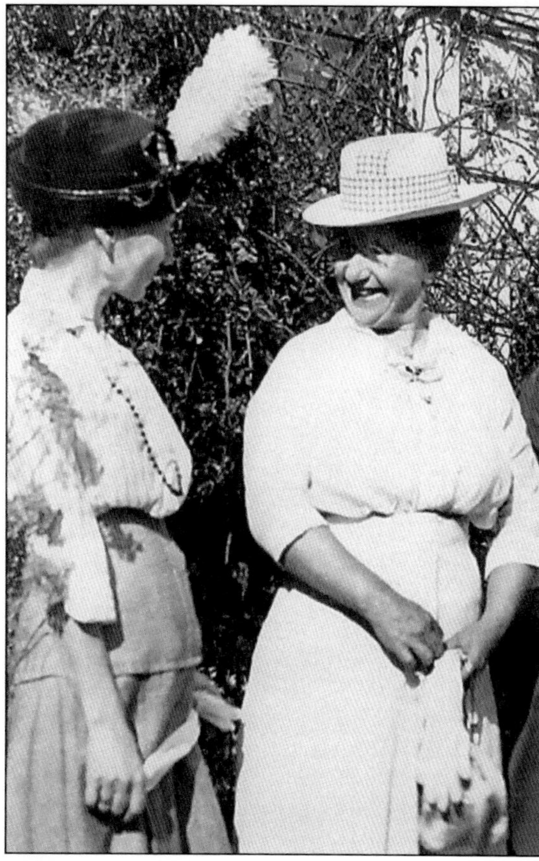

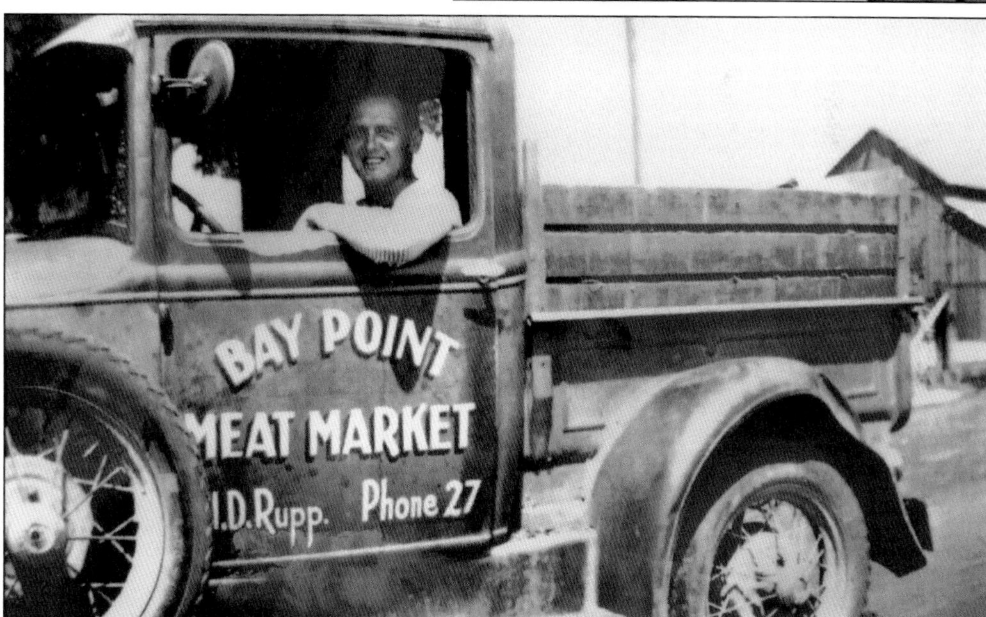

I.D. RUPP DELIVERING MEAT. When you phoned "27," the Bay Point Meat Company delivered your order anywhere in Bay Point.

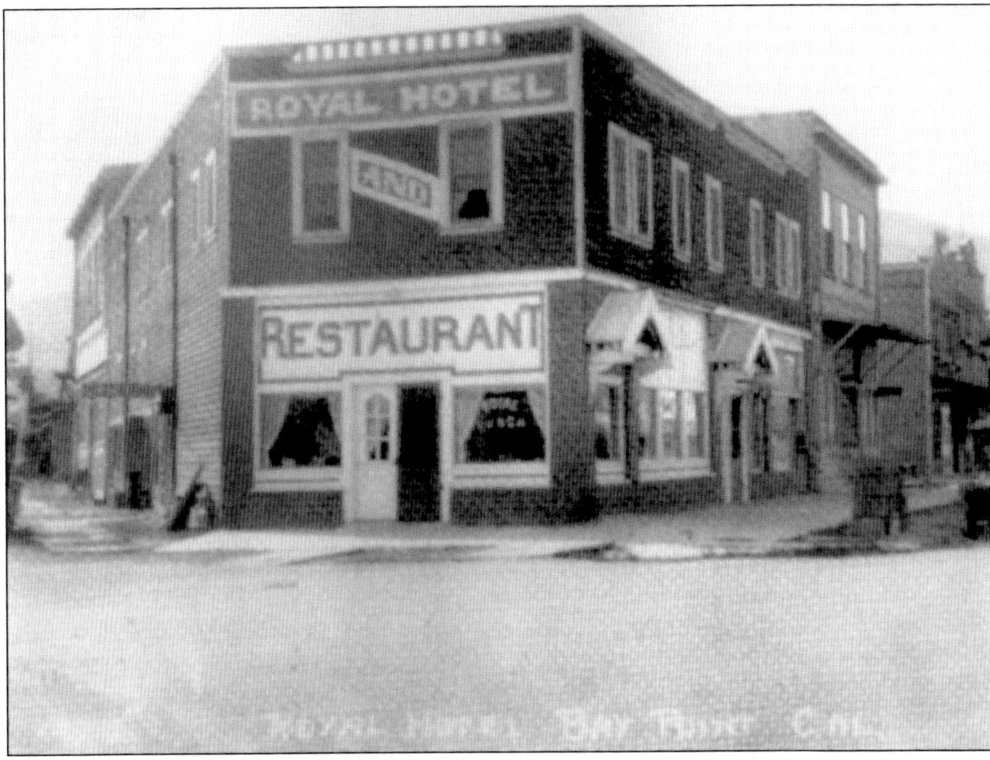

ROYAL HOTEL AND RESTAURANT. Located at the foot of Main Street, the hotel and restaurant was convenient for working men on the dock, as well as passengers getting off trains nearby. Note the newly paved roadway and the late-1920s cars.

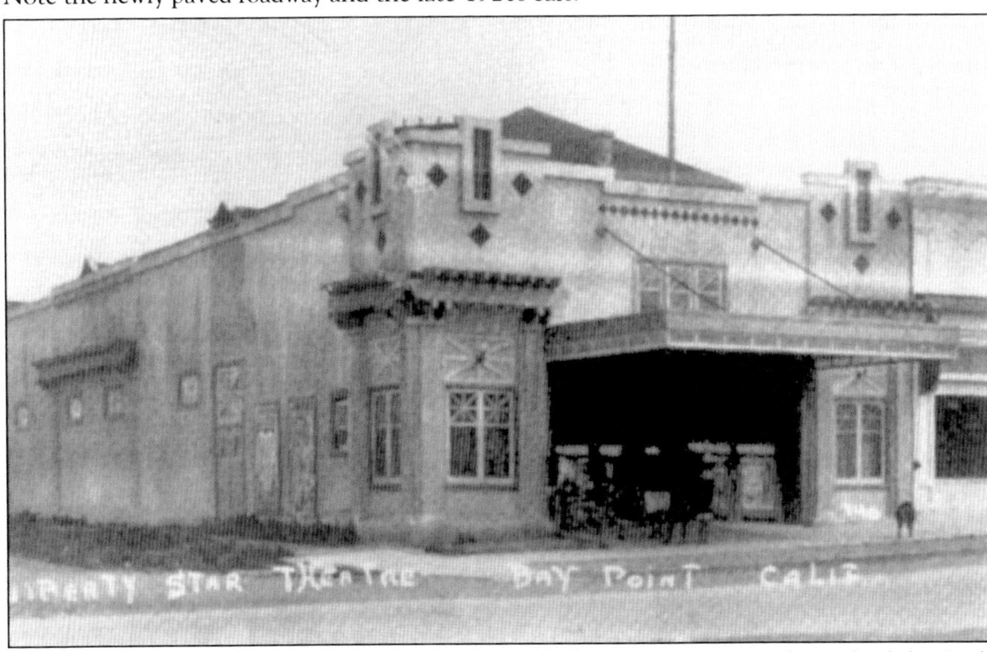

FAMOUS LIBERTY STAR THEATRE. Built by Meyer, this theatre competed with one built by Andy Shirpke in 1911.

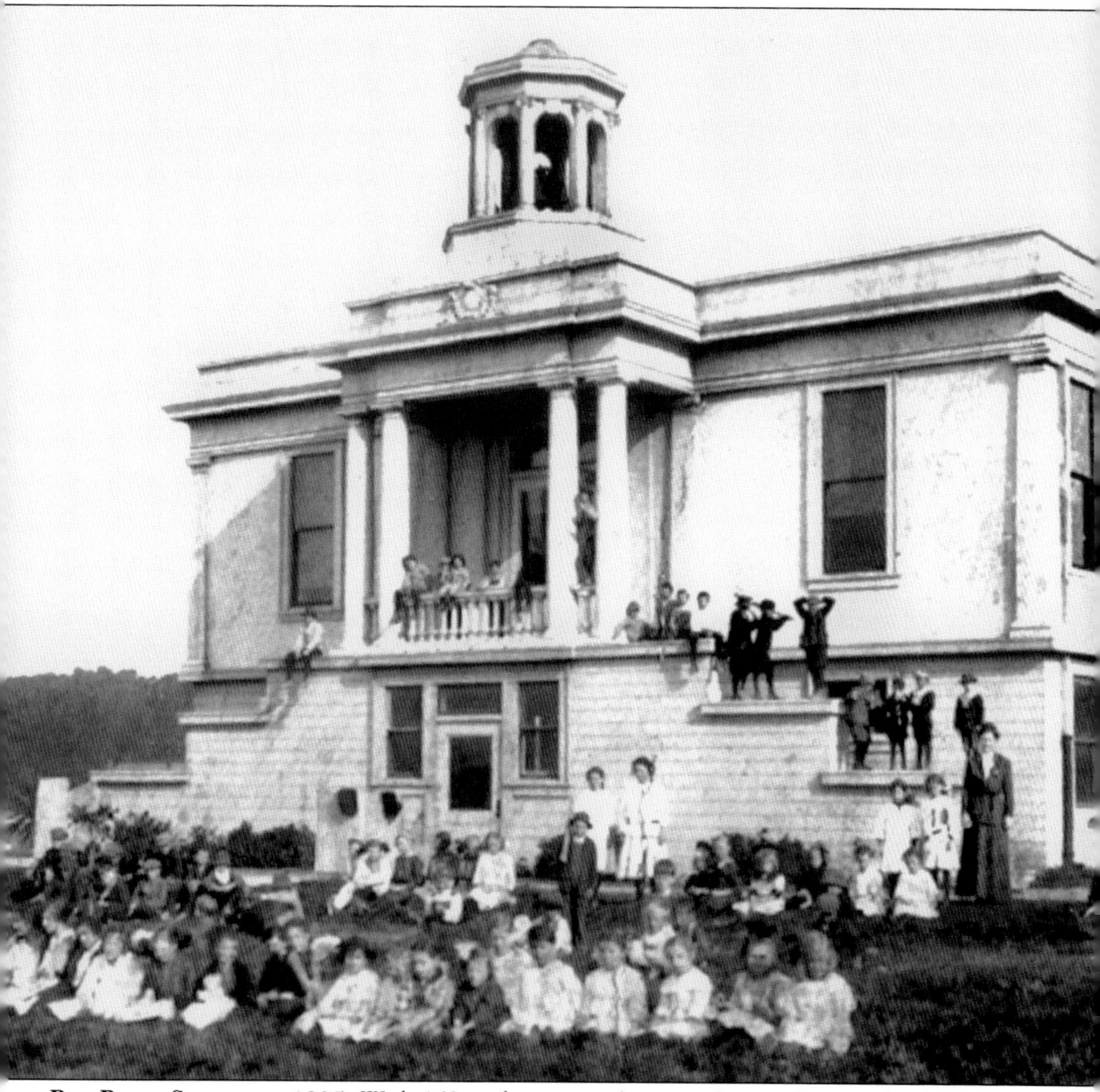

Bay Point School, c. 1925. With 168 students, it took six teachers to keep track of all the kids. Teachers were paid up to $135 per month for 12 months, but had to pay $5 a day for their own substitutes. The top floor of the school was used by grades 5–8. The bottom floor housed the lower grades, a wood shop for the boys, and a sewing room for the girls. This image shows an interesting level of self-expression among the students. The girls were sitting in groups by age, class, and friendships; the boys could show off. One boy posed as a soldier, one a boxer, two as baseball players, and one as an individualist.

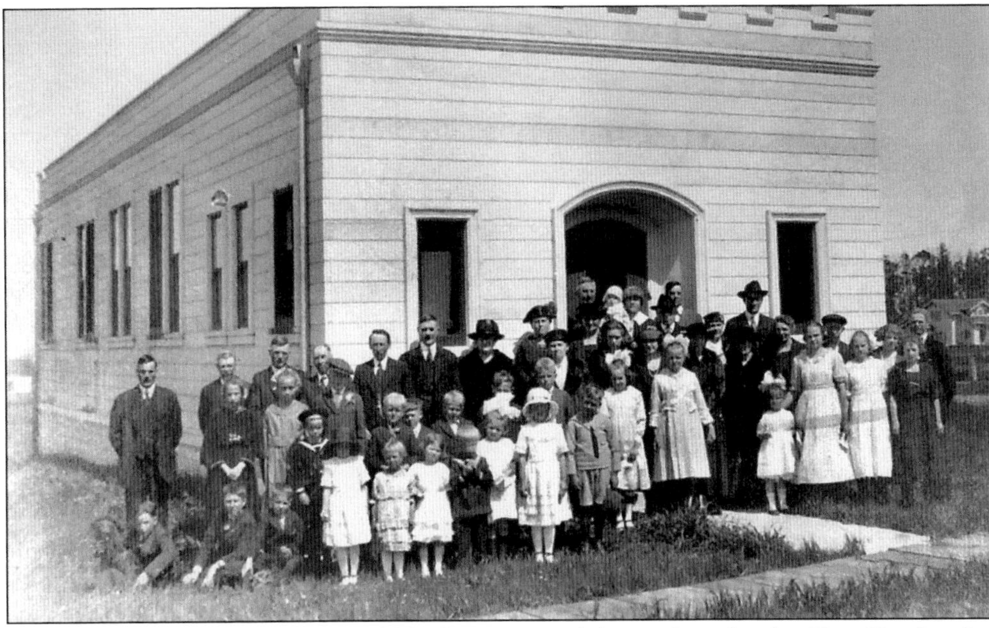

Sharon Lutheran Church, c. 1924. A majority of the workers for the Coos Bay Lumber Company were of Scandinavian descent. Here, we see some 11 or 12 families dressed up in their Sunday best. Notice that the sidewalks are still wooden planks.

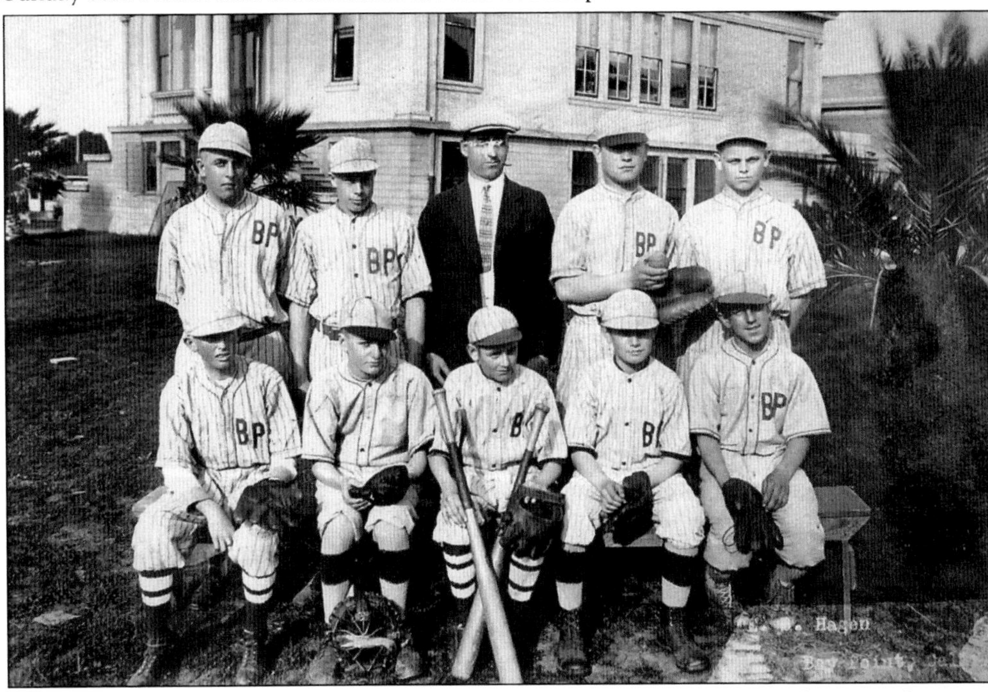

Bay Point School Baseball Team. County champions in 1925 and 1926, the team posed in front of the school on March 9, 1926. Pictured, from left to right, are (front row) Vernon Shaunberg, Ward Shideler, Ted Reese, Tony Lombardi, and Manuel Espinole; and (back row) Leo Reese, Frank Carroll, Principal Robert E. Lee, August "Lard Head" Grossi, and Walter Ganderr.

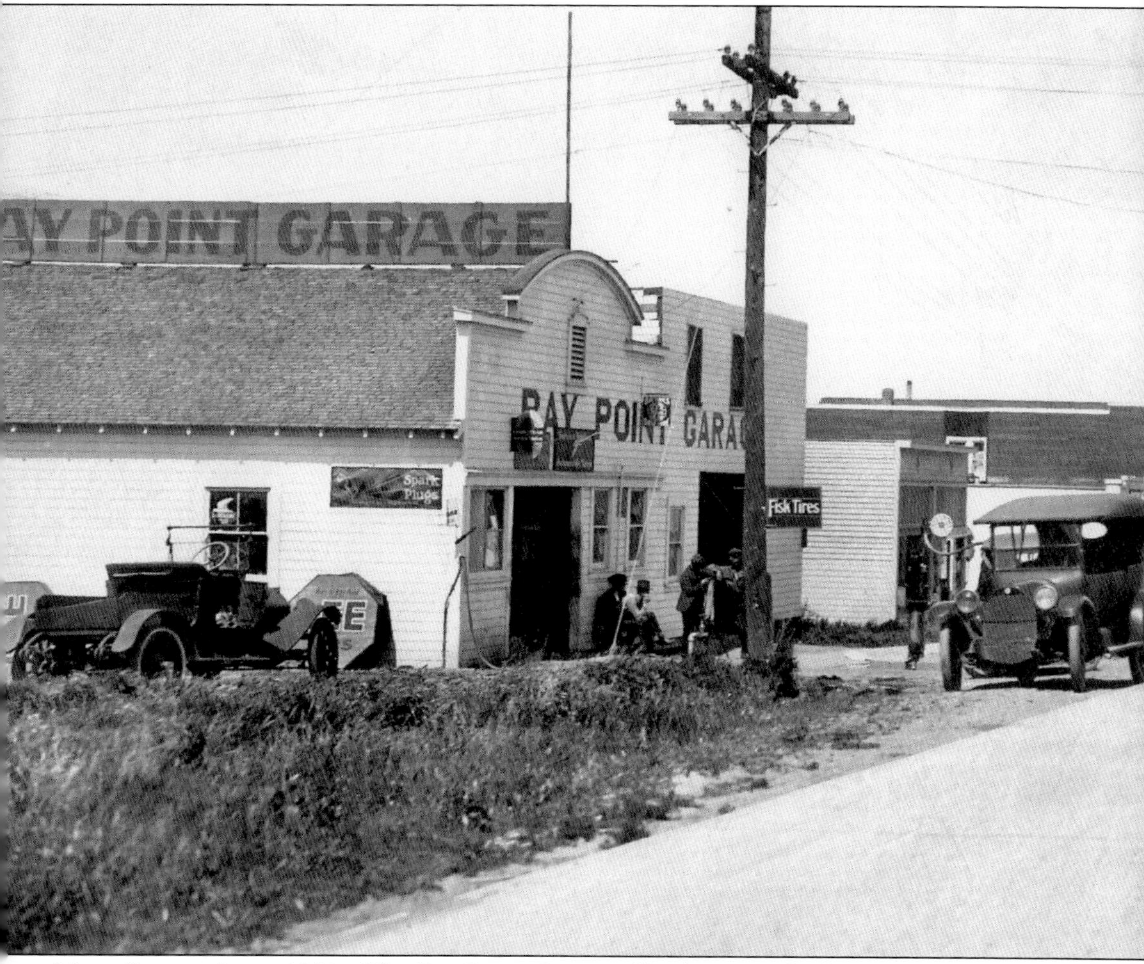

MAIN STREET, LATE 1920S. The Bay Point Garage offered ice, spark plugs, Fiske Tires, and a place to hang out. The newly paved street led to factories and the waterfront.

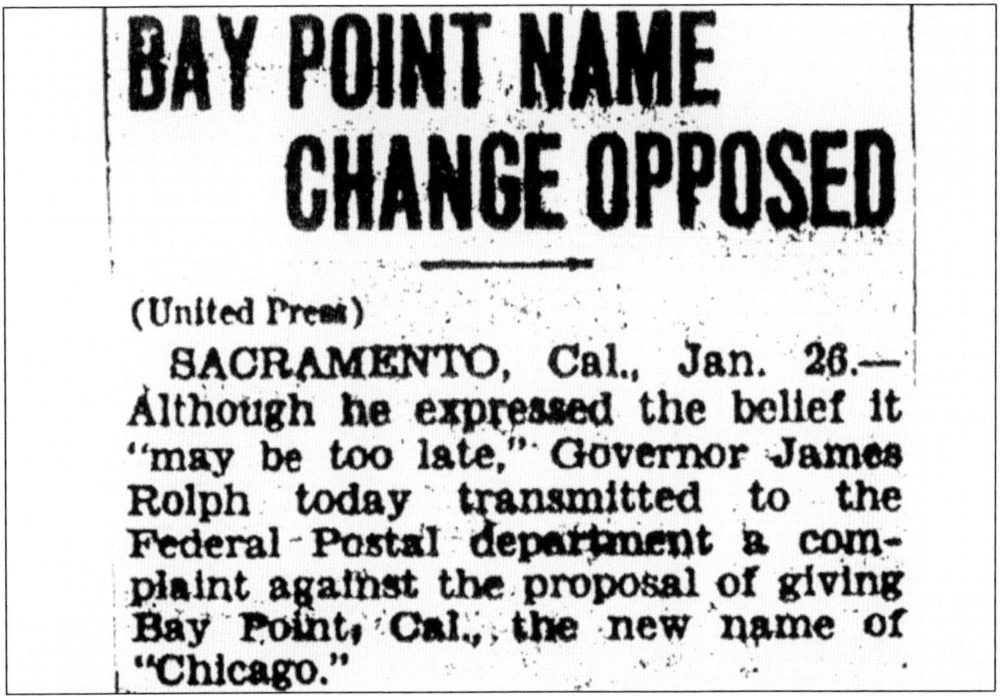

BAY POINT NAME CHANGE OPPOSED

(United Press)

SACRAMENTO, Cal., Jan. 26.—Although he expressed the belief it "may be too late," Governor James Rolph today transmitted to the Federal Postal department a complaint against the proposal of giving Bay Point, Cal., the new name of "Chicago."

BAY POINT OUT, PORT CHICAGO IN, 1931. Suffering mightily from the growing Great Depression, the town was losing jobs at an alarming pace and business was in steep decline. Walter Van Winkle, major property owner and president of the chamber of commerce, spearheaded the drive to enhance the industrial image of the town. The chamber put into place a grand public relations plan to rename the community Chicago. Not everyone in town was eager for the change. The U.S. postmaster disallowed the name, but accepted "Port Chicago."

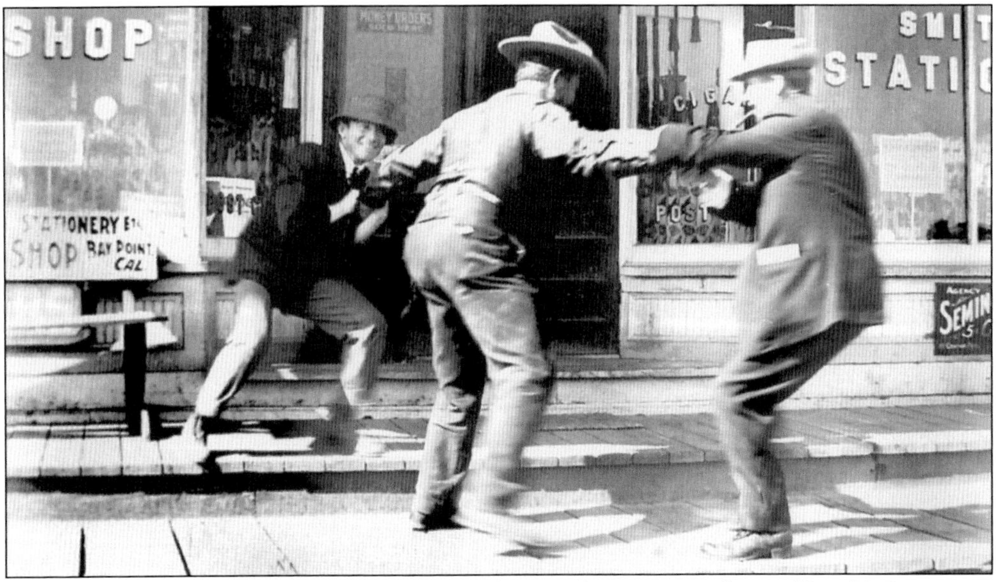

ROUGH-HOUSING IN "GUN POINT." This image shows police action in front of Smith's Stationery Store. The constable breaks up a mock fight on the boardwalk. The combatant on the right keeps a tight grip on his 5¢ Seminole cigar.

Four

Bay Point/ Port Chicago

Matters of Life and Death

The end of shipbuilding at Bay Point after World War I didn't kill the town, but in pre-Depression days of the 1920s and early 1930s enticing industry to Bay Point was a difficult task. The largest Bay Area growth took place in San Francisco, Oakland, Richmond, and Martinez. Bay Point was just a little out of the way of the major industrial growth of the Bay Area.

It was in this environment, when smokestacks meant prosperity, that Walter Van Winkle, president of the Bay Point Chamber of Commerce, conceived and executed a plan to reenergize the town. It was January of 1931, two years after the stock market crash. Although business was off, there was no mention of the Depression in the *Contra Costa Times*. Predictions were that 1931 would be better than the year before.

Van Winkle formed a coalition of business interests intent on initiating "one of the biggest civic programs that has ever been attempted on the Pacific Coast." In elaborate civic meetings, and accompanied by loud proclamations from the *Contra Costa Gazette*, the Bay Point Chamber of Commerce outlined a five-year program of building homes and industry in Bay Point. The prediction was that the town would grow from a population of 1,500 to 5,000 within 3 years.

A major part in revitalization was a clean-up effort that called for an entirely new image for Bay Point. Since industrialization was the goal, F.G. Cox suggested that the town change its name to reflect what it was to become. He suggested the name Chicago, since the Illinois city's industry was world-renowned. Van Winkle and his cohorts undertook a massive marketing effort and on Saturday, March 2, 1931:

> 250 volunteers moved 300 loads of rubbish from city lots and back yards to the municipal dock and dumped them into the bay. Every sign reading "Bay Point" was demolished, re-painted or obliterated. That night a fireworks display lit up a huge "CHICAGO" sign carved out of the hillside against which the town nestles. There was also a free dance that night.

The town sent a petition to the Postmaster General in Washington, D.C., requesting the name be officially changed. The request was refused because a larger city already claimed the name, to the extreme embarrassment of the chamber of commerce. A compromise was worked out to rename the town Port Chicago. Government leaders throughout Contra Costa County lent support to the name change and it stuck.

A year later, the largest employer in town, the Coos Bay Lumber Company, moved out of Bay Point and settled in Oakland. The five-year growth plan became a dead issue as the Depression gradually increased its strangle hold on the nation. Bay Point/Port Chicago, Clyde, and Nichols struggled on.

By 1936, the industries in the area consisted of Edith Fisheries, Bay Point Light and Power Company, California Water Service, Pacific Coast Shipbuilding, and in Nichols, the General Chemical Company. There was also the light rail line for hauling cement the 11 miles between Bay Point and the quarry at Cowell.

As in the rest of the nation, prosperity returned with the outbreak of World War II. In June of 1942, the War Department established what became the Concord Naval Weapons Station. During the early part of the war, Port Chicago's waterfront was the debarkation site for millions of tons of explosives.

The Port Chicago Disaster of July 17, 1944 is now an infamous part of U.S. naval history. Three hundred and thirty two sailors, most of them African Americans, were killed when two fully loaded ammunition ships exploded adjacent to the dock. At the time of the blast Port Chicago had over 650 homes and every one was damaged. Windows were reported blown out from the blast as far away as San Leandro. The "Port Chicago Mutiny" that followed brought national attention to the town, and had a major impact on race relations in the United States military. Among the final bombs shipped from Port Chicago were two atomic bombs delivered to Hiroshima and Nagasaki. After the war (and the reparations), the greatly expanded Naval Weapons Station began a decades-long war of attrition with the town of Port Chicago. Naval expansion plans included the whole town.

Finally, with the coming of the Vietnam War, the Navy acted "to protect the interests of the people of Port Chicago." Between 1966 and 1968, under eminent domain, the federal government bought 5,000 acres as a buffer zone. The following year it condemned the whole town, put up barbed wire fences, and obliterated every home. Nothing is left now but the trees and tracings of the streets of Bay Point/Port Chicago.

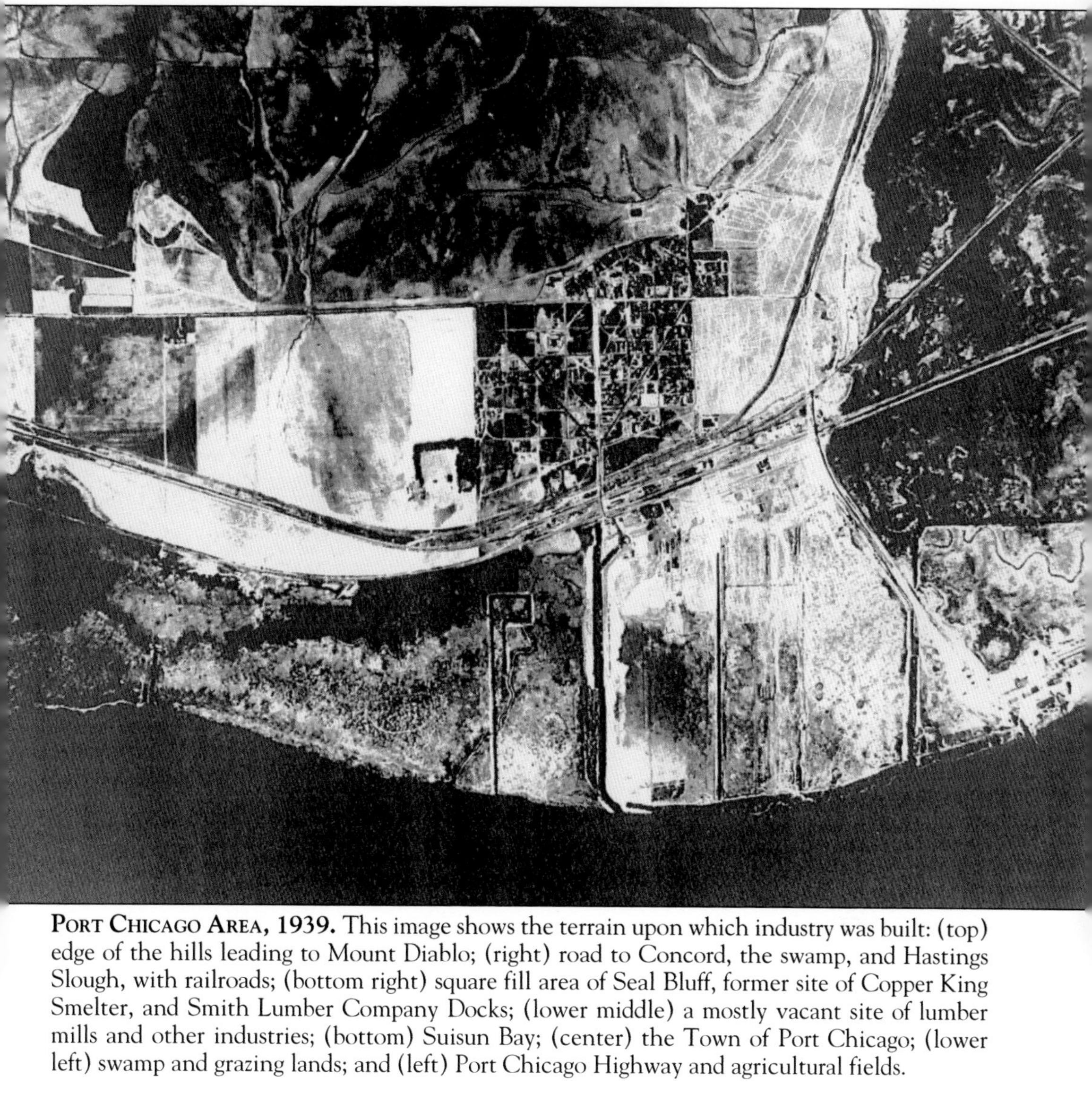

PORT CHICAGO AREA, 1939. This image shows the terrain upon which industry was built: (top) edge of the hills leading to Mount Diablo; (right) road to Concord, the swamp, and Hastings Slough, with railroads; (bottom right) square fill area of Seal Bluff, former site of Copper King Smelter, and Smith Lumber Company Docks; (lower middle) a mostly vacant site of lumber mills and other industries; (bottom) Suisun Bay; (center) the Town of Port Chicago; (lower left) swamp and grazing lands; and (left) Port Chicago Highway and agricultural fields.

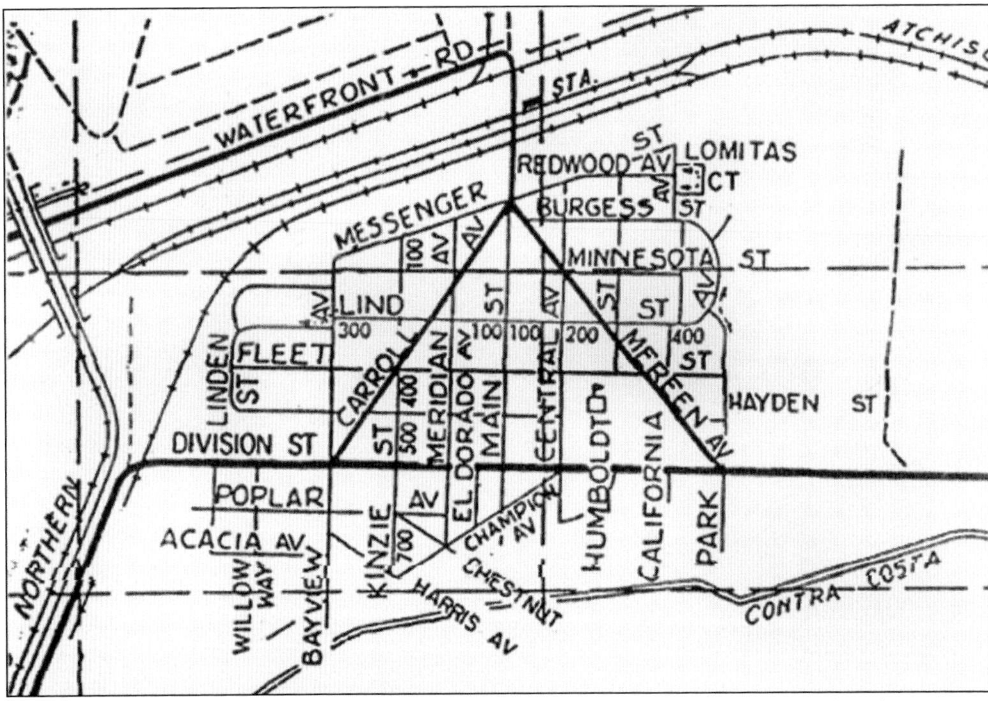

Port Chicago, Facing North. This depicts the town as it was before the mid-20th century.

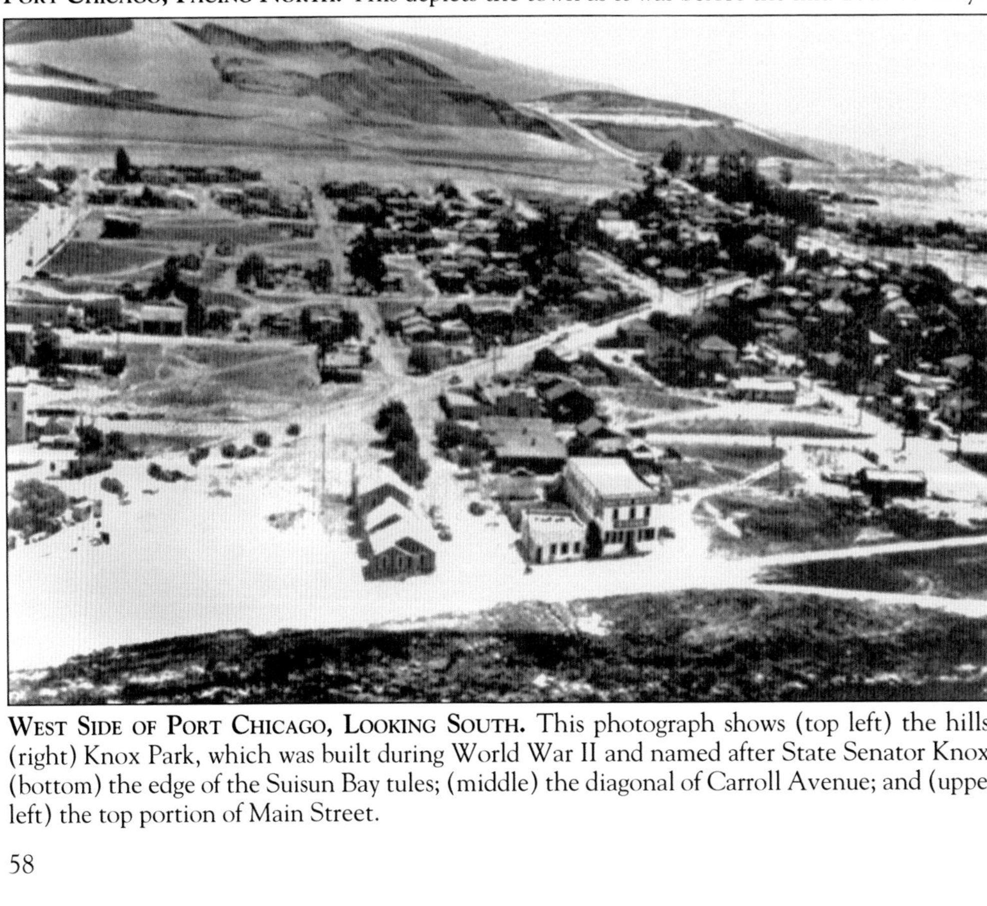

West Side of Port Chicago, Looking South. This photograph shows (top left) the hills; (right) Knox Park, which was built during World War II and named after State Senator Knox; (bottom) the edge of the Suisun Bay tules; (middle) the diagonal of Carroll Avenue; and (upper left) the top portion of Main Street.

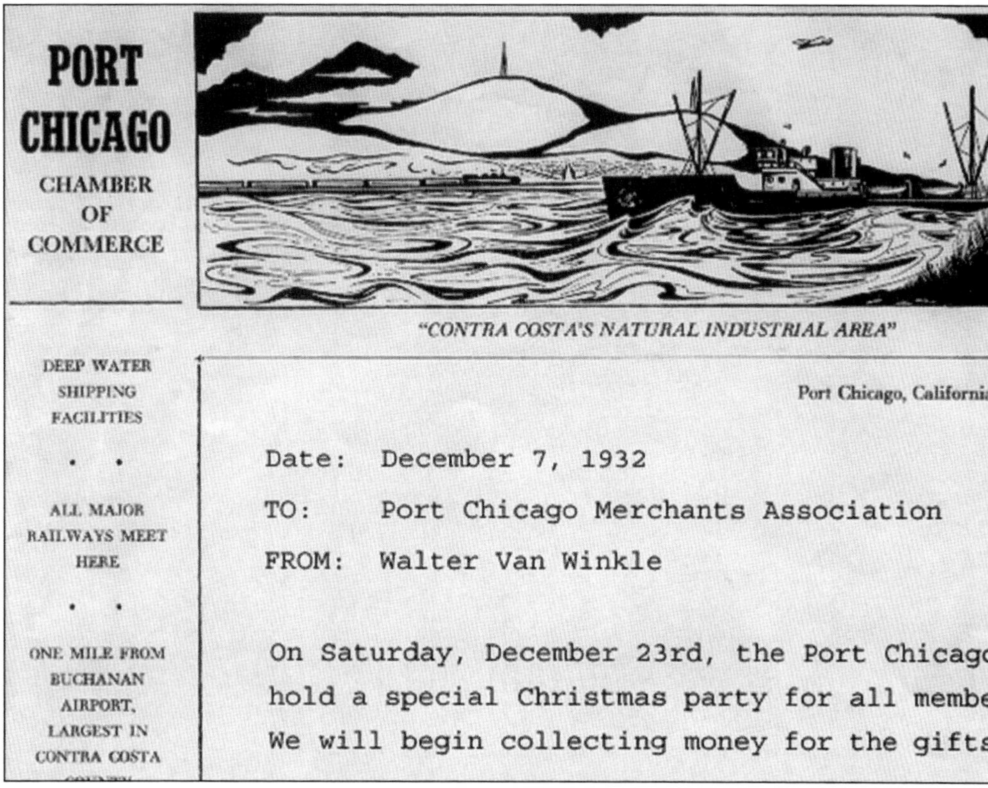

PORT CHICAGO
CHAMBER OF COMMERCE

"CONTRA COSTA'S NATURAL INDUSTRIAL AREA"

DEEP WATER SHIPPING FACILITIES

• •

ALL MAJOR RAILWAYS MEET HERE

• •

ONE MILE FROM BUCHANAN AIRPORT, LARGEST IN CONTRA COSTA

Port Chicago, California

Date: December 7, 1932

TO: Port Chicago Merchants Association

FROM: Walter Van Winkle

On Saturday, December 23rd, the Port Chicago
hold a special Christmas party for all membe
We will begin collecting money for the gifts

PORT CHICAGO CHAMBER OF COMMERCE. A year after the name change, the chamber planned its Christmas party. This was during the lowest part of the Great Depression.

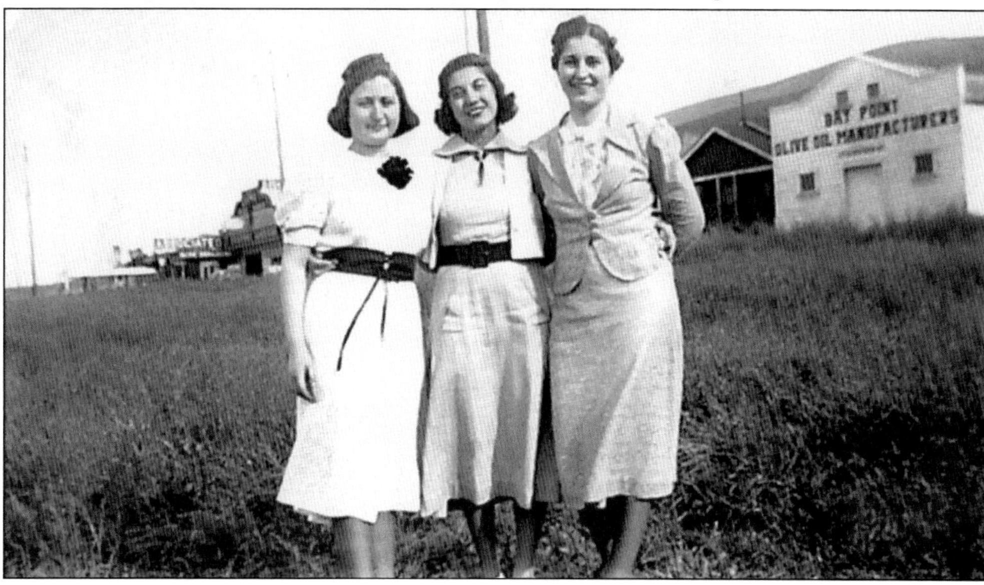

BAY POINT OLIVE OIL MANUFACTURERS, APRIL 24, 1938. Pictured here are three young Port Chicago girls: Zampia, Urania, and Christine. Numerous olive groves prospered in the rural vicinity of Port Chicago, providing a nearby supply for the Bay Point Olive Manufacturers' plant.

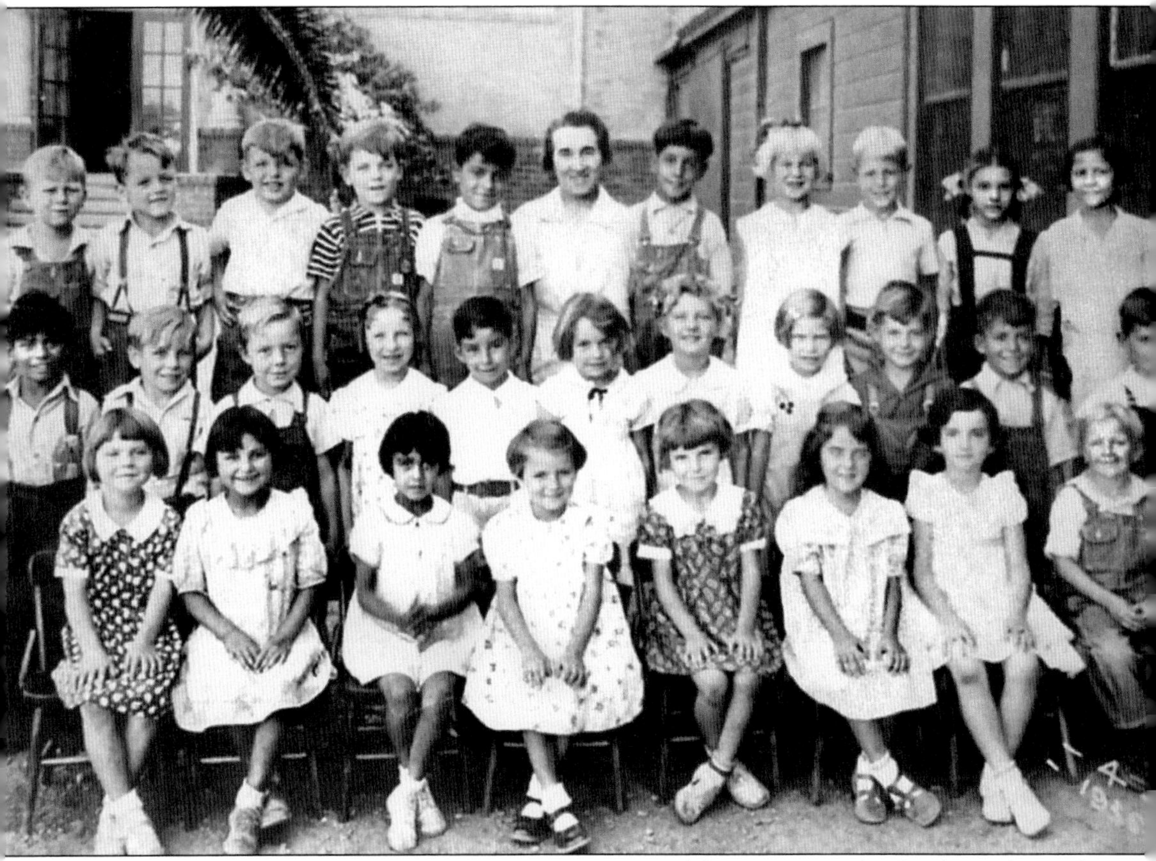

Miss Brennan's Bay Point School Class, 1936. Madeline Brennan, the daughter of an Irish immigrant father and a Swiss/Australian mother, graduated from Riverview High School in Antioch in 1913. She taught at the Bay Point School from 1917 to 1957. Of the hundreds of Bay Point/Port Chicago children she influenced, 29 well-dressed and well-scrubbed students are pictured here, all with smiles.

CONTRA COSTA COUNTY FREE LIBRARY. The Port Chicago Branch on Carroll Avenue and Fleet Street proved the adage "If you build it, they will come." Notice the 14 x 14 ft. dimensions.

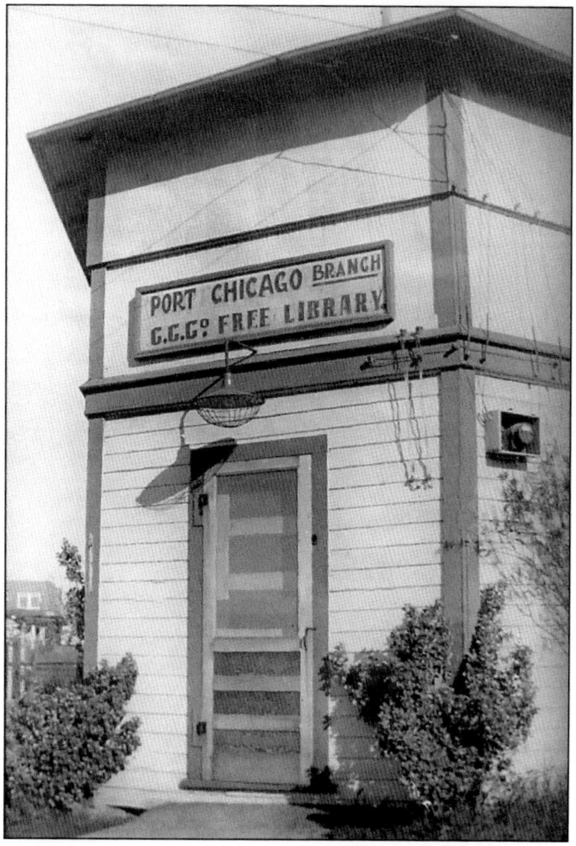

THE LOCAL NEWS RAG. The town had its own news and advertiser, the *Bay Point Breeze*. Obviously named euphemistically for the regular high winds in the area, it later became the *Sun of Contra Costa County*, providing information of local events and gossip.

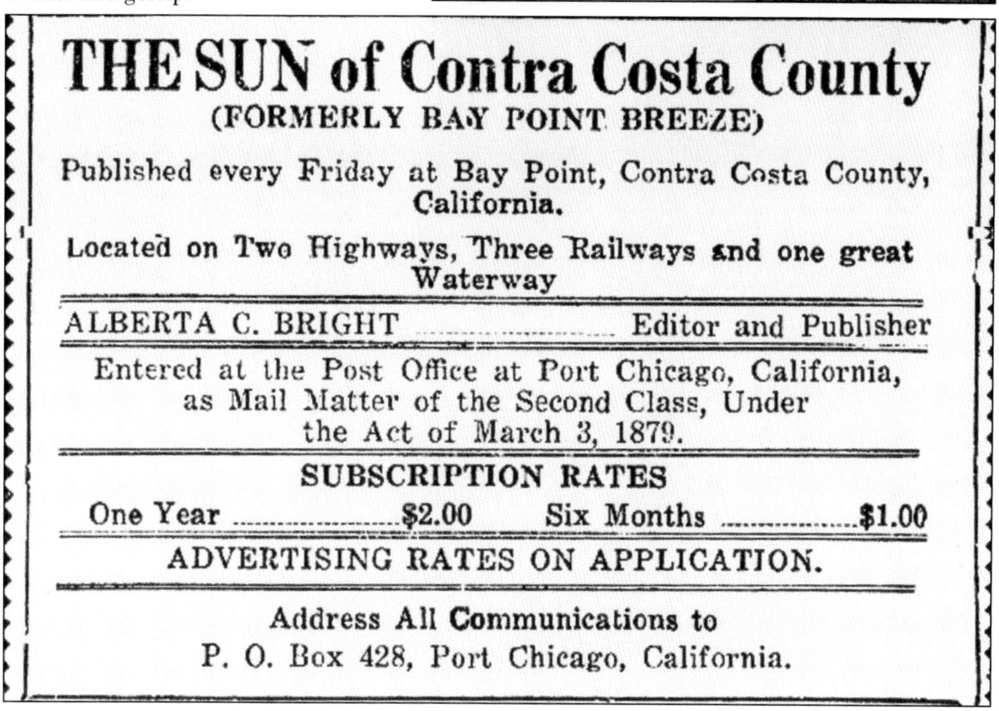

THE SUN of Contra Costa County

(FORMERLY BAY POINT BREEZE)

Published every Friday at Bay Point, Contra Costa County, California.

Located on Two Highways, Three Railways and one great Waterway

ALBERTA C. BRIGHT .... Editor and Publisher

Entered at the Post Office at Port Chicago, California, as Mail Matter of the Second Class, Under the Act of March 3, 1879.

SUBSCRIPTION RATES

One Year ....$2.00 Six Months $1.00

ADVERTISING RATES ON APPLICATION.

Address All Communications to

P. O. Box 428, Port Chicago, California.

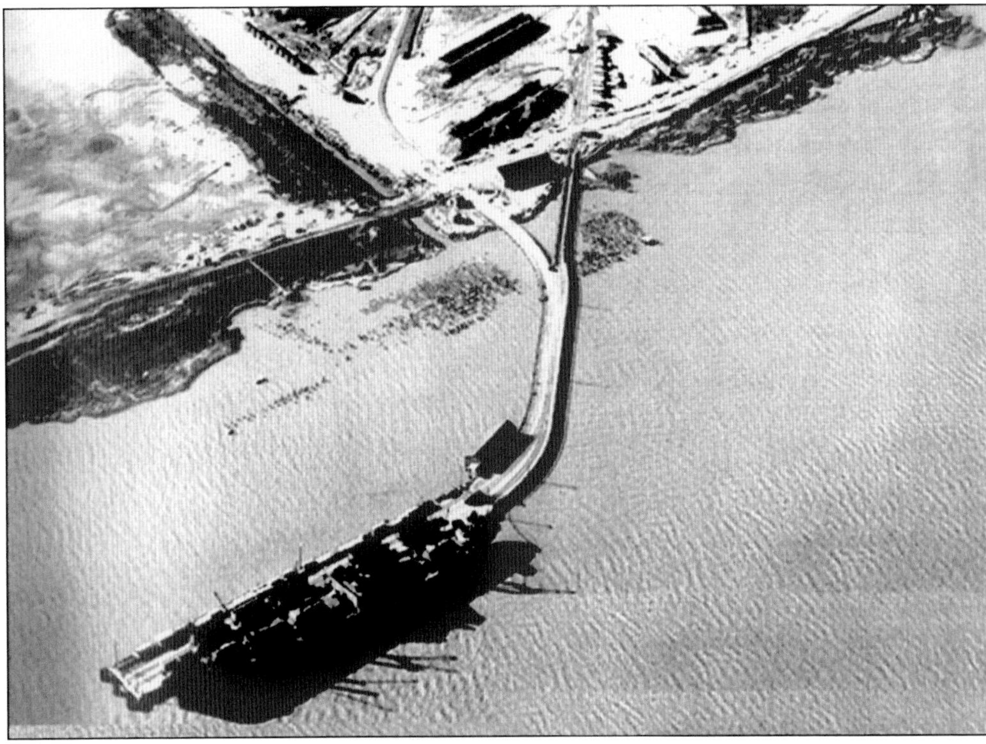

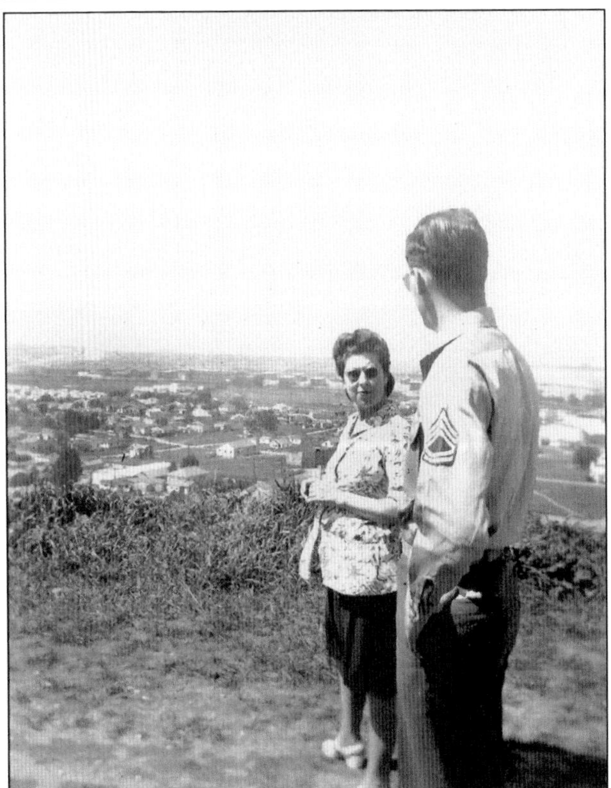

THE NAVY DOCK AT PORT CHICAGO. Situated on Suisun Bay, a half mile north of the town of Port Chicago, the navy docks shipped a large share of munitions to the Pacific Theater during the 1940s. In the upper right-hand corner is the vacant land once part of the Bay Point Yacht Harbor, taken by eminent domain from P.M. Ballomo.

VIEWING A PROSPEROUS FUTURE IN PORT CHICAGO. World War II brought families from around the world, seeking opportunity. Harlan Bailey Sr. and his pregnant wife, Josephine Grossi Bailey, imagine their future in the town.

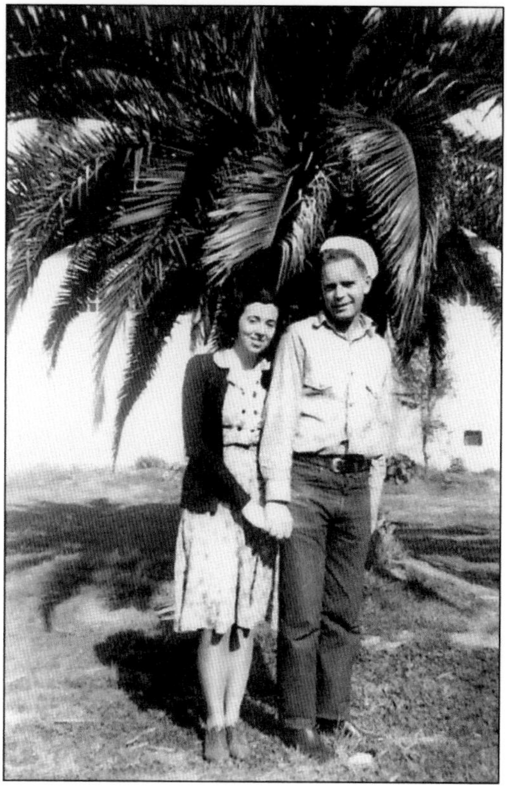

A Loving Couple Dreams of War's End. A majority of the 322 sailors and stevedores killed at the docks on July 17, 1944 were African Americans. Yet, many whites were also killed, including Jim Barn (pictured) of Port Chicago.

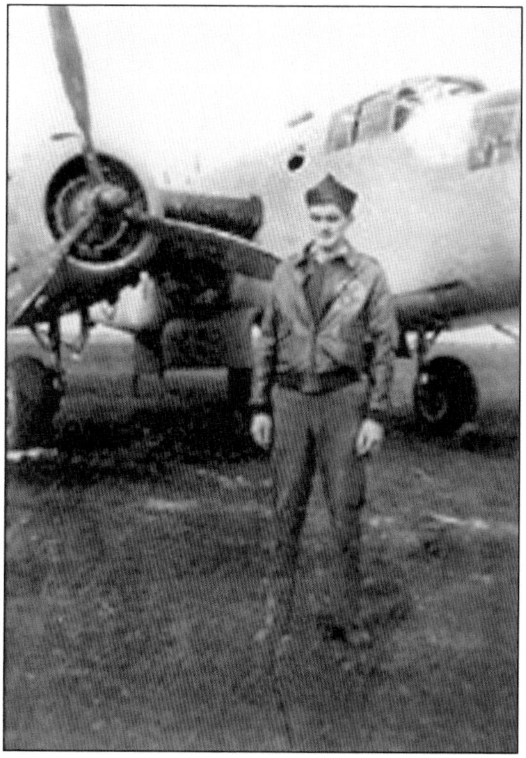

Passion for Flying B-25s. The journey was long for H.P. Bailey as it took him from Cisco, Texas; to North Africa; Italy; Hamilton Field; French Hospital in San Francisco; and finally to Port Chicago.

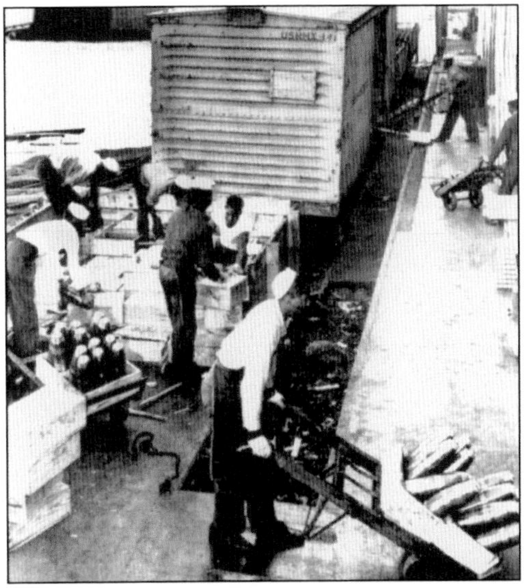

LOADING AMMUNITION FROM RAILCARS. Of the millions of tons of munitions that passed through Port Chicago, most got through safely. Protecting the loaders with gloves and aprons, the military felt pressure to demand breakneck work flows.

UNIDENTIFIED CIVILIAN VICTIM OF EXPLOSION. Within hours, many of the county emergency resources responded for the dead, dying, and injured. Here, late-night first aid is administered to a Port Chicago resident hit by flying debris.

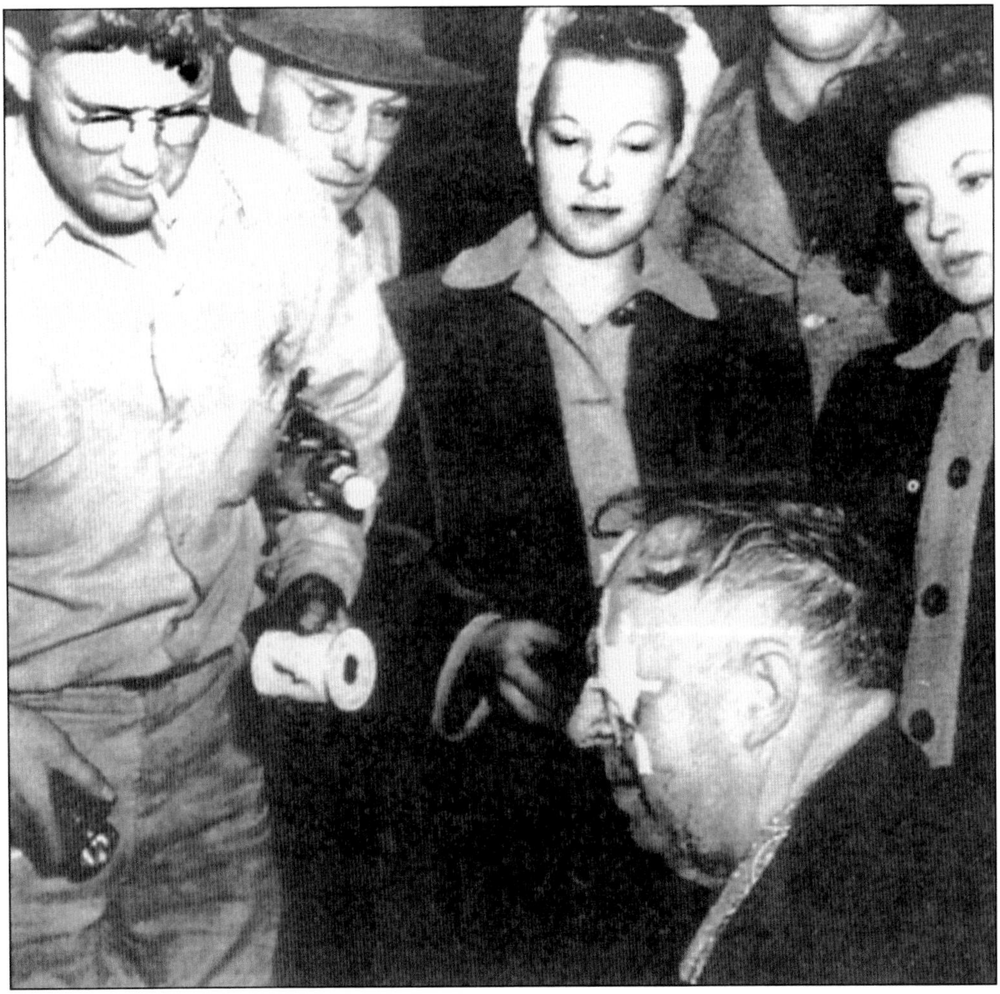

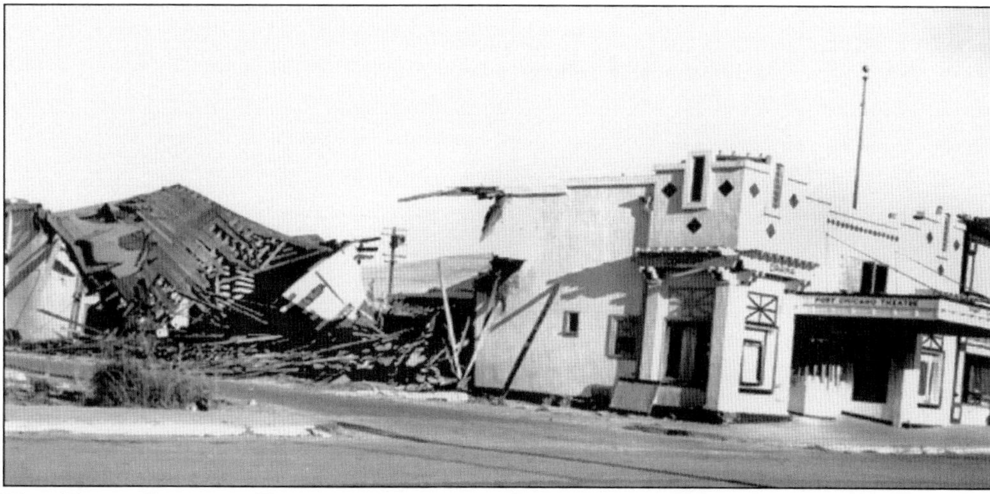

THE PORT CHICAGO THEATER AFTER THE EXPLOSION. Despite the theater being full of moviegoers at the time of the explosion, no one was killed. However, many injuries were treated.

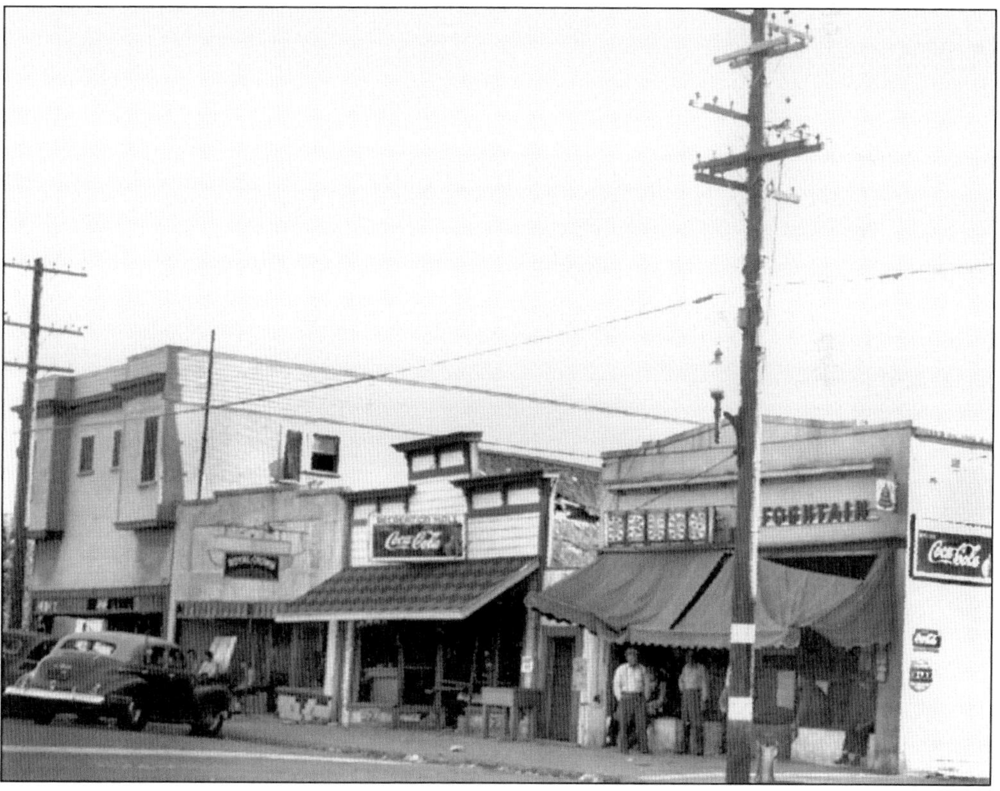

THE MORNING AFTER. Random damage on Main Street is visible from the explosion as Lichti's Drug on the right lost its awning and the recreation hall next door had a big hole in its roof. Outside of the dockyards damage was also scattered. The Navy received 10,000 claims for shockwave damage from points as distant as Vacaville, Petaluma, San Mateo, Brentwood, and Rio Vista.

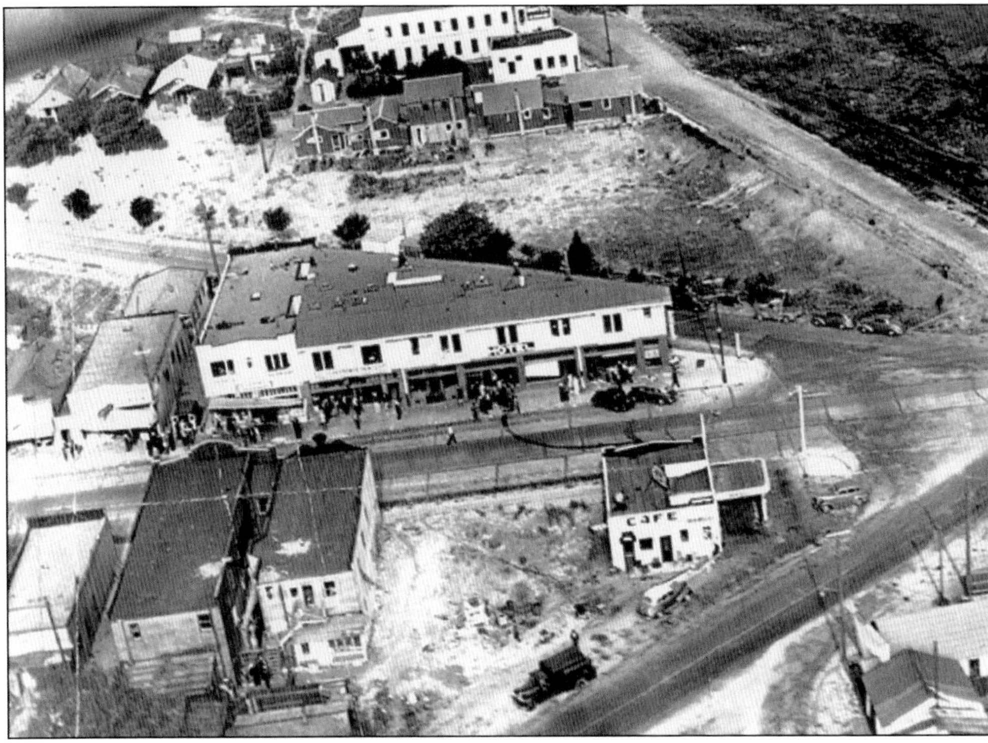

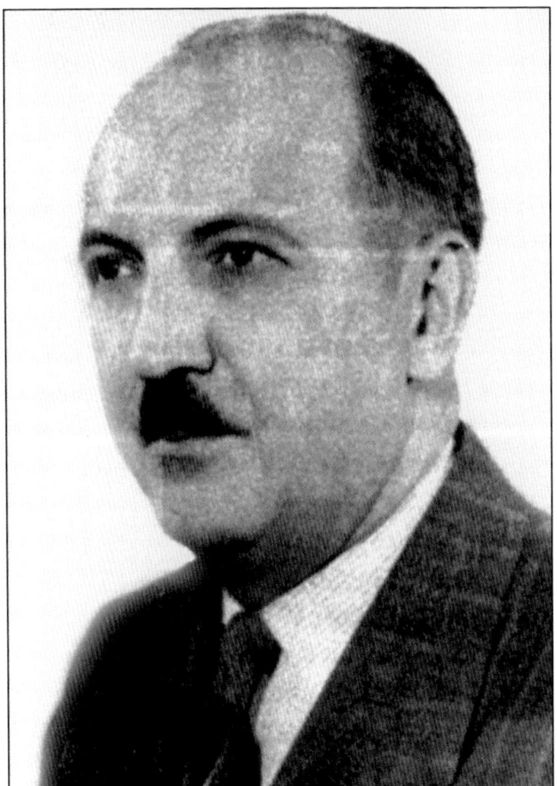

ANOTHER VIEW OF MAIN STREET DAMAGE. Here, the immediate damage is inspected with a focus on the hotel, the café, and two shops in the left center of the photograph.

JUDGE OTTO LICHTI, LEADING LIGHT OF THE COMMUNITY. Appointed justice of the peace on September 1, 1938, Judge Lichti served the community for many years. In his first case, he suspended the sentence of Arnold Kane for dining and dashing at the Peterson Pool Hall. Kane was required to report every two weeks on good behavior. Lichti's court had jurisdiction over misdemeanors with maximum penalties of $500 fines and 6 months in the county jail. Felony convictions in those years, handled by Superior Court, resulted in sentencing to San Quentin or execution.

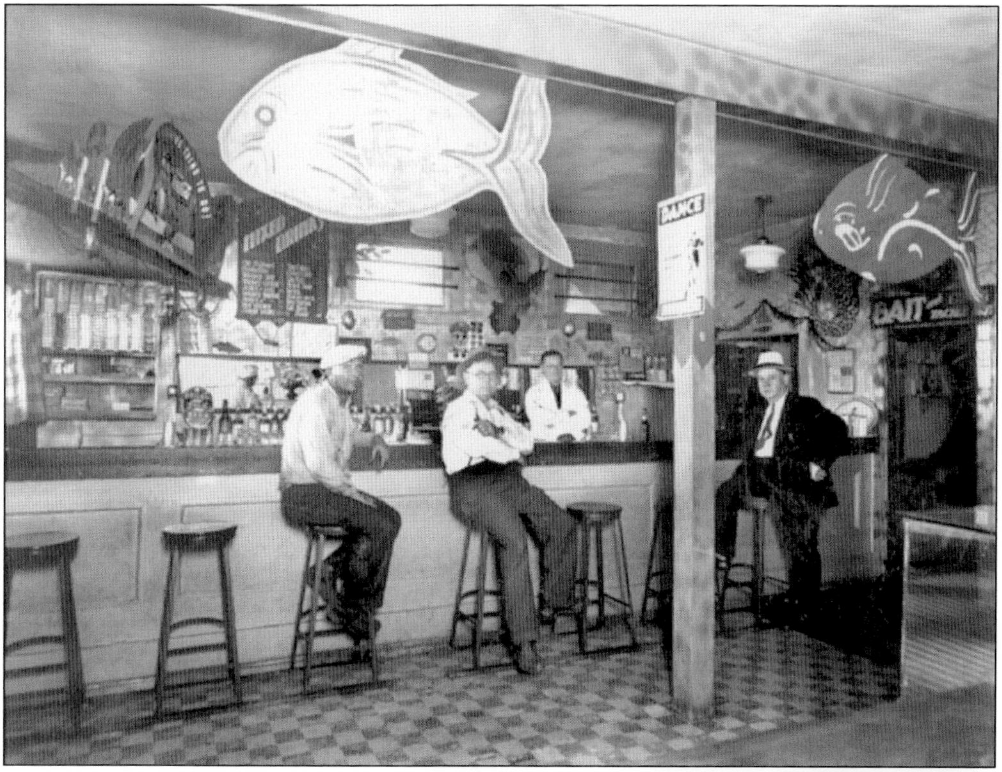

Scene of the Crime. Peterson's Pool Hall was the local source for bait, cigarettes, mixed drinks, and Saturday night dancing. According to a local informant, "None of the rough reputation Port Chicago had throughout the county was ever witnessed here!" Pictured are some of the local hard guys. Depression-era kids hung out here during the day and played pool.

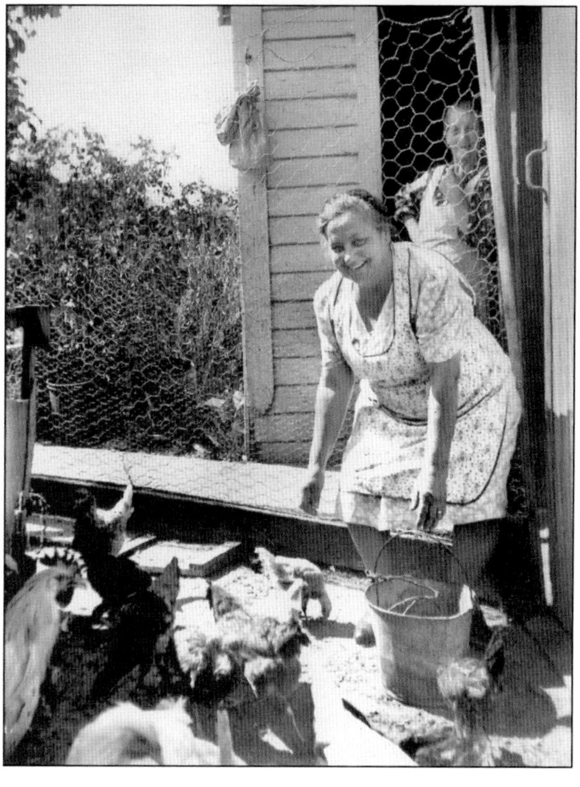

Domestic Tranquility at the Chicken Coop. Guilia Grossi is caught here in a graceful pose with the chickens at her home in Port Chicago (Lucia Montenegro inside). She was locally famous for her old-country method of making capons. The method is best shared orally.

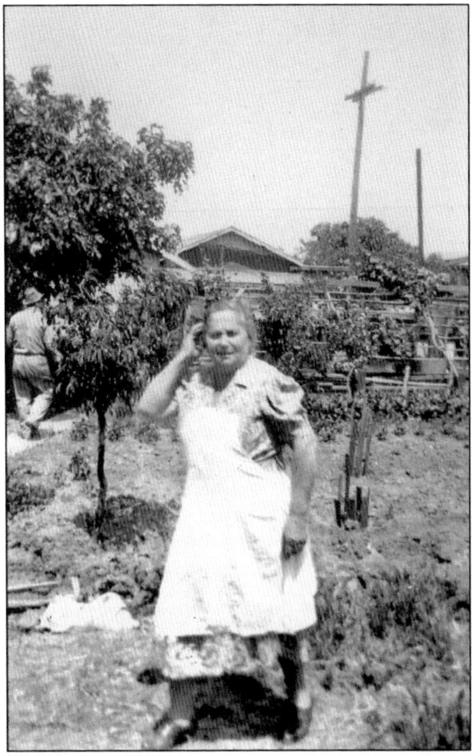

Primping for the Camera. Guilia Grossi protests candid photos during a 1950s working day. Most families in Port Chicago had their Victory Gardens. Not only did the homegrown food supplement income, but the harvests also prompted sharing and trading with neighbors, family, and friends.

Port Chicago Lions. This group picture was taken sometime mid-century. The Lions Club was one of the service organizations long associated with the town. Along with the chamber of commerce, the American Legion, Boy Scouts, and others, these organizations fostered community activity on many levels. The club hosted a 1933 New Year's dinner and dance at the Clyde Inn for Lions Clubs from all over the East Bay. They planned for about 300 to attend.

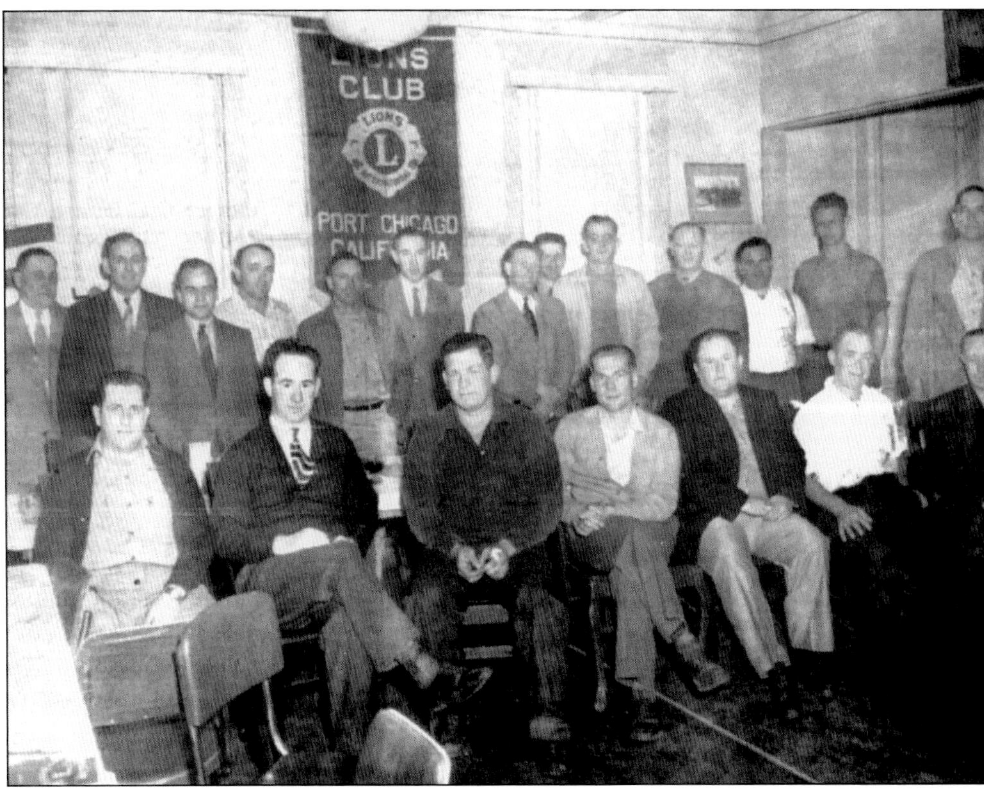

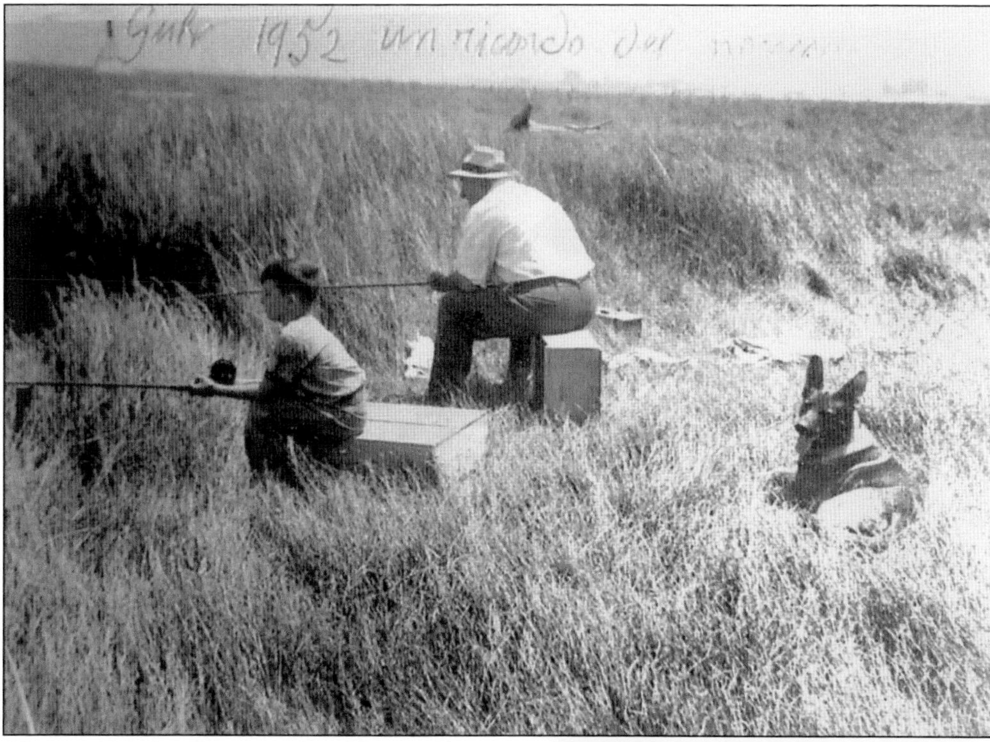

"Guli 1952, Un Ricordo Del Nono" This is an example of summer slough fishing near General Chemical. Domenico Grossi, his grandson, Harlan Bailey, and Fritz spend quality time doing what kids and grandpas did in 1952. Domenico, a "contodino" in San Giovanni, Italy, found a different life fueling the California post-war automobile boom.

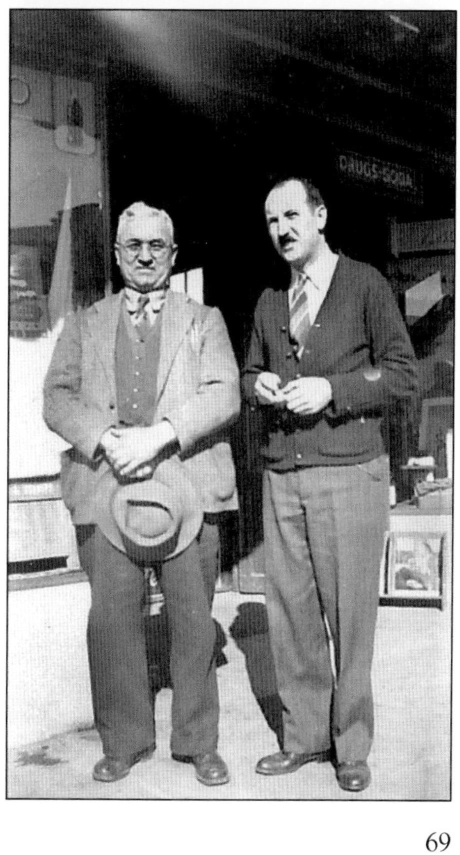

Meeting of the Minds. Judge Otto Lichti (right) conducts informal court outside of his pharmacy.

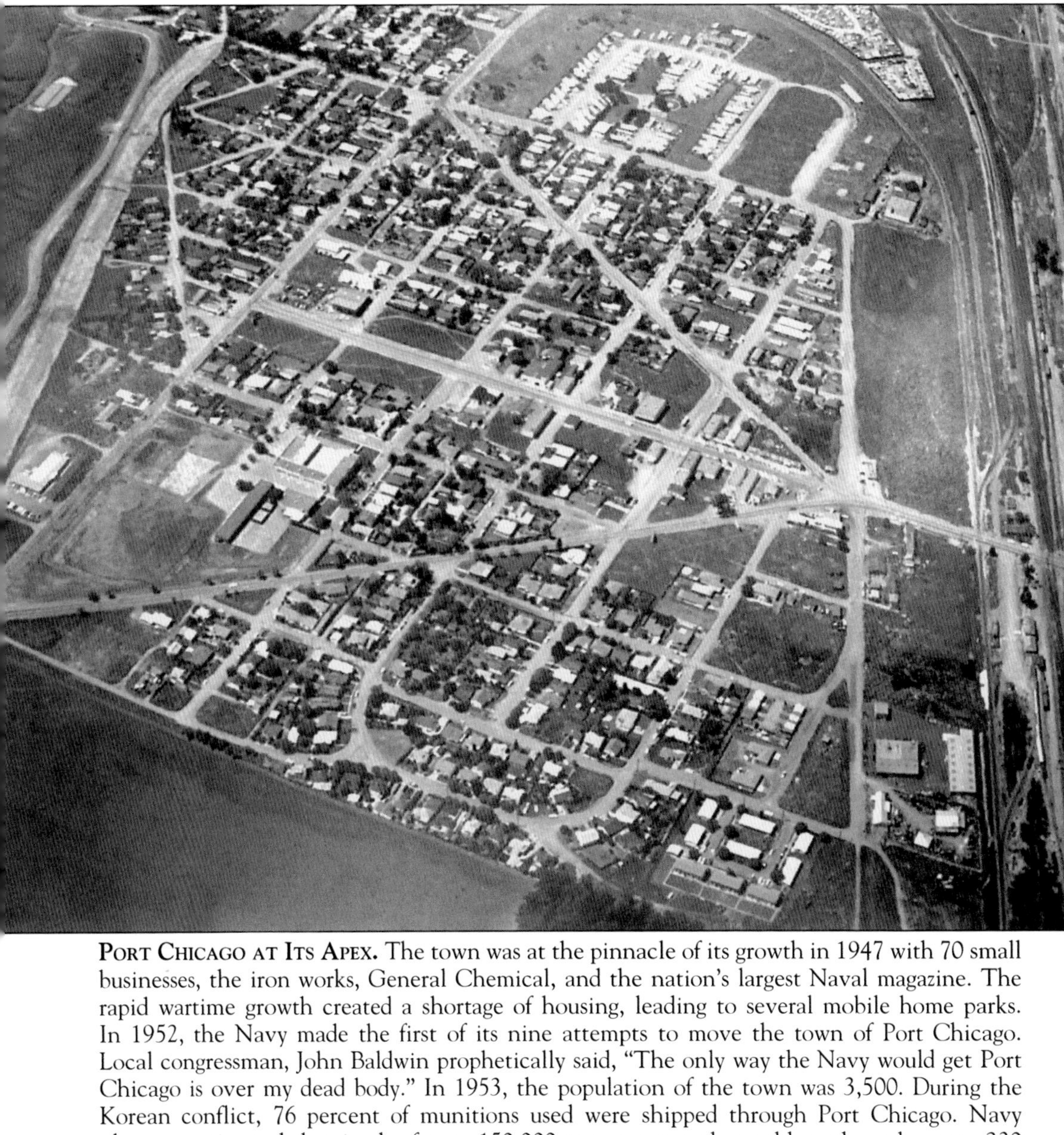

Port Chicago at Its Apex. The town was at the pinnacle of its growth in 1947 with 70 small businesses, the iron works, General Chemical, and the nation's largest Naval magazine. The rapid wartime growth created a shortage of housing, leading to several mobile home parks. In 1952, the Navy made the first of its nine attempts to move the town of Port Chicago. Local congressman, John Baldwin prophetically said, "The only way the Navy would get Port Chicago is over my dead body." In 1953, the population of the town was 3,500. During the Korean conflict, 76 percent of munitions used were shipped through Port Chicago. Navy planners estimated that in the future 150,000 tons per month would go through town, 230 percent more than during World War II. That year, the same Navy planners reported that Port Chicago, Nichols, and Clyde had "remained static with little or no economic change, increase in population or structural improvement." They were "considered in the low income group." The following year Navy planners wrote: "The imminent possibility of industrial development is predicted to 'greatly enhance land values,' hence acquisition should be expedited 'to control future development and limit density of population.' "

RADICALS PROTEST NAVY TAKEOVER. Eunice Van Winkle, widow of one of the leading lights, supports Judge Lichti in a town protest. Moments later, Eunice took the bullhorn in hand. Sixth graders from Bay Point Elementary sang "God Bless America."

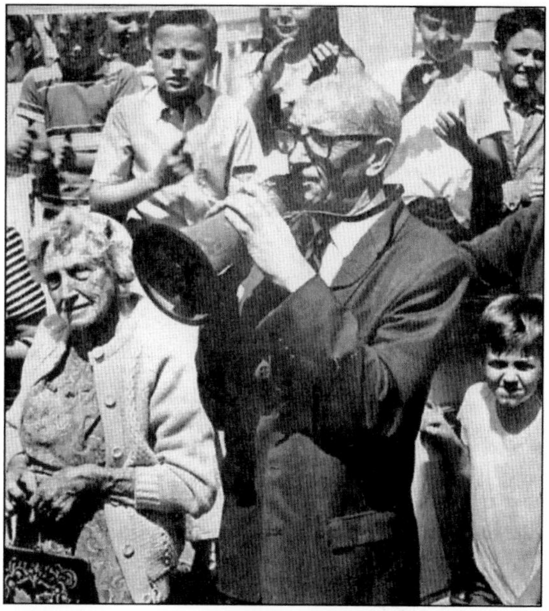

"BATTLE OF PORT CHICAGO" ENDS. After a 15-year regional and national public relations effort, combined with the hammer of Eminent Domain, the U.S. Navy was successful in getting congressional budget approval to purchase additional land "on the Sacramento River, 45 miles from San Francisco." The *Wall Street Journal* reported Port Chicago's defeat three days before the assassination of Martin Luther King.

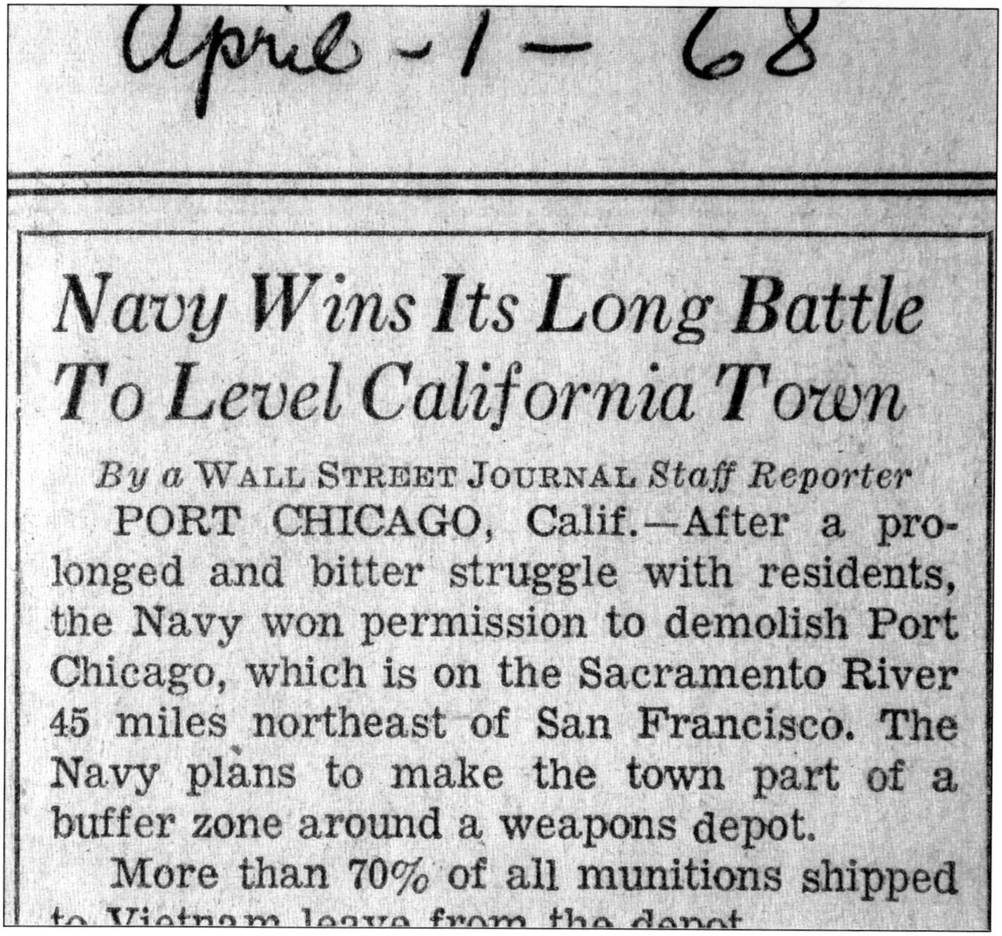

April-1-68

Navy Wins Its Long Battle To Level California Town

By a WALL STREET JOURNAL *Staff Reporter*

PORT CHICAGO, Calif.—After a prolonged and bitter struggle with residents, the Navy won permission to demolish Port Chicago, which is on the Sacramento River 45 miles northeast of San Francisco. The Navy plans to make the town part of a buffer zone around a weapons depot.

More than 70% of all munitions shipped to Vietnam leave from the depot.

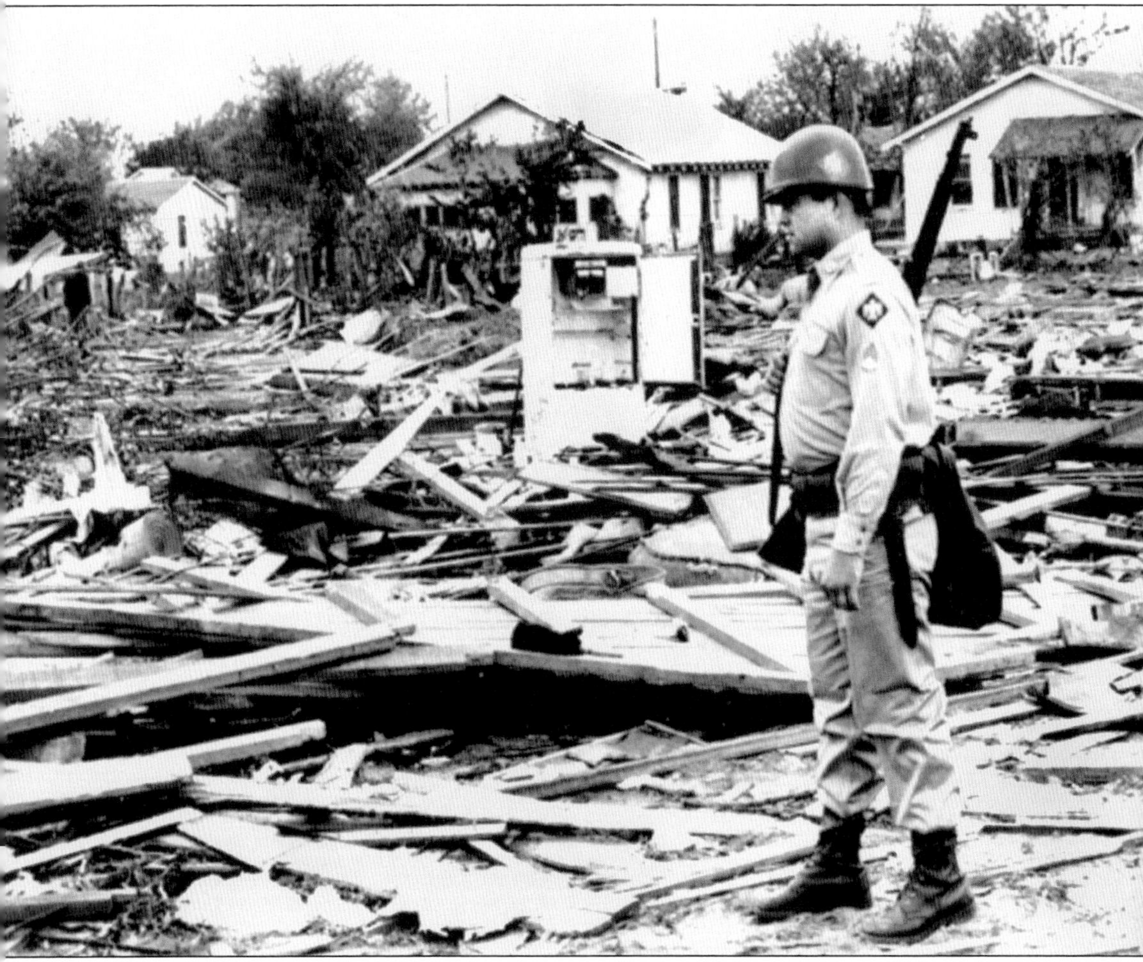

DOING WHAT IT DOES BEST. Military guards protect debris from Port Chicago homes just demolished by Navy contractors. Most residents accepted the distressed market prices offered by the Navy and walked away with what cash they could. Some moved their homes to other nearby locations outside the two-mile buffer zone in unincorporated West Pittsburg. A few of the more prosperous business owners engaged in lawsuits in an attempt to recoup their losses. Terry Bidelman, a World War II Navy veteran, barricaded himself in his home and was the last civilian resident to leave in November 1969.

Five

In the Country Livestock to Chemistry

So what to do with the rural east side of township Two North, Range One West? The better farm and ranch land areas were spared the early urbanization and heavy industry that came to the town of Bay Point/Port Chicago. Three distinct waves of settlers ranched and farmed in the early Bay Point School District. The first group, mentioned in chapter 1, was made up of gold rush–era refugees from around the United States. Many became discouraged because they couldn't get clear title to their Bay Point lands. A few, like the Wights, stayed on.

The second wave arrived after 1870. When the railroad returned the lands to the public domain in 1870, there was an influx of Irish families. Of those who came, at least three have descendants in the area to this day.

Henry O'Hara was born in Ireland about 1802. He and his wife Nancy came to the area, settling in Section 14 near Charles Pramberg. The O'Hara family eventually occupied several ranches and farms in the area, and fifth generation descendents still live here.

The Tormey family has roots in the county beginning in the 1860s. John Tormey's branch settled in the 1880s near what became Nichols, and has descendents in modern Bay Point.

James Kennerly, perhaps of British military beginnings, left England for Australia first, and then settled in 1866 in Sections 10 and 15. He was a very successful stock raiser and blacksmith. His family was a strong influence in the community for several generations, providing teachers to the community. His descendants still live in Bay Point.

In the last couple of decades of the 19th century, there was a third influx of settlers into the ranching areas of the township. Portuguese families began to find their way to the farm and grazing lands of the Bay Point School District. They included the Evoras and the Enes.

John Enes came to American from the Azores on a whaling ship about 1857. He fought in the Civil War and eventually settled in Contra Costa County, farming in the San Pablo area. He and his wife, Emma Vargas, had 13 children. They settled here in 1884 on a ranch in the hilly area whose streets still bear the family names. They bought the ranch, raised prize horses, and grew household crops. John later bought another farm in northern Concord on Grant Street.

His son, Antone, acquired flat land to the east, in what is now the geographic center of Bay Point. Antone Enes became the first housing developer in modern Bay Point.

Francisco Evora came to California in 1860 and was a potato farmer in Half Moon Bay. After four years he returned to the Azores. Three of his sons came to this county right after 1900. They worked at farms around the county for nearly 20 years before one of the sons, Manuel, was able to buy the hilly ranch of John Enes. Much of their ranch was developed into housing in the 1980s, but some of the acreage is still home to descendents. Part of the Portuguese impact in Bay Point is reflected in street names. Other Portuguese who came early were the Dutras, the Noias, and the Farias.

PIONEER PORTUGUESE. John Enes was born in the Azores, spent his early years on a whaling ship, and came to America in 1857. After the Civil War, he met Filomena Vargas in the San Pablo area of Contra Costa County. "Mena" is said to have sailed to Panama as a young child with her two sisters, ridden a donkey across the Isthmus, and sailed up to San Francisco. The couple bought a farm in the hills near the Willow Pass road between Concord and Black Diamond in 1884.

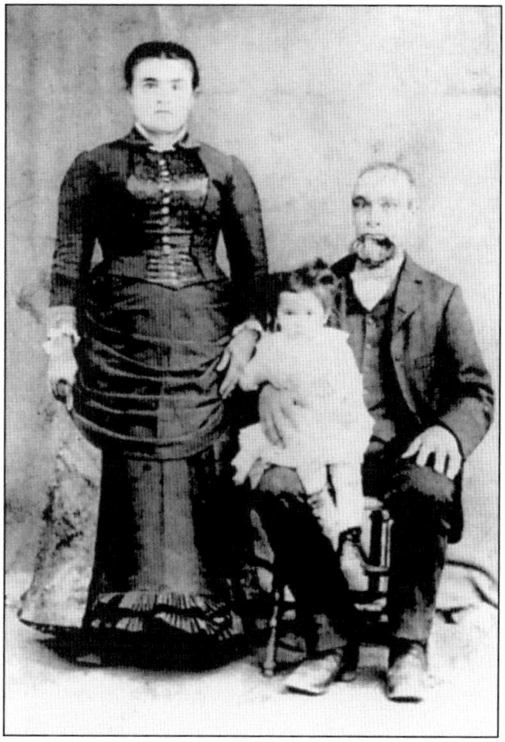

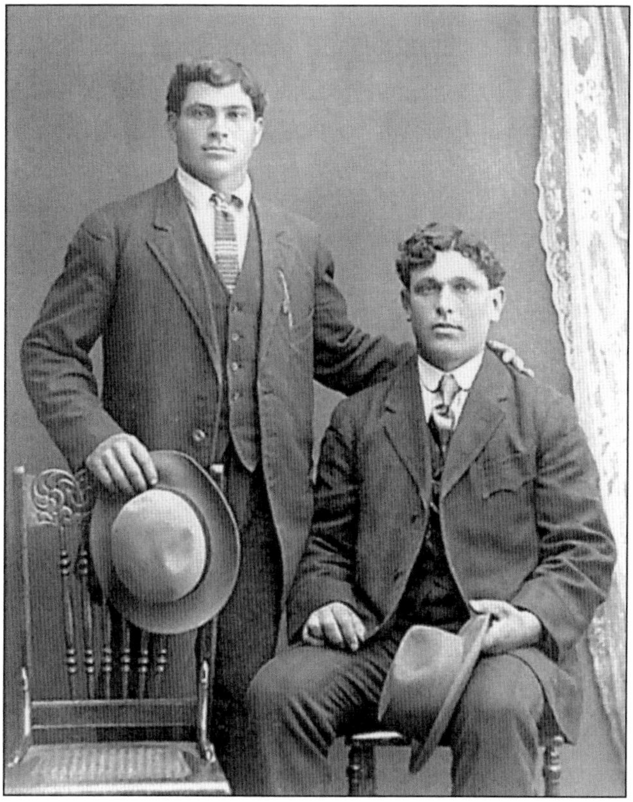

SECOND-GENERATION PORTUGUESE. Manuel and Francisco Evora came to California about 1860. After trying to farm in Half Moon Bay, he returned to the Azores. Three of his sons, Frank, Manuel, and Joseph came to the Bay Area soon after the turn of the 20th Century. In 1921, Manuel bought the Enes ranch on the Willow Pass and passed it to his daughters Clara and Ida.

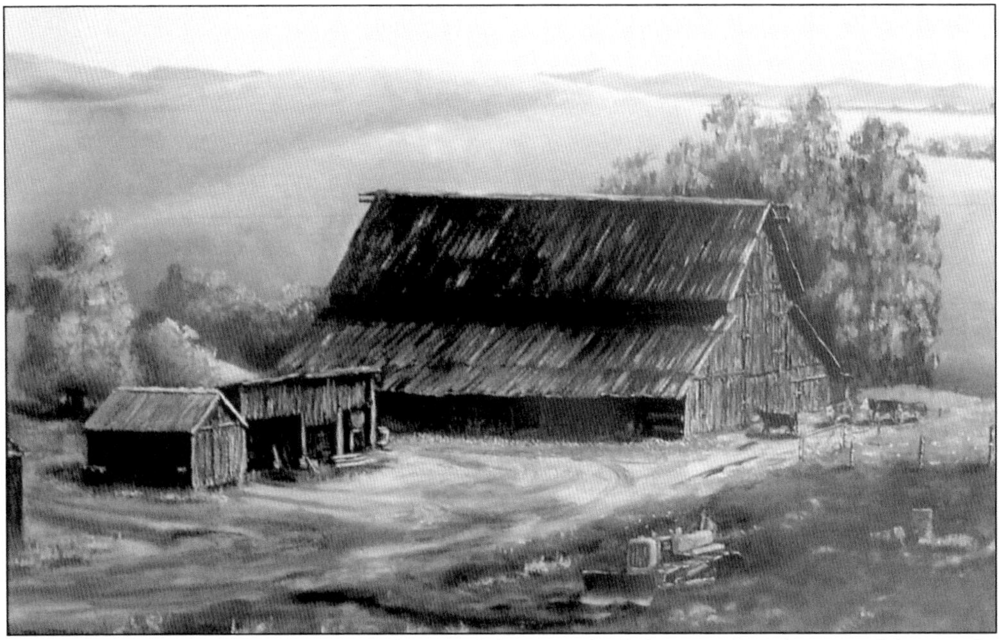

THE MOTA RANCH. This artist's rendition of the 1884 built barn and outhouses of the ranch, shows Suisun Bay and Solano County in the background. Clara Mota and Ida Enes sold most of the ranch in the 1980s to developer Kaufmann and Broad, now KB Homes. The hill in the foreground was removed, creating a flat where some 400 homes now sit overlooking the bay. A small parcel on Mota Drive is still in the family.

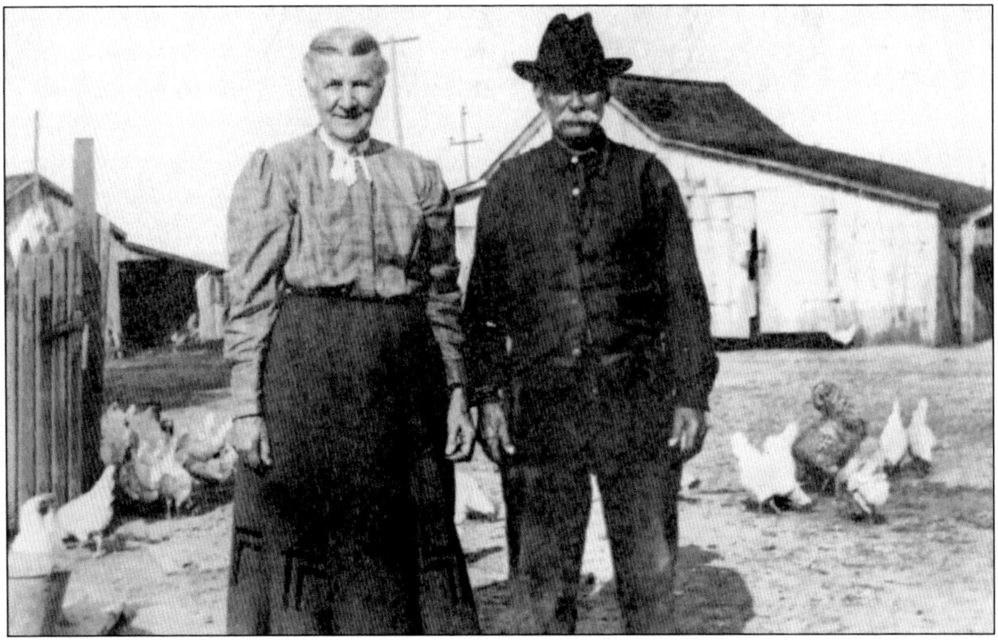

SECOND-GENERATION IRISH-ENGLISH. Frank and Alvina (Krumland) Kennerly pose outside the barnyard. Frank was born 1874 on the ranch on Willow Pass Road. Alvina was born 1878 in Byron. They lived their whole adult lives on two ranches on Bailey Road and Willow Pass Road.

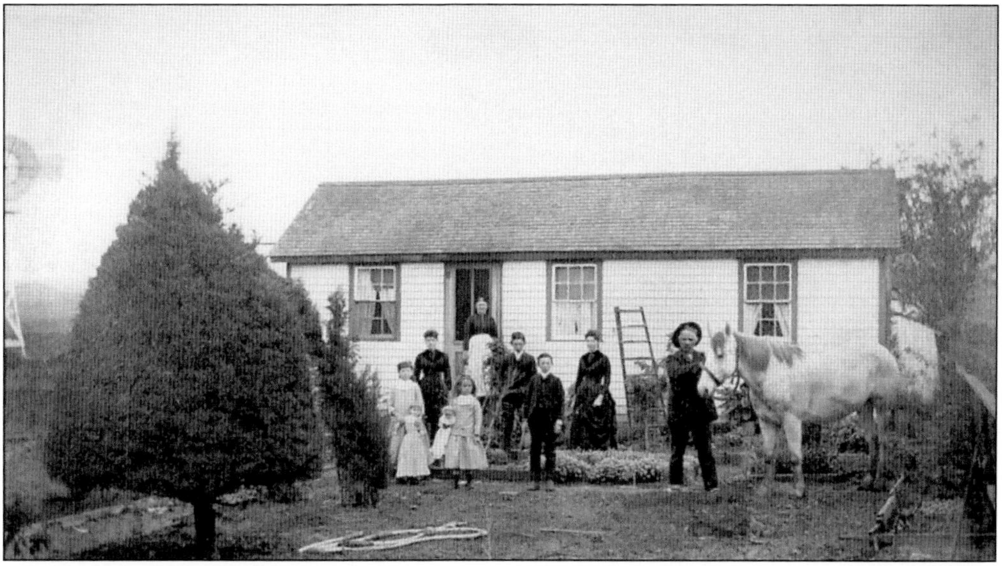

SECOND-GENERATION RANCHERS. The Frank Kennerly family is shown here at home on Willow Pass Road, c.1923. Shown here, from left to right, are Dohrs Elizabeth (with standing doll), Geraldine, Ella May, Alvina (on porch), Raymond, Alvin, unknown, and Frank (with horse). Most of the land between Pittsburg and Concord was still ranch land, except for Nichols and the town of Bay Point.

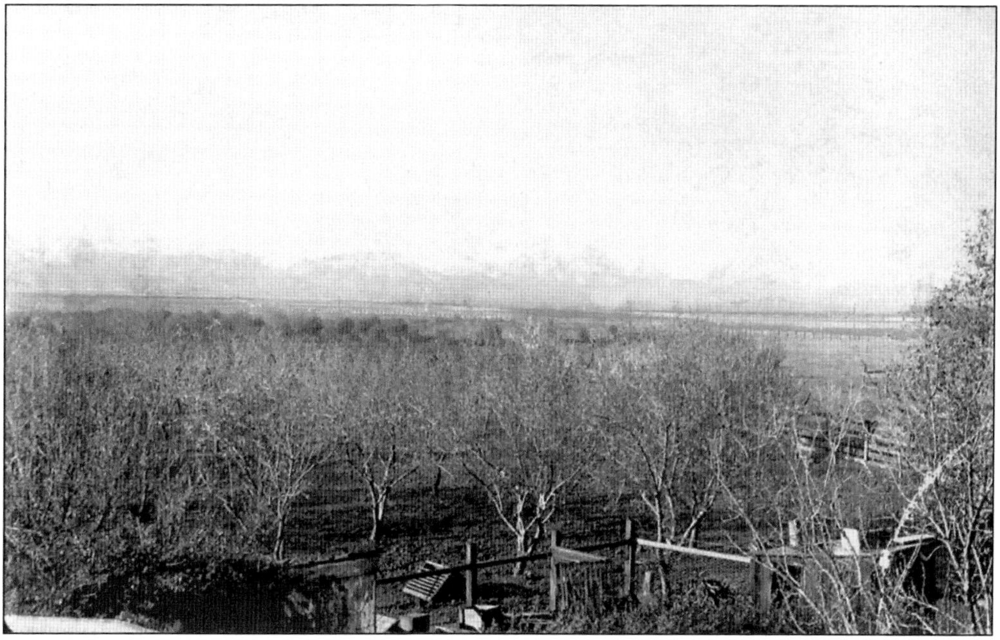

ORCHARDS AND SNOWY HILLS, 1896. This image shows the Kennerly ranch on Willow Pass Road.

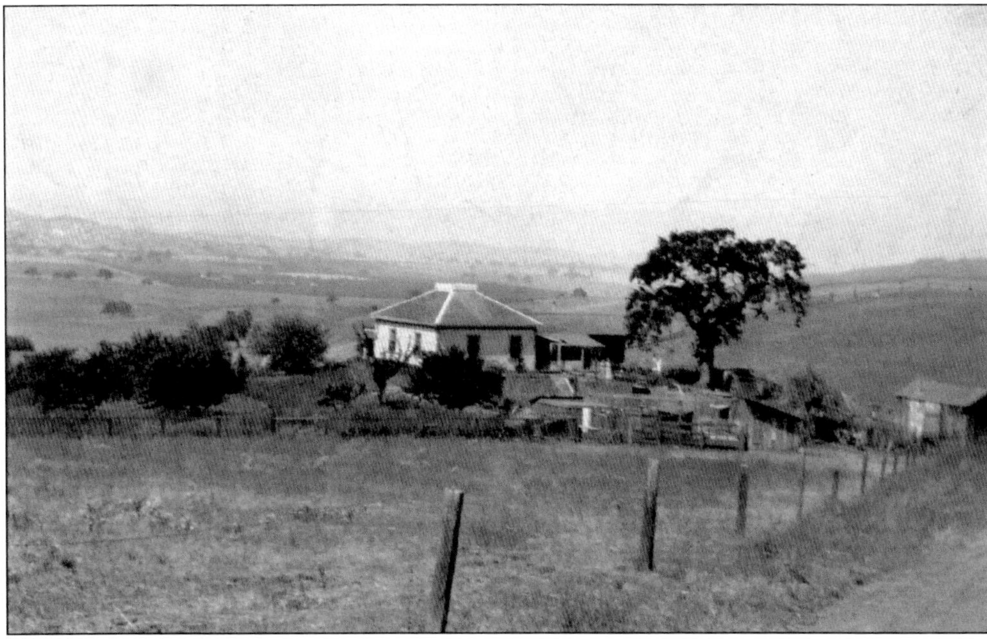

Bailey Road, Looking toward Rural Concord. This photograph is of the Frank Kennerly family home and the valley view looking west.

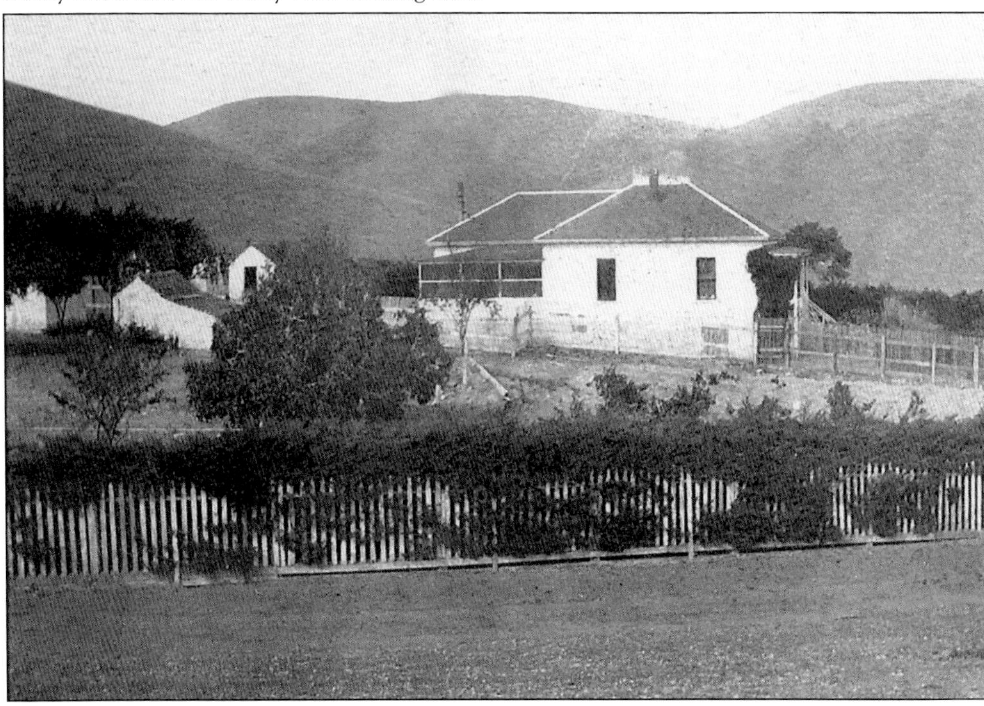

John Tormey Farming Bay Point. This image depicts the farmhouse and outbuildings built in the 1890s. The Tormeys originated in Westmeath County, Ireland, and came to Contra Costa County after the railroad was built. John married Frances (Fanny) Murray, who was related through marriage to the Cunninghams, large landowners in what became the town of Bay Point.

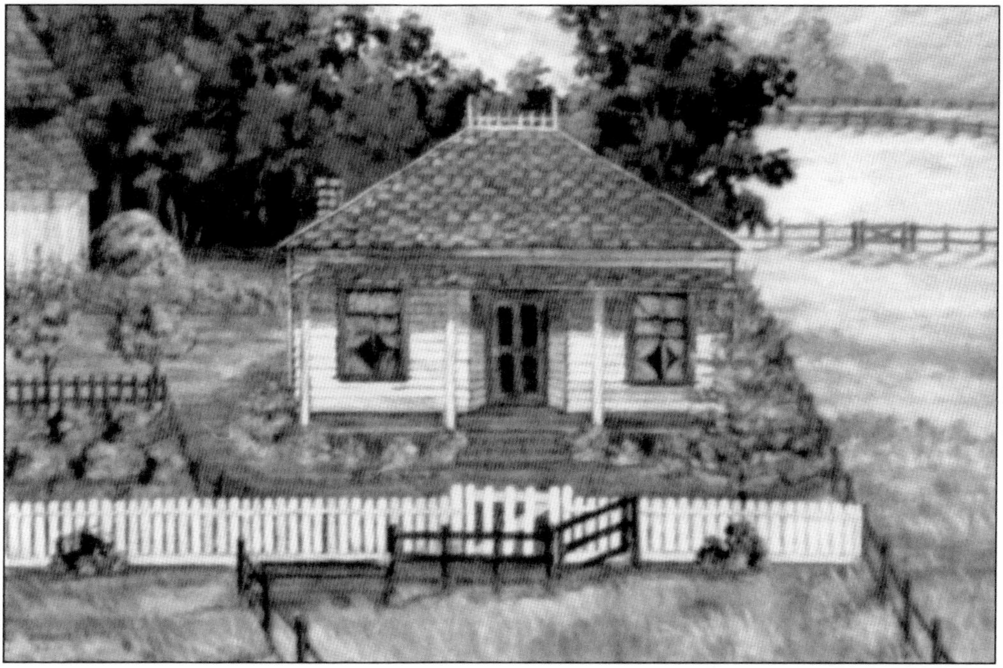

"Nothing But Good Things." This painting shows a front view of the Tormey house on Nichols Road, backed up to Nichols Creek. John Tormey died in 1908, but the family continued to live there until 1918 when the widow Fanny died.

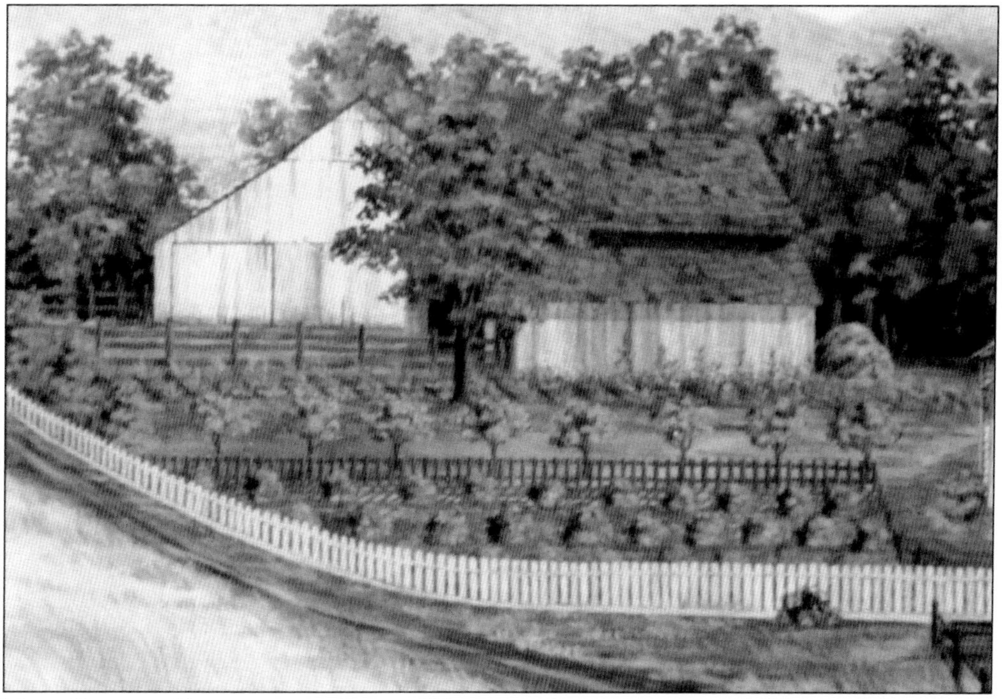

Neat Garden, Vineyard, and Barns. This is an idealized painting of the rear of the Tormey farm, painted *c.* 1906. After Fanny died, her orphaned niece then went to live with her cousin Loretta Vlach in Martinez and eventually settled in the Modesto area.

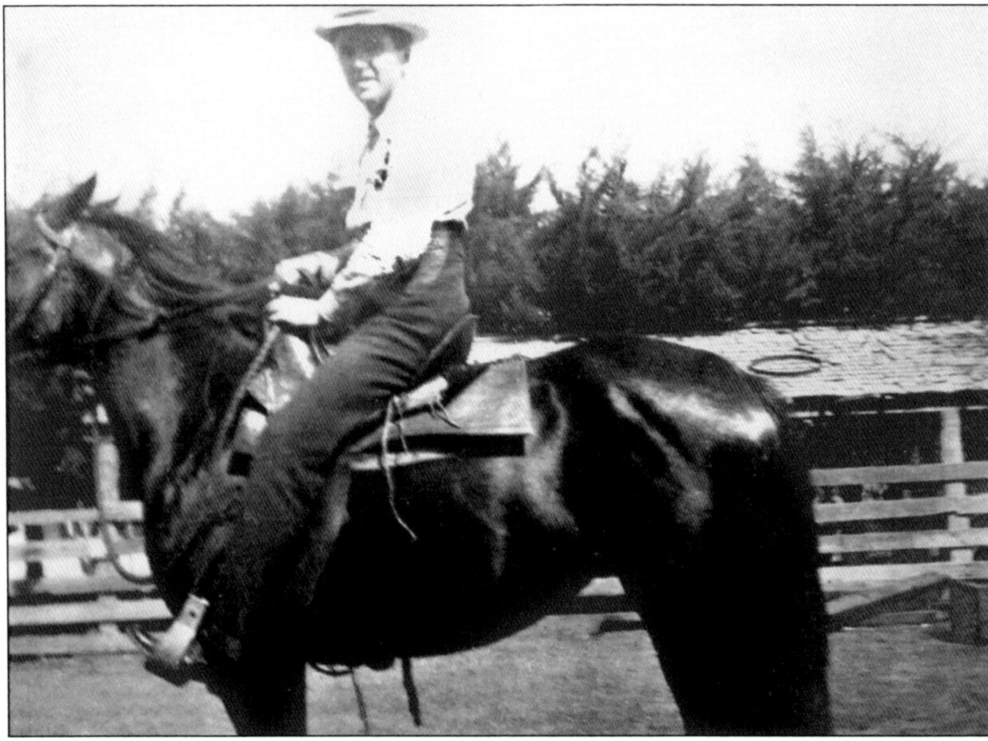

The Best Transportation Money Could Buy, 1906. Morgan O'Brien keeps a tight rein on the pride of the ranch at the John Tormey farm on Nichols Road, where he visited his relatives. The mount's ears signal mild displeasure posing for the camera.

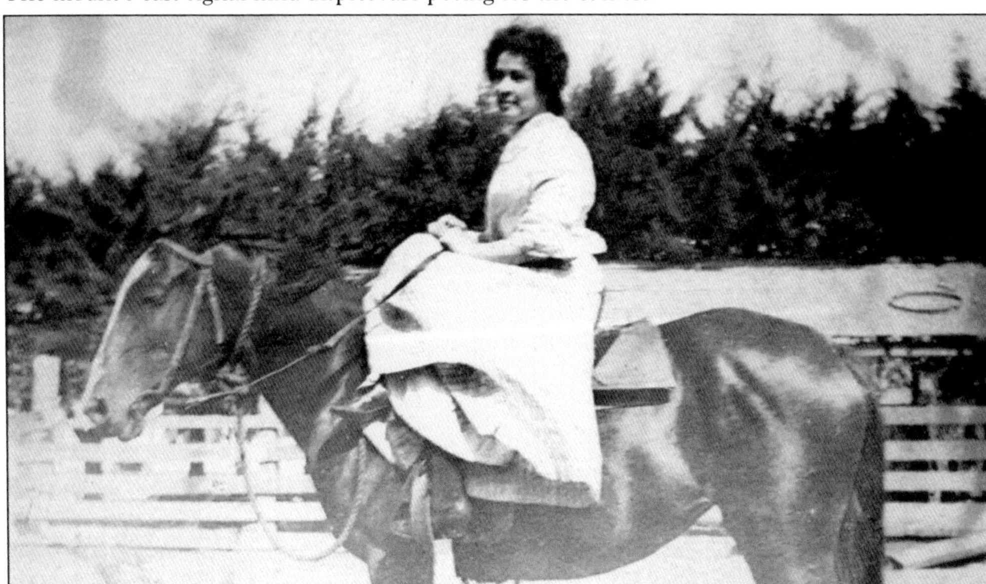

Mary Tormey at the Ranch. The extended Tormey family often met for holidays at the Thomas Tormey ranch on Nichols Creek. Here, his sister Mary poses on the family mount. The early deaths of Thomas and his wife left a niece and nephew, who were already orphaned, in a bereft condition. "Hellcat" Mary raised one of them.

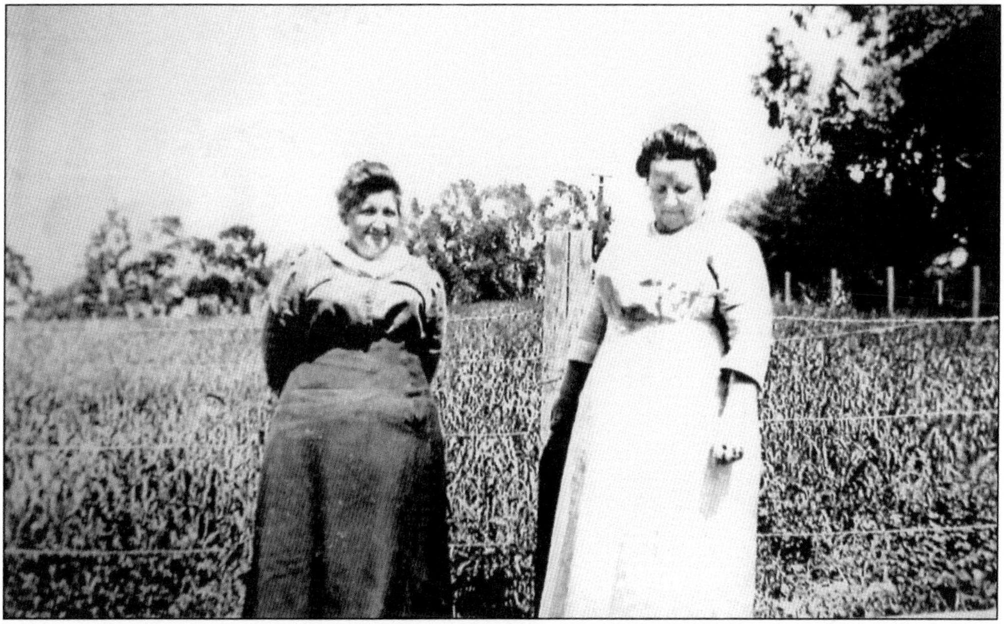

FAMILY GETTING TOGETHER. Fanny Tormey and her younger sister, Ann, pose in front of the field, in full bloom. It may have been a Fourth of July reunion.

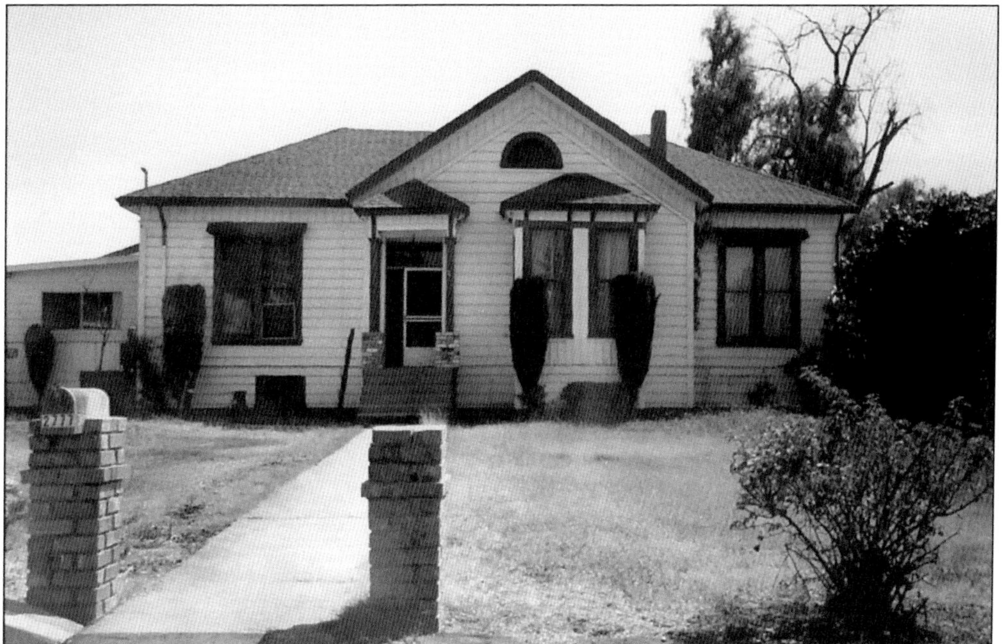

SELLERS HOUSE IN BAY POINT TODAY. This historic house on Willow pass Road is nearing 100 years old. It was a gathering place for many of the families on the eastern edge of the Bay Point School District at the turn of the 20th century.

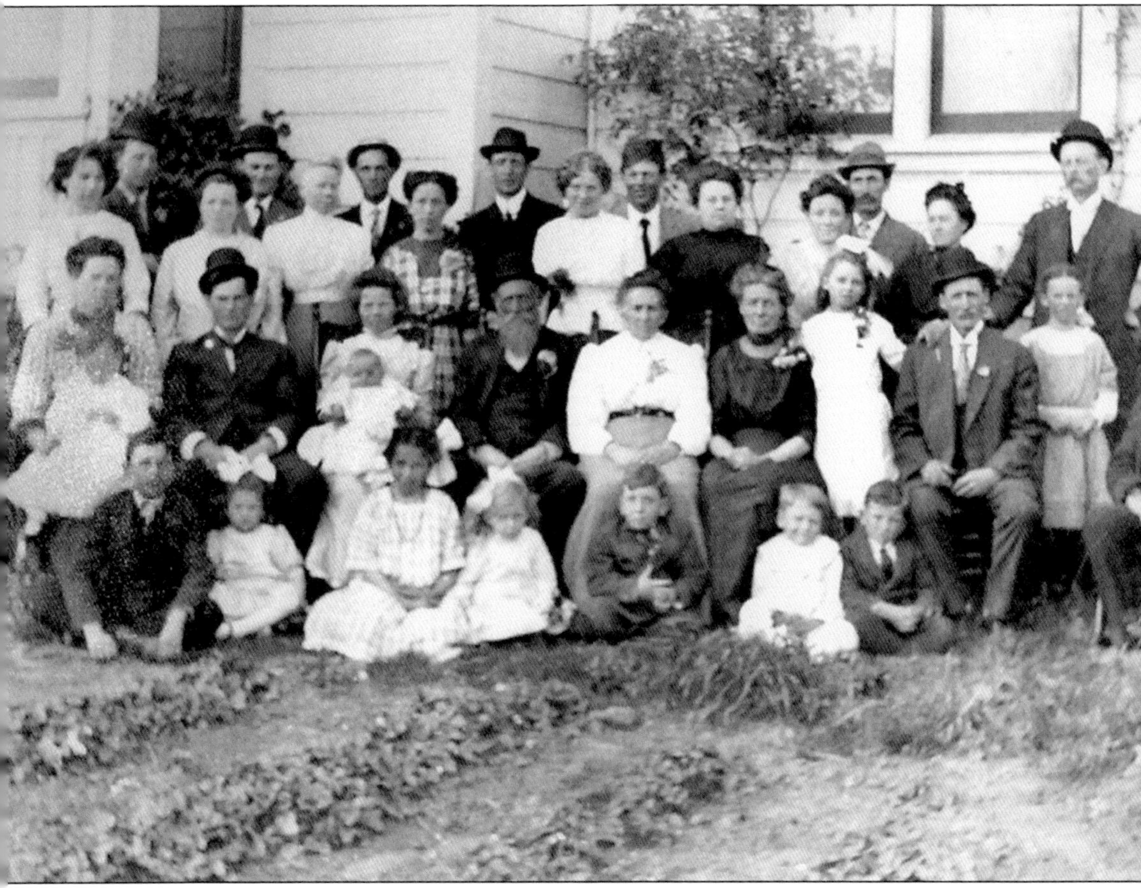

WILLOW PASS NEIGHBORS, FOURTH OF JULY, 1912. Posing in their holiday finery, 34 descendants of "grandpa Jeff Bailey", for whom Bailey Road is named, and "Grandpa Andrew Gore" pose behind the Willow Pass house. Dorothy Bailey Richards, sitting second from the left on the bottom row, provided the photo. The newest arrivals were infants Donald Bailey, second row on the left, and Marshall Gore, third from the left.

"FARMERETTES," C. 1918. Geraldine and Estelle Kennerly are pictured on the Frank Kennerly ranch on the road to Concord. Overalls and pointed buckle shoes were for the farm, and the high boots and dress for school.

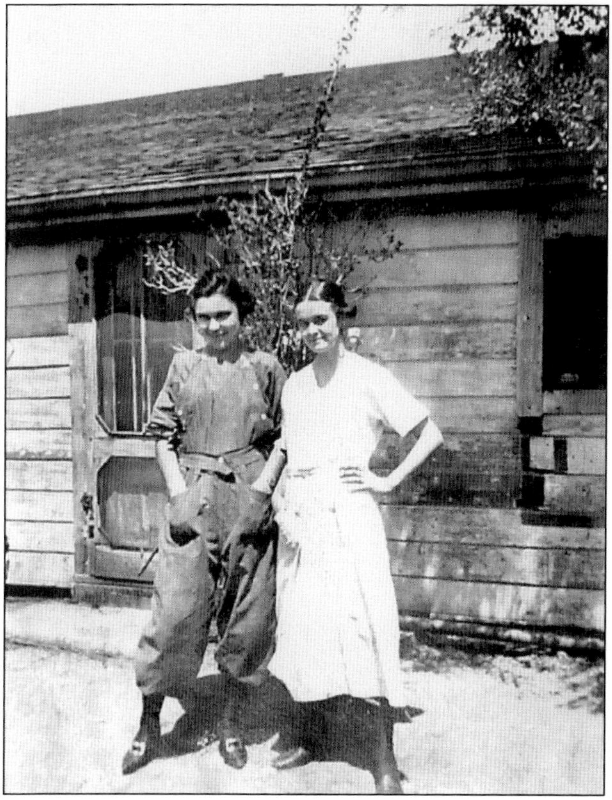

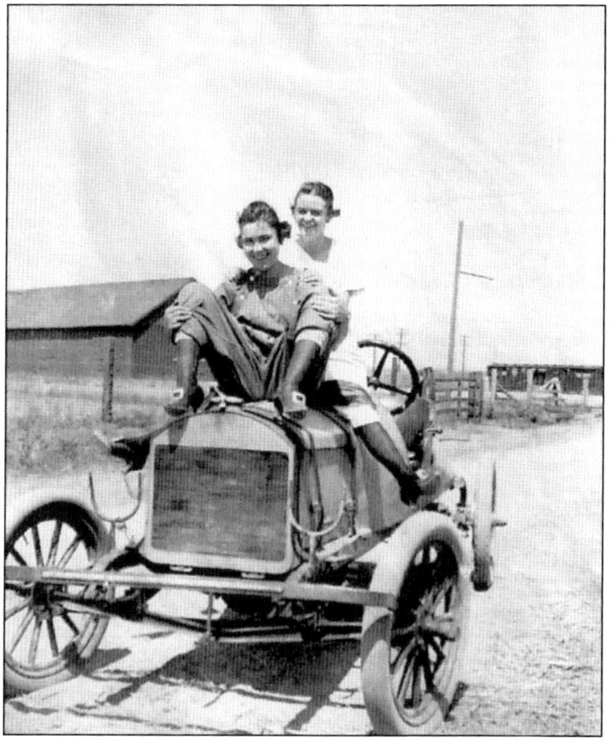

"FOR SALE," SAME DAY. The coltish 16-year-old Kennerly girls pose on the family convertible, behind the farmhouse.

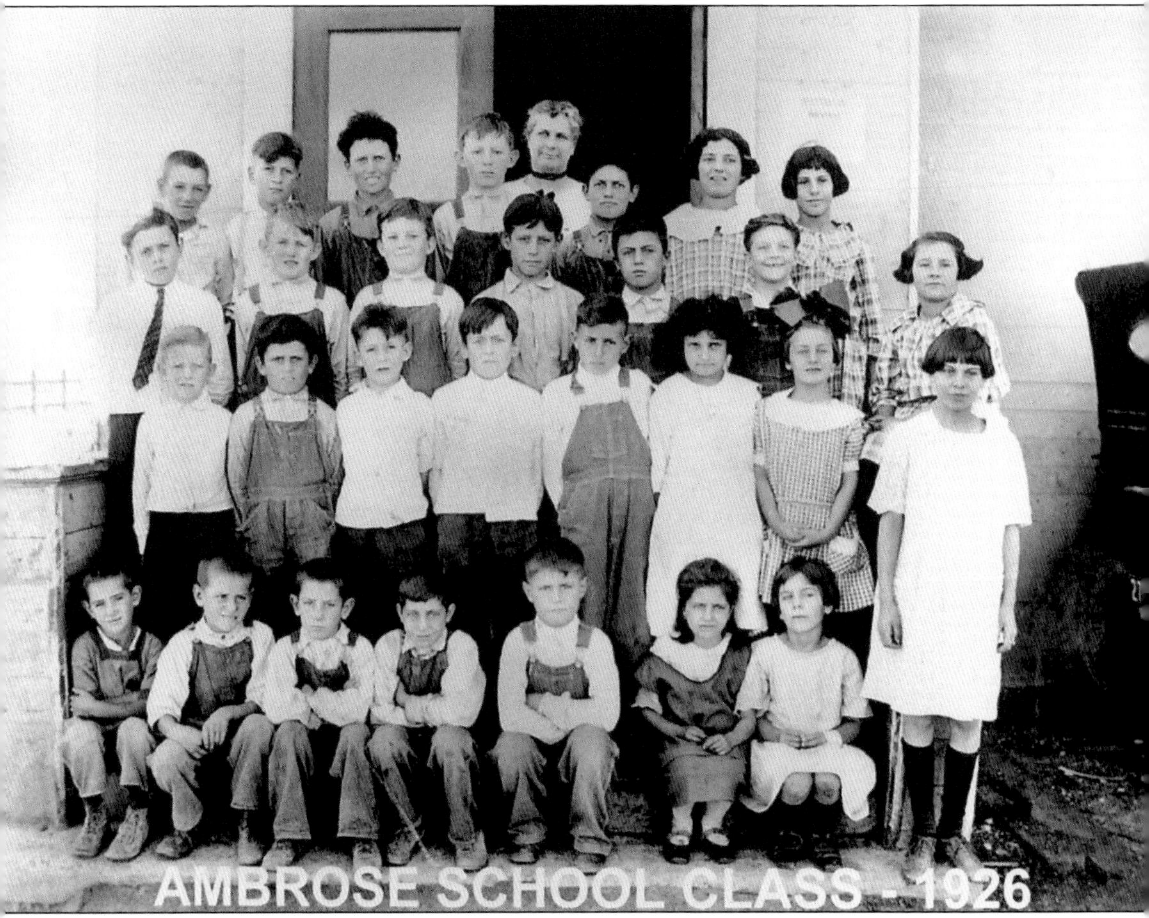

AMBROSE SCHOOL CLASS, 1926. With growing industry all over the district in 1909–1910, new school districts were created. The Bay Point schoolhouse was moved from its site on Riverview Drive to an acre of Seller's land on the Willow Pass Road. In 1912, it became the Ambrose School, named after the nearby Santa Fe flag station. There were 30 students. The school grew gradually, struggling with a low tax base during the 1920s. Ambrose tried to merge with the wealthier Pittsburg School district, but they were rejected. Shown are 29 students, with most of the boys in coveralls and the girls in their Sunday best. One budding executive wore his best white shirt and tie. Notice a mother's touch displayed in a big bow, second from right in the second row.

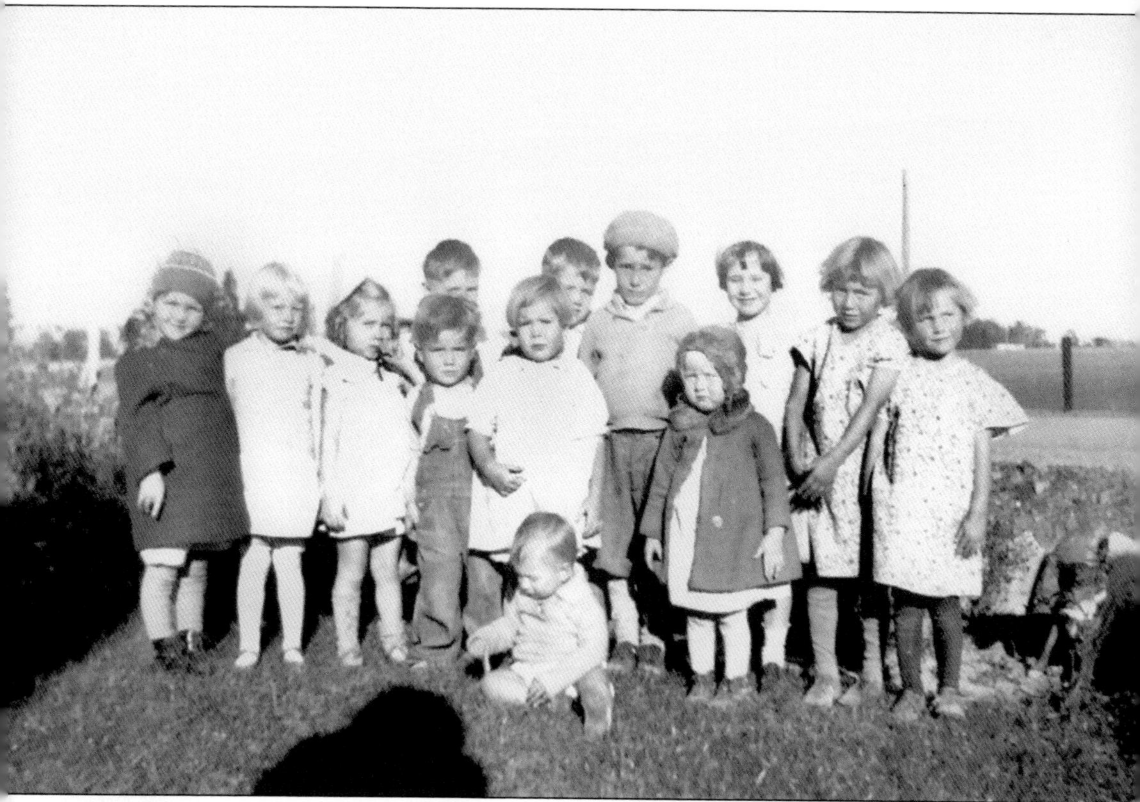

AMBROSE FIRST GRADERS, 1931–1932. Construction of the new Shell Chemical plant across the road and the Pittsburg Steel Mill four miles east of Bailey Road brought rapid growth to Willow Pass and the Ambrose School. With a higher tax base at Ambrose, the Pittsburg School District proposed a merger. Ambrose "rejected the overture." By 1930, the school had 77 students. Pictured, from left to right, are (front row) Nadine Morris, Florence (Flossie) Cawthorne, Wanda Collins, unknown boy, unknown girl, and Vivian Cawthorne; and (back row) Reggie Collins, unknown boy, Russell Anuda, Betty Anuda, Rosemarie Andrus, and Lois Andrus; and . Also pictured are the photographer's baby and a friendly calf. Russell was killed in World War II.

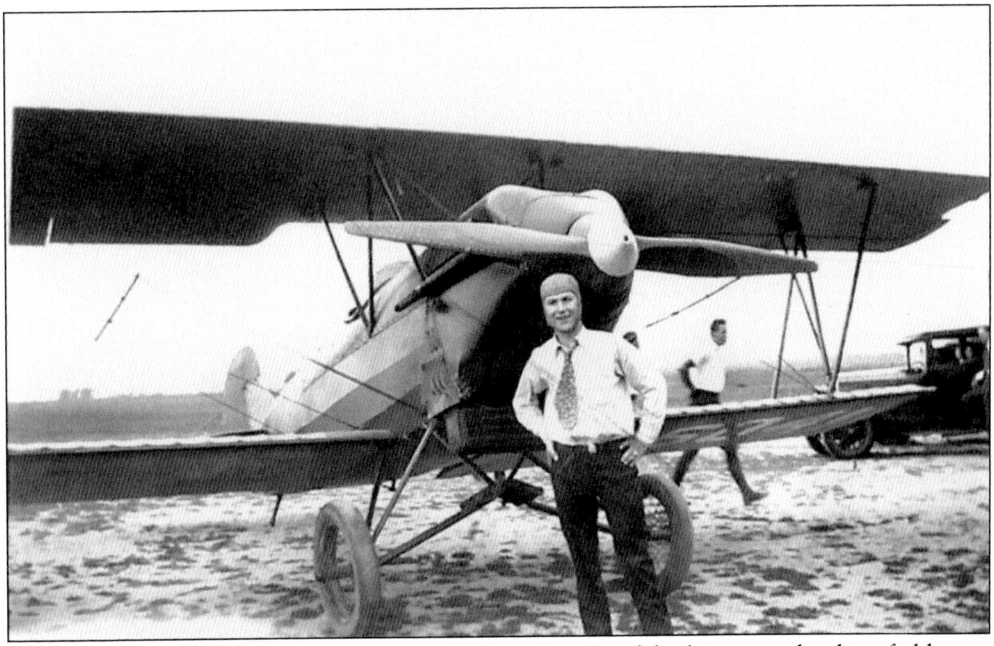

Early Bay Point Aviation c. 1930. Willow Pass Road had its own landing field next to Shell Chemical. Here, 18-year-old Gus Grossi poses before he is given a ride on the single-engine biplane. He died in 2002.

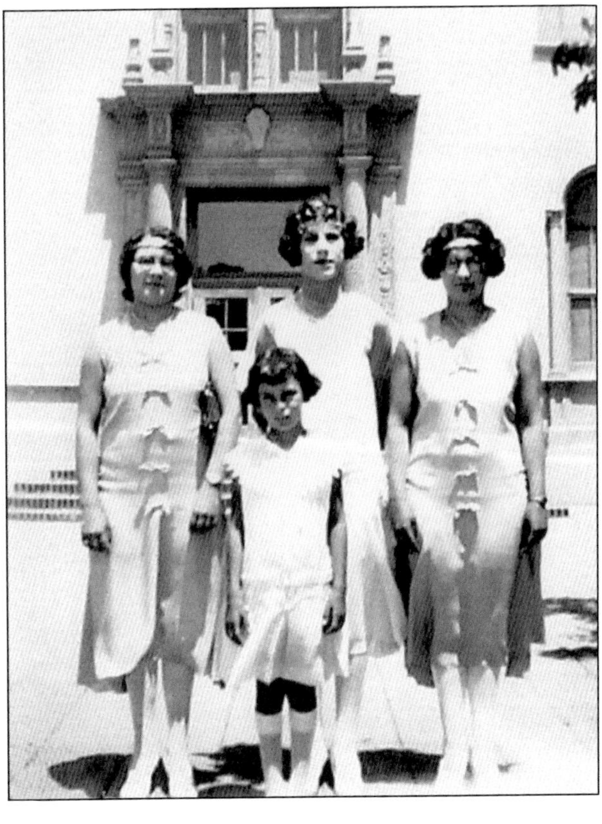

Enes Girls, 1930. The Holy Ghost Festival was a major Portuguese tradition. Here we have the queen and her attendants posing in front of Mt. Diablo High School. From left to right are Marion Alvernez, Ida Evora Enes, Dorothy Alvernez Culbertson, and Clara Evora Mota.

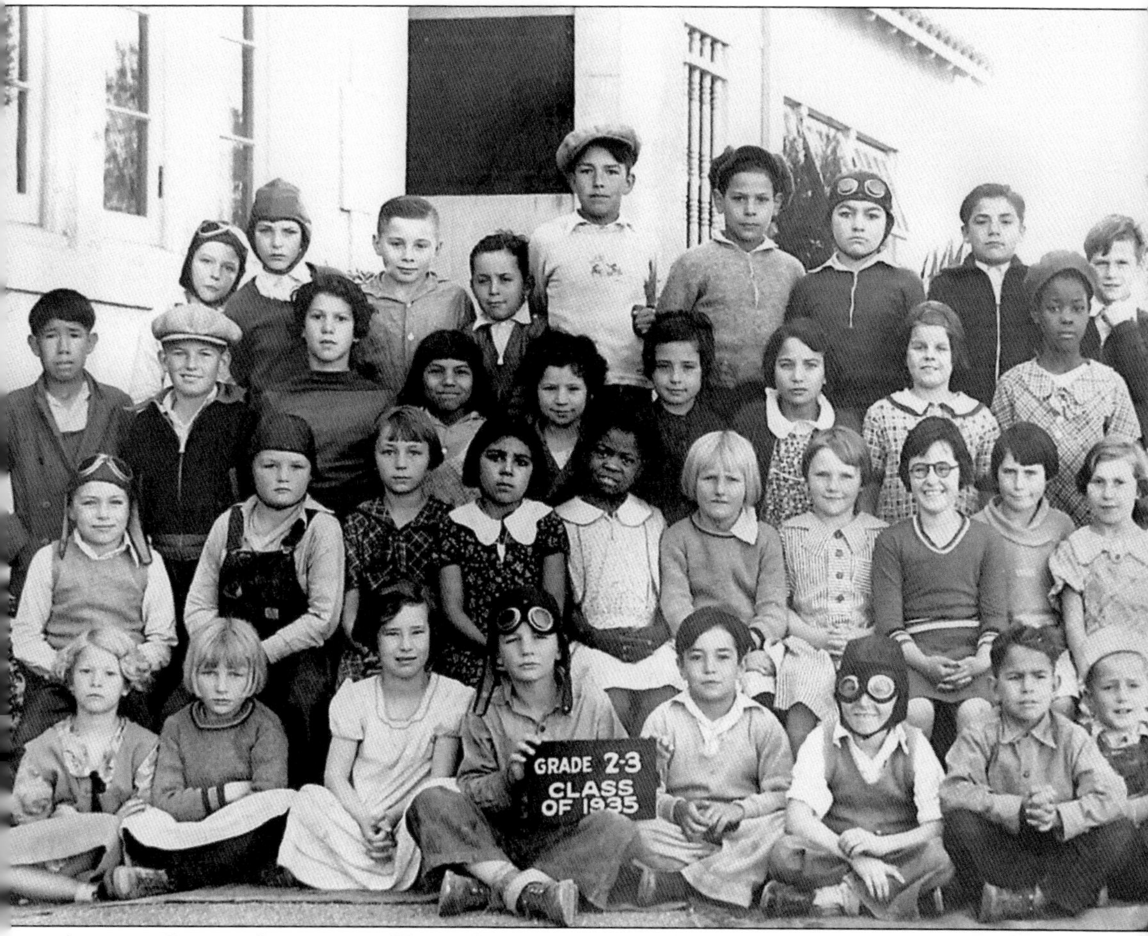

AMBROSE SCHOOL SECOND AND THIRD GRADERS, 1935. The Ambrose School hit a high-water mark in attendance in the mid-1930s. As seen, seven of the 18 boys were airplane enthusiasts, if their caps are any indication. Pictured, from left to right, are (front row) Florence (Flossie) Cawthorne, unknown, Betty Anuta, Bobbie Miller, unknown, redheaded Carlo Zocchi, Manuel Mendevil (killed in World War II), and Jimmy Black; (second row) Reggie Collins, Eddie Pool, Rosemary Andrus, Carmen Ramirez, Olive Lois Bean, Mavis ?, Nadine Morris, Marilyn Levada, Norma Hartsock, and Pearl Lehr; (third row) unknown, Paul Tilsche, Mary Cuellar, Carmen Sanchez, Alice ?, ? Marcus, Rosemary Mendevil, Katherine Vlach, and Mattie Mae Berkeley; and (top row) Roger Scott, Charles Smith, Russell Baden, unknown, Francisco Sanchez, Joe Cuellar ("meanest kid in school"), Leo Marcus, Benito Sanchez, and David Davies.

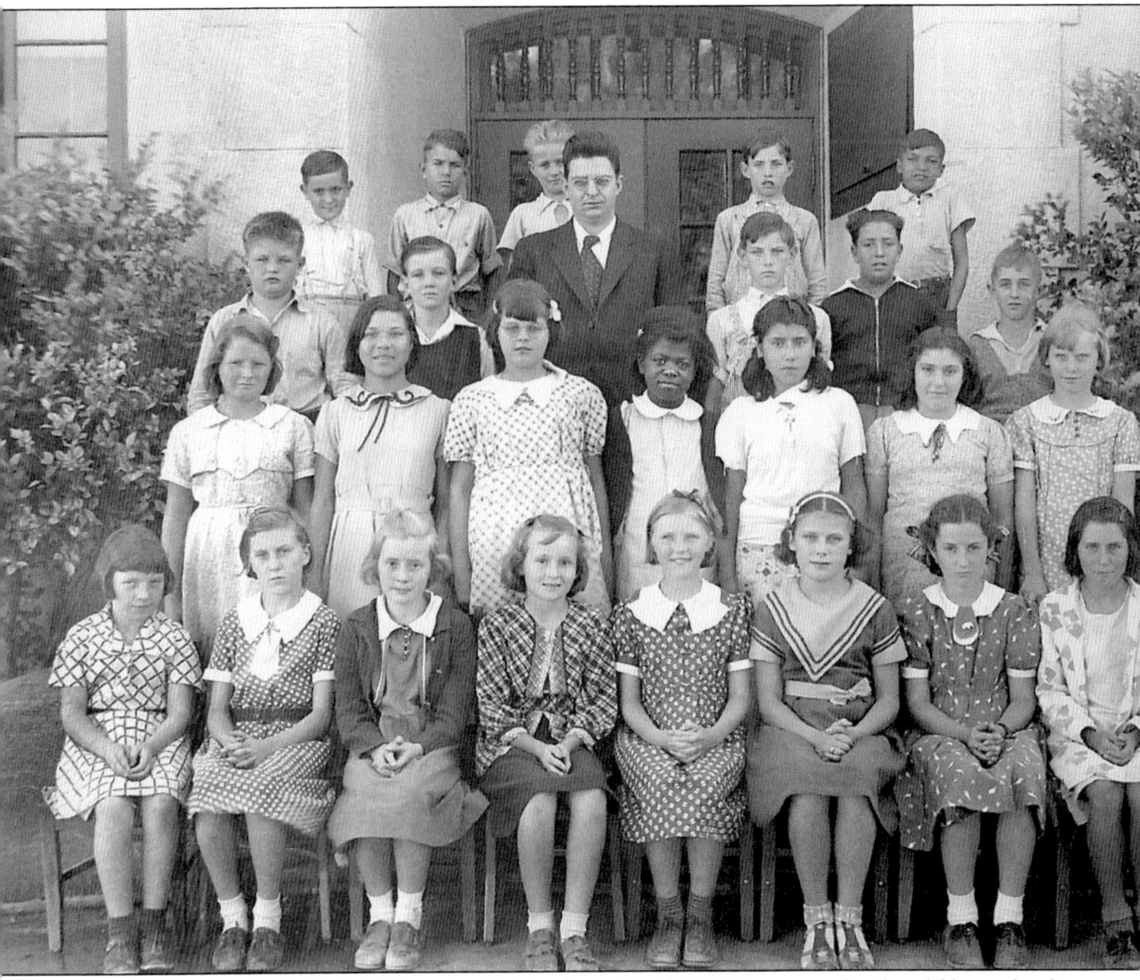

AMBROSE SCHOOL, C. 1937–1938. The teacher, Harold DeFraga, taught this fifth-grade class. The following year, he became the school principal. Pictured, from left to right, are (front row) Lorretta Soligney, Pearl Lehr, Beulah ?, Sarah Hayes, Nadine Morris, Alberta Rogers, Marilyn Levada, and Norma Hartsock; (second row) Loretta ?, unknown, Katherine Vlach, Olive Bean, Margarita Luna, Catherine Puglisi, and Colleen Ritchie; (third row) Eddie Pool, Bobbie Miller, Charles Smith, Jimmy Dias, and David Brown; (back row) unknown, Manuel Mendevil, Jimmy Black, Defraga, unknown, and Joaquin Costa.

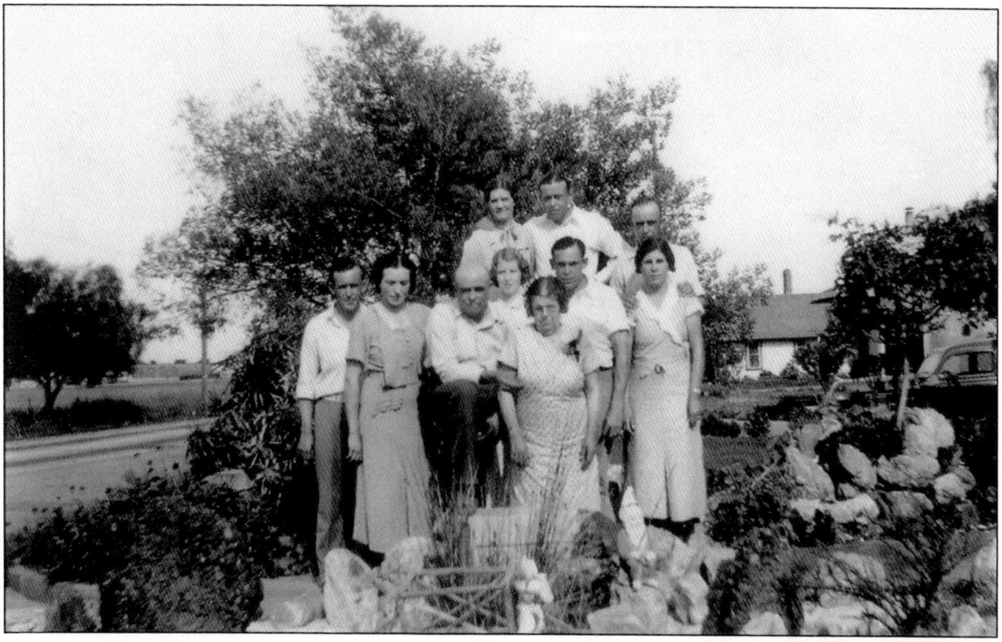

ANTONE ENES FAMILY, 1936. Ambitious and hard working, the Enes family built one of the first subdivisions in what became West Pittsburg, later Bay Point (notice the male Enes stare). Pictured, from left to right, are (front row) Chris, Mamie Enes (later Meister), Antone, Evelyn (Barker) Enes, Clementine (Monduncy) Enes, Lennard, and Ida (Evora) Enes; and (back row) Madalyn (McClure) Enes, Bernard, and Albert.

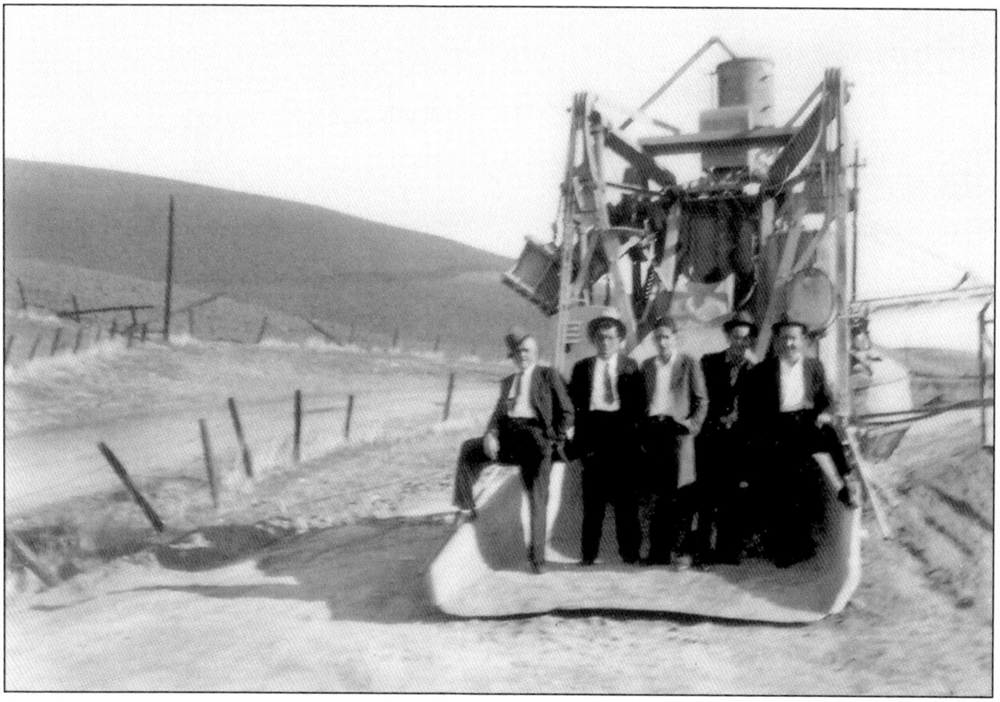

EARTHMOVER FOR ENES TRACT. Pictured, from left to right, are Antone Enes, Joseph Monduncy, and other partners of Burkhard Investment Company.

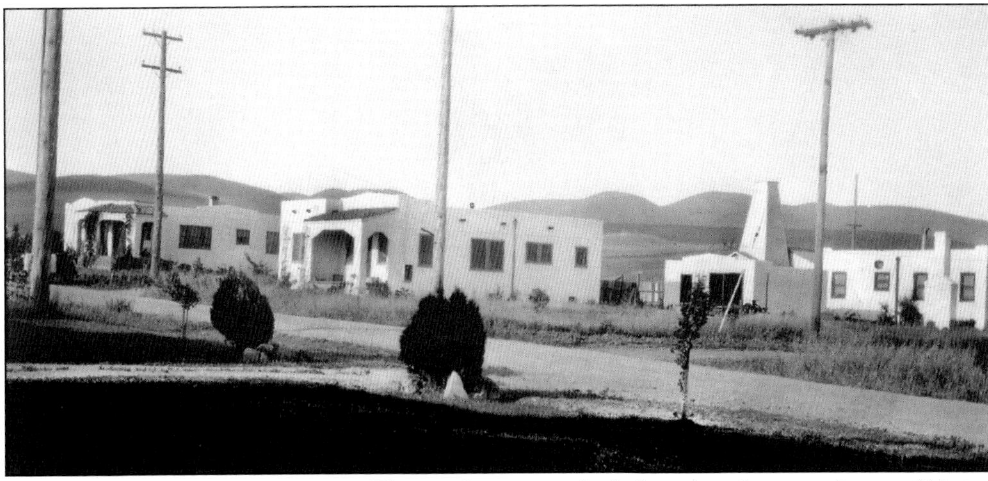

First Homes, Enes Tract, 1932. The two homes on the left in this photograph are still being used in 2005. Pictured, from left to right, are the homes of Bernardand Madeline Enes, Stephen and Rosalie Reynolds, and Albert and Ida Enes. The small tower coming from Albert's garage was a well that furnished water for the whole subdivision.

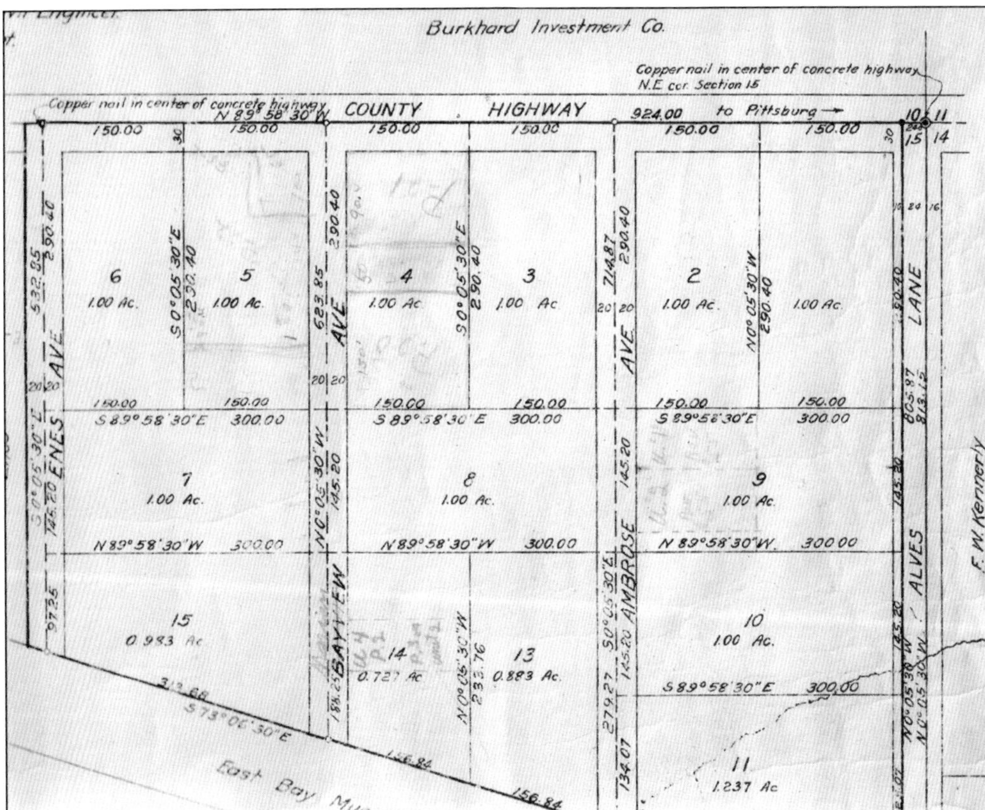

Plan of Enes Tract. Partially funded by the Burkhard Investment Company, the Enes boys built the homes on Enes Avenue, Bayview Avenue, Ambrose Avenue, and Alves Lane. Situated on County Highway, now Willow Pass Road, the tract was adjacent to Frank Kennerly's ranch, now Ambrose Recreation Center. Bayview was later renamed Marin.

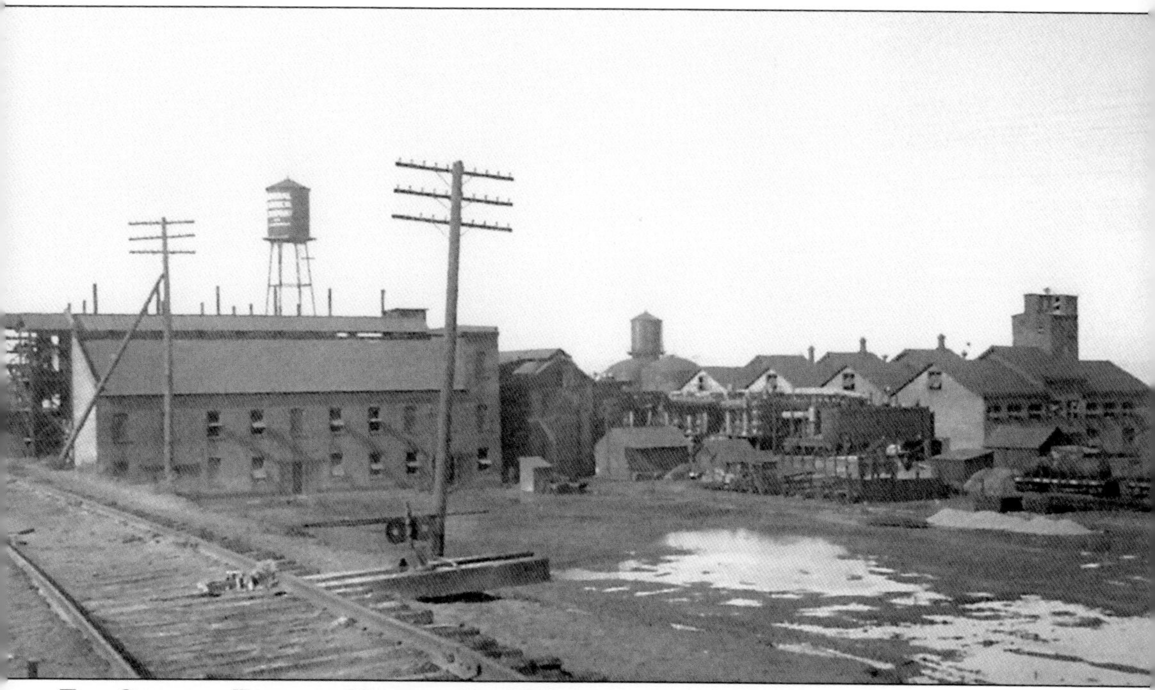

The Company Town of Nichols. Dr. William H. Nichols began his career in 1870 by producing sulfuric acid. He was a charter member of the American Chemical Society in New York. In 1902, he created the annual Nichols Award, for original research in the chemical field. The award is still given in 2005. In 1910, his syndicate built the General Chemical Bay Point Works on Port Chicago Highway, two miles from the town of Bay Point. That year he built about 50 homes and 10 bunkhouses for plant workers across the road from the factory. Built on land originally owned by Emer Sailes in the 1870s, the company town eventually grew to a population of 600.

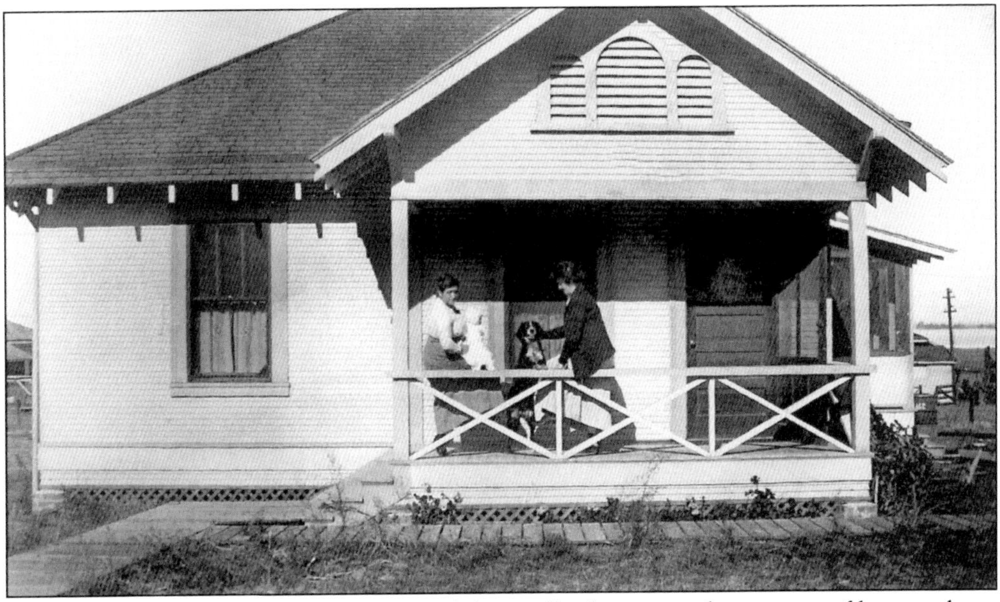

A Middle-sized Nichols House. "One of the smaller houses in the top row of houses above the road [Port Chicago Highway], it had two bedrooms, one bath and a kitchen. There were front and side porches and a wooden sidewalk around the house. Rents were said to be 'very low.' " Pictured from left to right are Teresa Steccati, baby Hugo, the dog, and Mrs. Bob Ramsey.

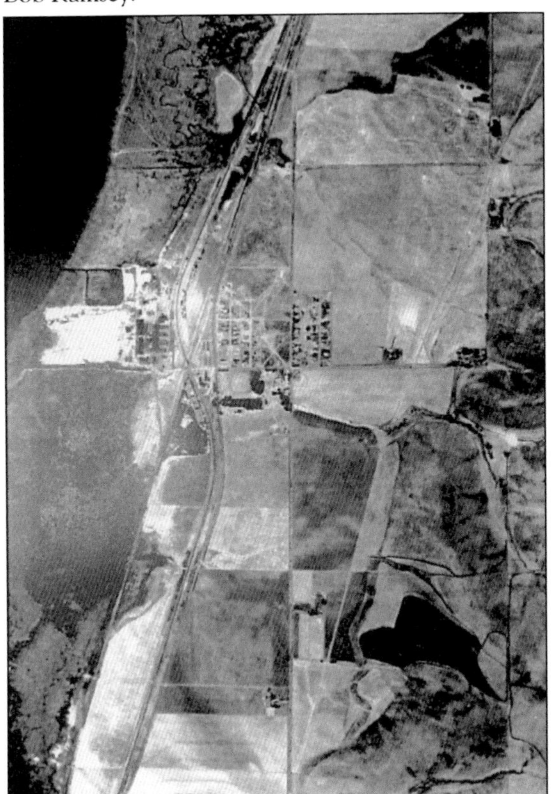

Aerial View of Nichols. The long vertical line in the center of the photo is Port Chicago Highway. Visible are the houses of Nichols to the right, the General Chemical Plant to the left, and the Nichols School below the intersection.

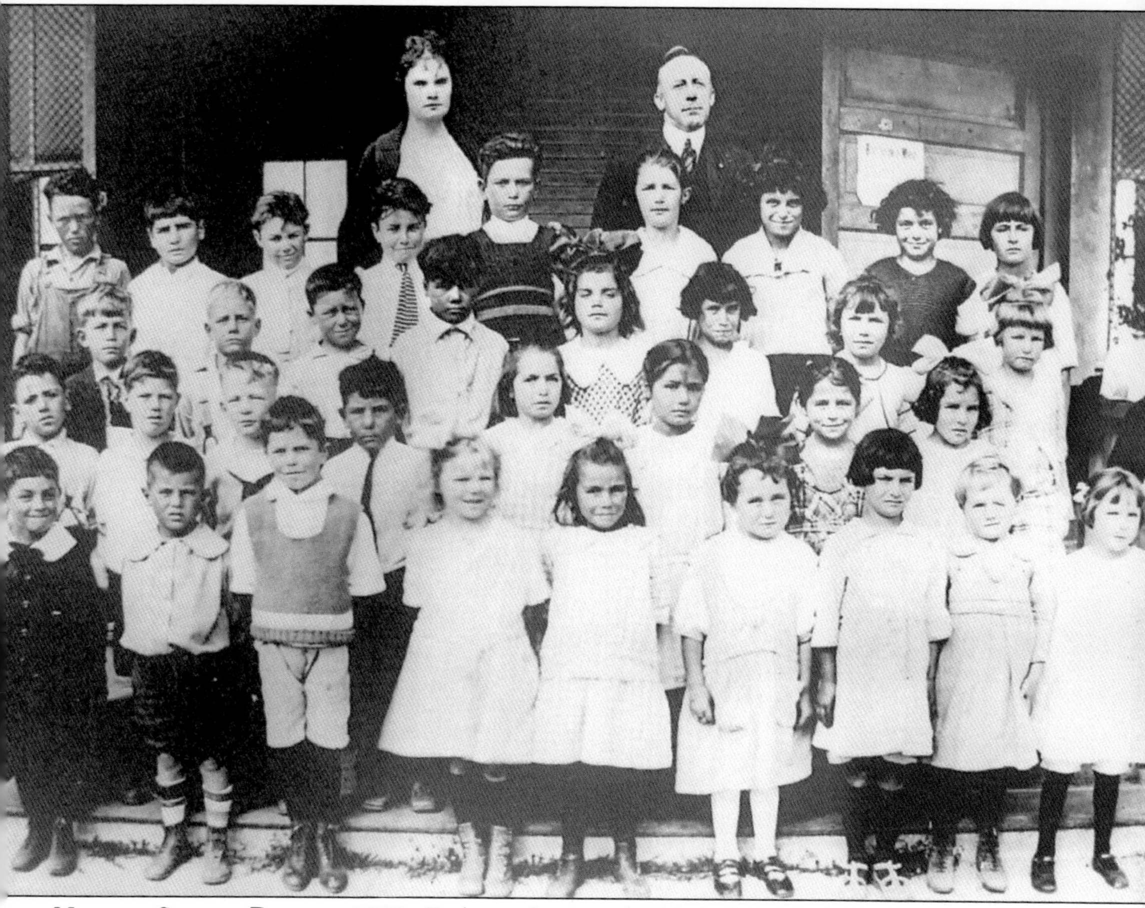

Nichols School Picture 1922. Early teachers at the Nichols School were Isabel A. Nay in 1915 and Itha K. Jones in 1916. By 1920, another classroom and a second teacher were added to the school. Pictured, from left to right, are (front row) Hugo Steccati (ready to burst), Charles Vimini, unknown, Jean Fuller, unknown, Olivia Allesandrelli, unknown, Stella Biagi, and unknown; (second row) two unknowns, Fred Clark, unknown, Zita Biagi, two unknowns, and Virginia Black; (third row) Richard Dow, unknown, Louis Allesandrelli, unknown, Barbara Tonti, and three unknowns; (fourth row) Tino Marazani, Joe Ferry, unknown, Joe Avila, August Grossi, Annie Dow, and three unknowns; and (back row) Miss Limmini (substitute) and Mr. White (county worker).

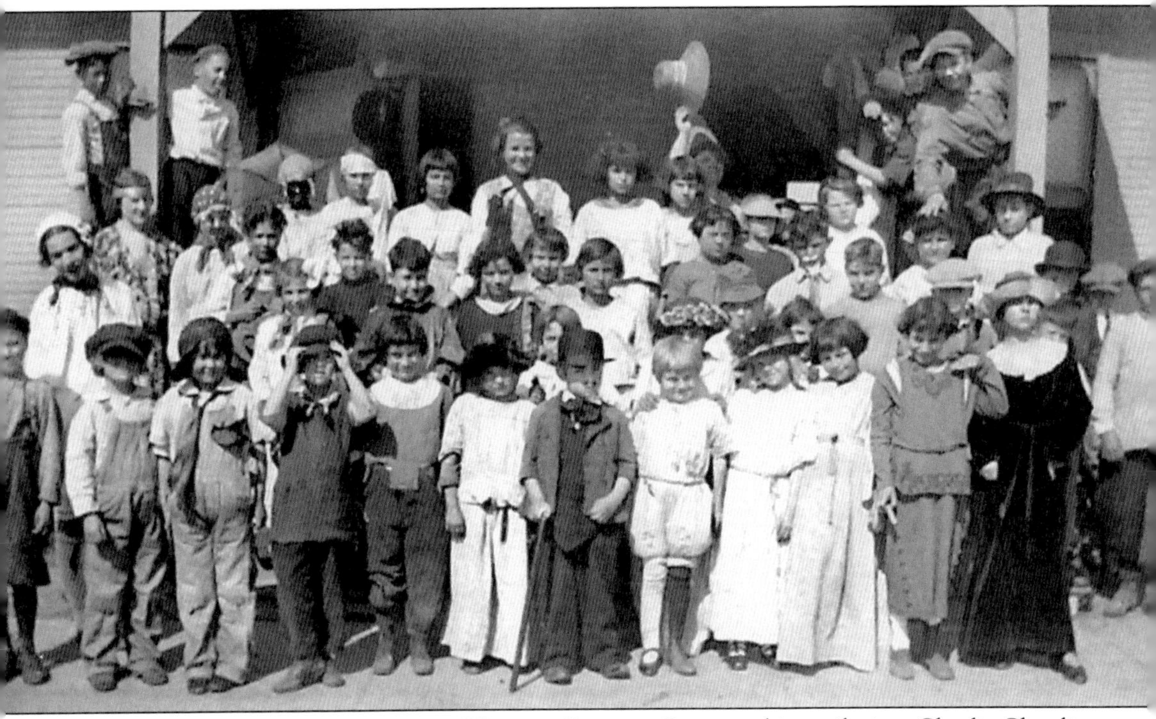

"RUBE'S DAY," APRIL 1, 1923, AT NICHOLS SCHOOL. Street urchins, pilgrims, Charlie Chaplin, Elizabethans, Victorians, thespians, pirates, banditos, and general roustabouts showed up for school in full regalia. Only they know the tomfoolery that went on.

SERRANUS CLINTON HASTINGS, EARLY FOUNDING FATHER OF CLYDE. The first Chief Justice of the California Supreme Court in 1850, Judge Hastings lived for many years in Benicia. He built his ranch, called "Government Ranch," in 1860 on the future town site of Clyde. On the way to making his fortune in land acquisition, he played a key role in the violent removal of Native Americans in Round Valley, Mendocino County, and likely from the Indian Rancheria at Pacheco. He was later the founder of the Hastings School of Law in San Francisco.

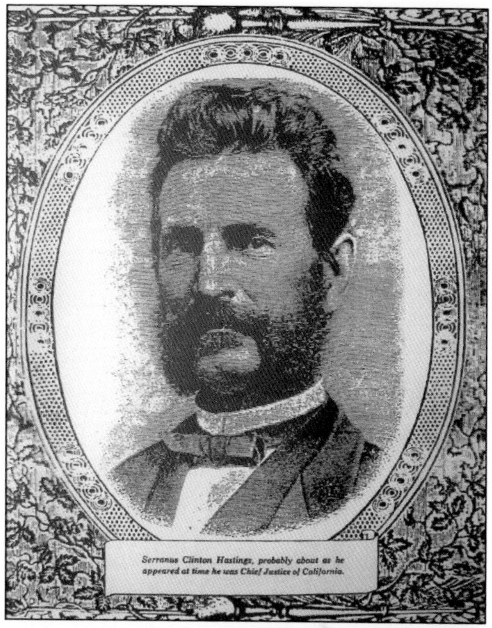

Serranus Clinton Hastings, probably about as he appeared at time he was Chief Justice of California.

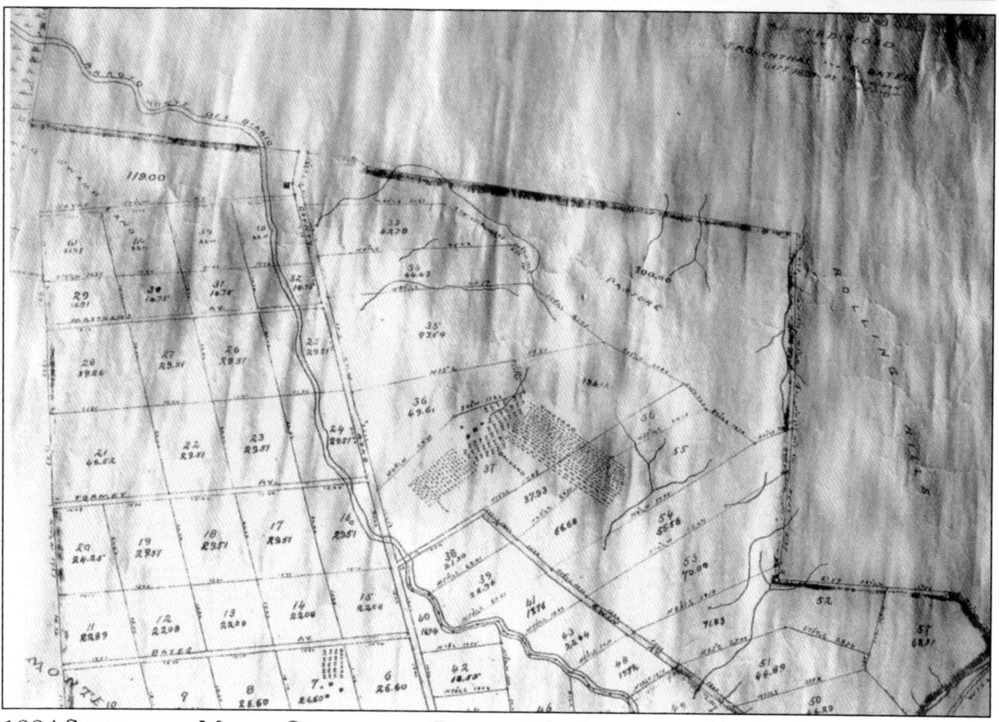

1884 SUBDIVISION MAP OF GOVERNMENT RANCH. After being owned by the first Chief Justice of the California Supreme Court, two of Guadalupe Vallejo's sons-in-law, a governor of California, and one of the major founders of the Transcontinental Railroad, the land that became the village of Clyde was subdivided. At the time, in 1884, Governor William Gwin's son owned the property. Visible, in addition to the subdivision lines, are Diablo Creek, Willow Pass Road, the late 19th-century watercourses coming out of the hills, and the layout of the ranch. An orchard and large vineyard are visible.

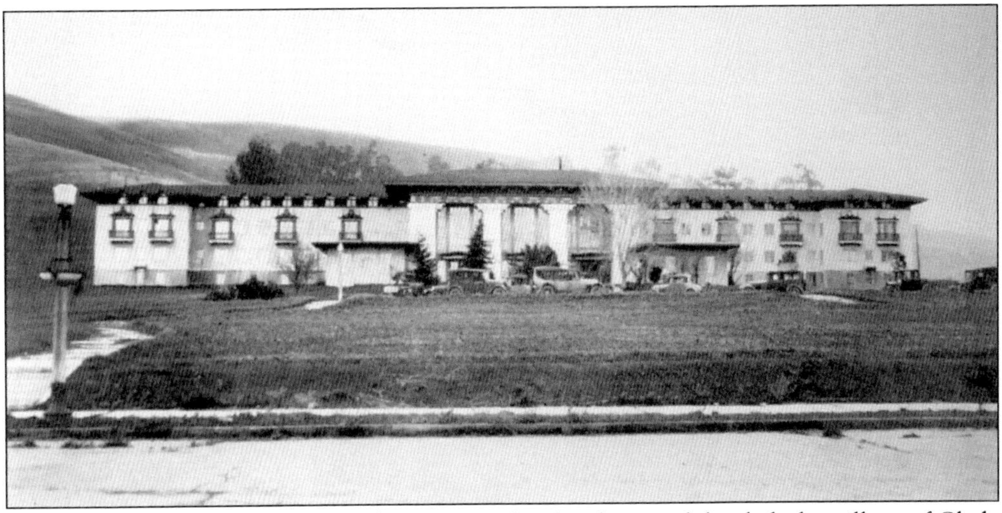

The Pride of Clyde, 1930s. Nearly 33 years after first being subdivided, the village of Clyde was built. Walnut Creek entrepreneur Robert Burgess obtained a government grant to build the Pacific Coast Shipbuilding Company. There was a shortage of housing in Bay Point and in 1918, Burgess was able to get federal funding to build houses for his shipyard workers. Since he owned Government Ranch rather than any land in Bay Point, he built the housing where Clyde now stands. The high-water mark of construction in Clyde was the Clyde hotel, built in the late 1920s. Pictured here in the 1930s, it was a retreat for social elites from San Francisco and Hollywood.

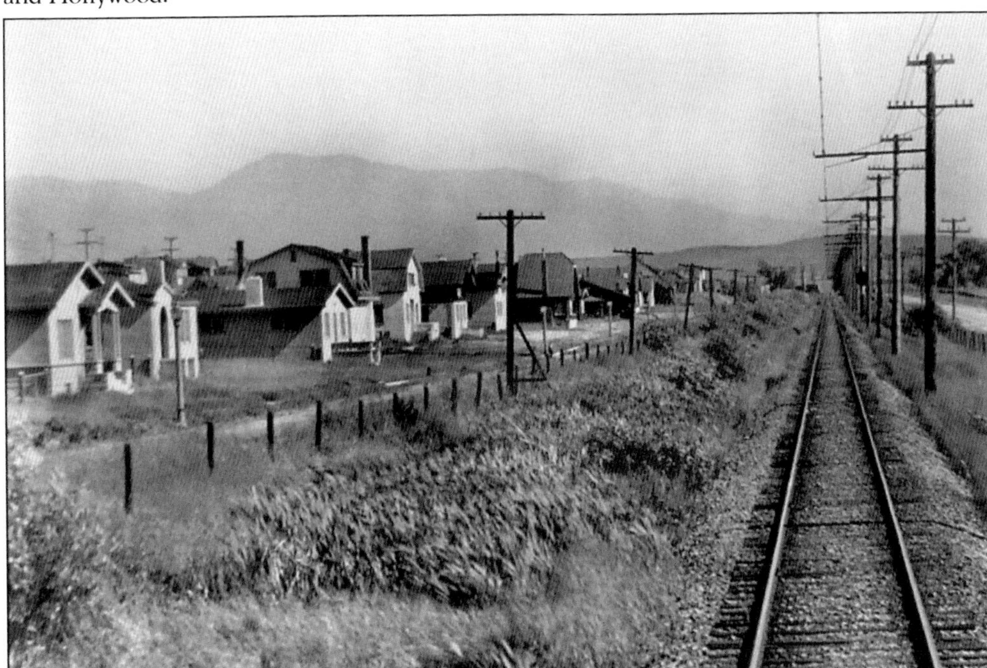

New Clyde From the North. In the distance, Mount Diablo, source of the hills behind Clyde, stands watch. This appears to be new, modern housing, built before World War II. There is no sign of military fencing along the railroad tracks that became property of the Concord Naval Weapons Station.

Six

West Pittsburg Backyard of Contra Costa County

While all of the excitement was going on at the West end of the area during the first seven decades of this century, gradual growth and change was occurring on the rural east side closer to the Pittsburg border.

The coming of the electric train from Sacramento to Oakland in 1912 created a tiny spurt of prosperity on the far western edge of Pittsburg. The train was ferried across Suisun Bay and formed a crossroad where the rails went east and west. By 1914, the name West Pittsburg appeared on a county map. Actually located outside of the township, several homes and businesses grew around the station. Later, when the train ceased operation, decline set in.

In 1928, Shell Chemical Company built a large plant on what had been Ambrose Ranch. By the end of the war, housing tracts had sprung up on three sides of it. Neighborhoods were built in the North Broadway area, the Enes tract, and later a huge subdivision was built called Shore Acres near McAvoy Crossing. Neighborhoods grew up around the new Ambrose Park.

Not attached to Pittsburg, Concord, or any other incorporated town, the early neighborhoods were part of a national trend of inexpensive suburban housing. Most residents worked at the nearby Shell Chemical plant, and commuted to factories in Pittsburg, Nichols, Port Chicago, Avon, or Martinez. These were neighborhoods of working people. They valued home, family, church, and the industrial jobs that made life possible.

Not an area known for wealth or higher education, the neighborhoods nevertheless provided a generation with experiences and memories that longtime residents remember fondly. A major turning point for the community can be traced to the donation of acreage by Enes in 1947 for the creation of the Ambrose Park and recreation district.

The end of the Vietnam War brought overwhelming change to the neighborhoods west of Pittsburg. The evacuation after "The Battle of Port Chicago" brought newcomers into the remaining neighborhoods. The completion of Highway 4 through the Willow Pass opened the area up for more development. Not unlike other industrial areas after Vietnam, there was an increase of negative factors here. Being unincorporated, West Pittsburg had no city government to protect the interests of local citizens. Greater Contra Costa County considered the area Wild West Pittsburg.

Services declined and the high school closed. The budding business section along Willow Pass Road languished. During the 1970s and 1980s crime increased substantially. The population of West Pittsburg nearly doubled between 1980 and 1990. West Pittsburg became known primarily in the county press for drugs and prostitution. Though the reputation was unfair to thousands of law-abiding citizens of West Pittsburg, the crime statistics were quite high. Yet, there was a strong sense of community pride. A few fought for better things.

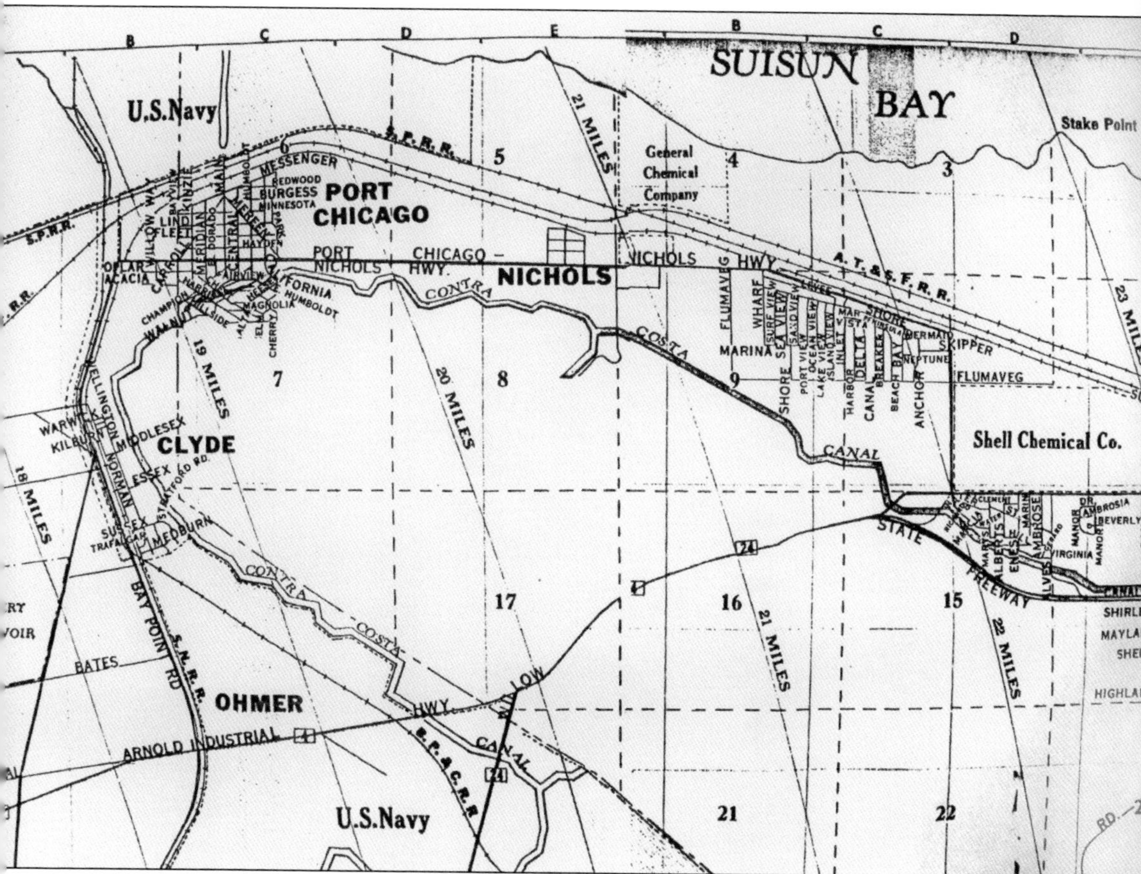

Unincorporated Contra Costa, 1950s. By the 1920s, housing had been built for the lumber workers at Port Chicago, shipbuilders at Clyde, and chemical workers at Nichols. The construction of Shell Chemical Company further east led to the construction of homes along the Concord to Antioch highway. Each, in its own way, was a "company town" community with economic and social activities centered on the plant. After World War II ended, the large subdivision of Shore Acres was built. It was the beginning of a homebuilding boom that continues unabated along Highway 4 today. In this map, State Freeway 4 had been completed west to what is now the junction of Port Chicago Highway and Willow Pass Road. Each subdivision grew from a ranch or farm that had been first worked and settled in the 1850s and 1860s.

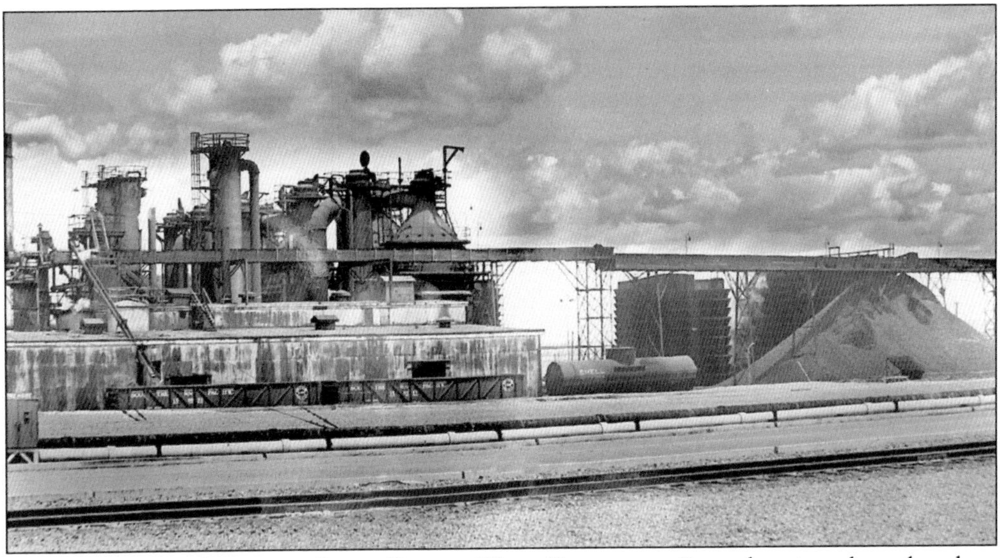

Shell Chemical Company, Shell Point, West Pittsburg. Petrochemistry has played an essential role in the community now known as Bay Point. Pictured here is part of the plant in the 1940s. The plant was sold and now operates as Criterion Catalysts. Their largest industrial use is now in the making of silicon chips for the computer industry.

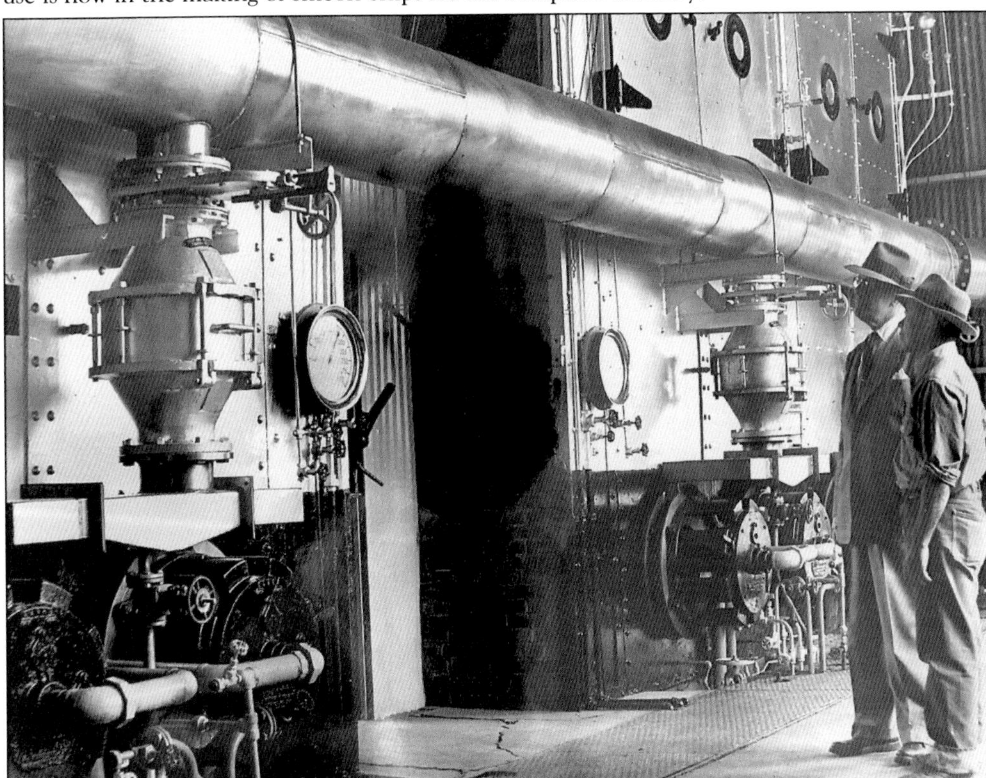

Dials, Knobs, and Wheels. Valves, levers, and pressure gauges all served to manage the chemical processes at the plant. This is the control room and panel for the ammonia synthesis plant. A single technician could observe and control any step in the synthesis process.

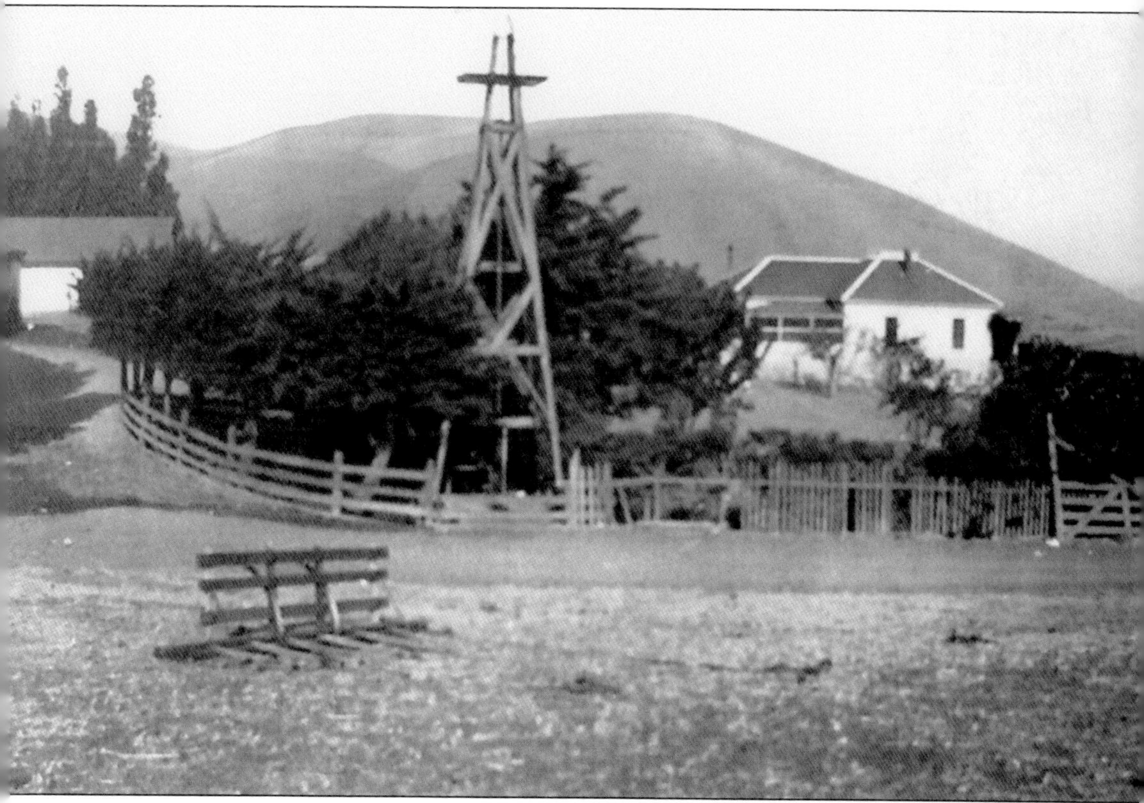

Ranches in the Country. For 50 years after the 1930s, the ranches and farms of the Bay Point School District gave way to housing subdivisions. This photo of the Tormey Ranch just off Port Chicago Highway gives a sense of the rural way of life that gradually yielded to the suburban lifestyle. This ranchland, originally owned by Charles Murray, passed to William Tormey in the early 20th century.

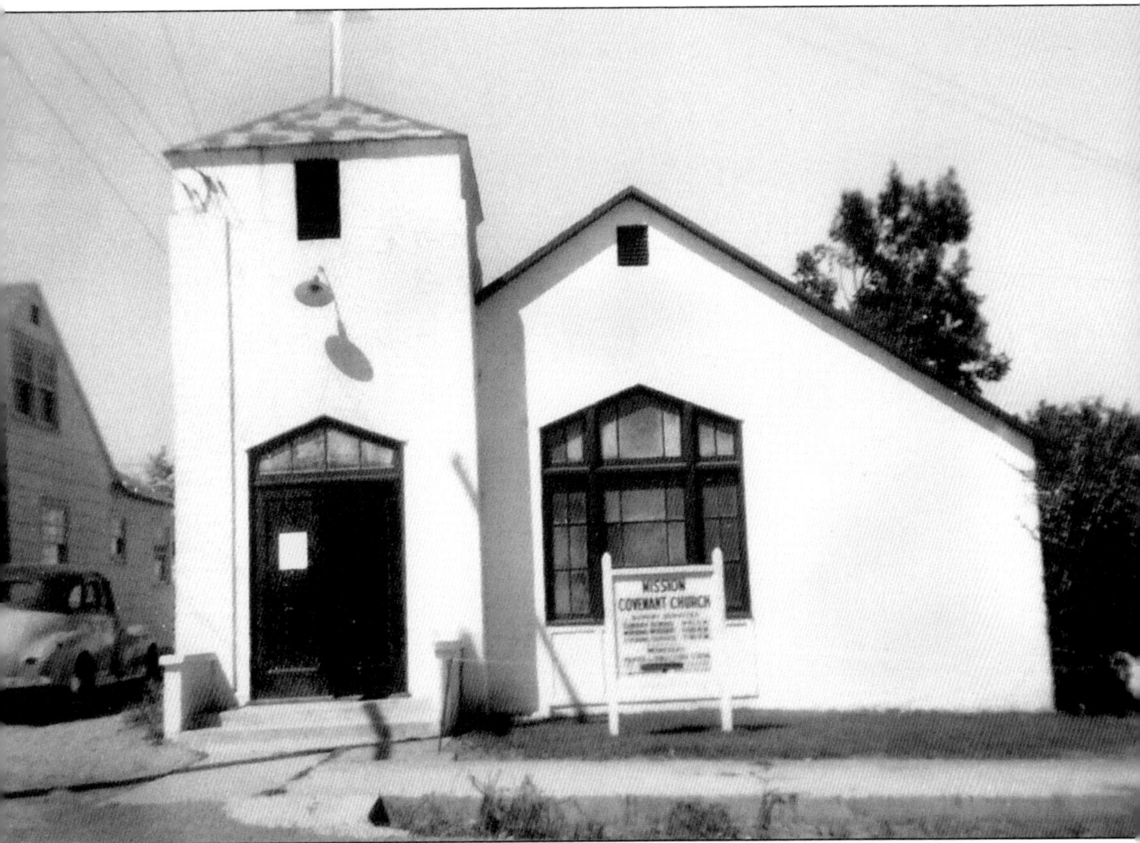

SWEDISH MISSION COVENANT CHURCH, "OUR CHURCH." Pictured is of one of the earliest churches of West Pittsburg. Still located on Alves Lane, today's church serves a close-knit congregation.

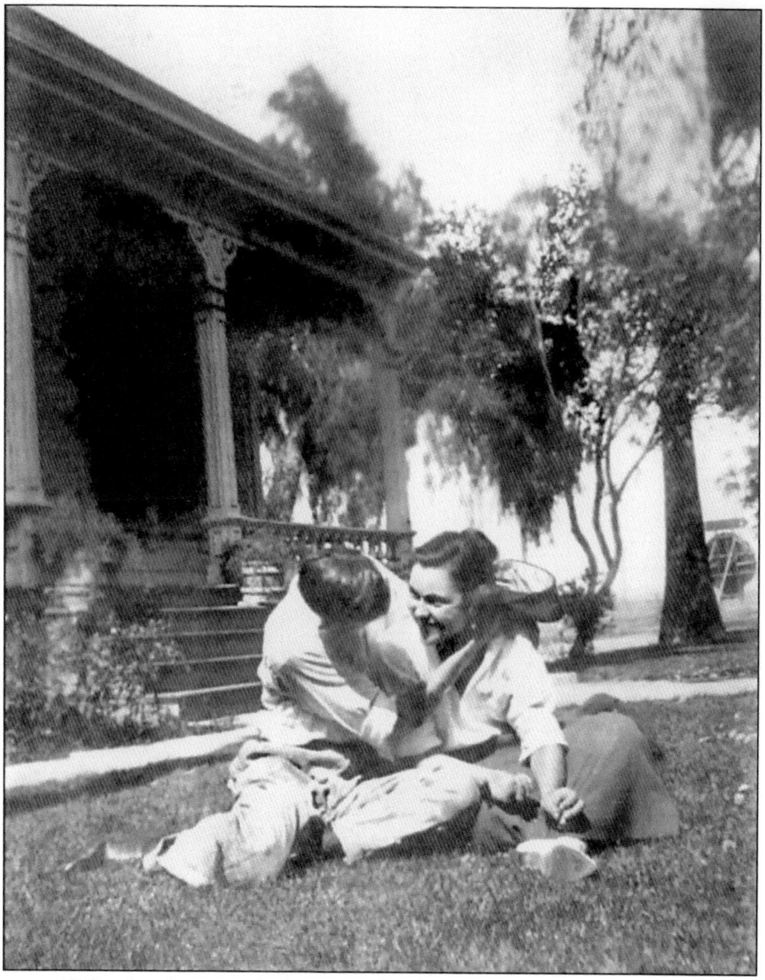

"WHY HESITATE?" In the days just before poodle skirts, courting and romancing took place on the front lawn. Here, Geraldine Kennerly puts up a minimal amount of resistance. For many years a teacher at Ambrose, little did her students know that she had once "spooned" on the school lawn.

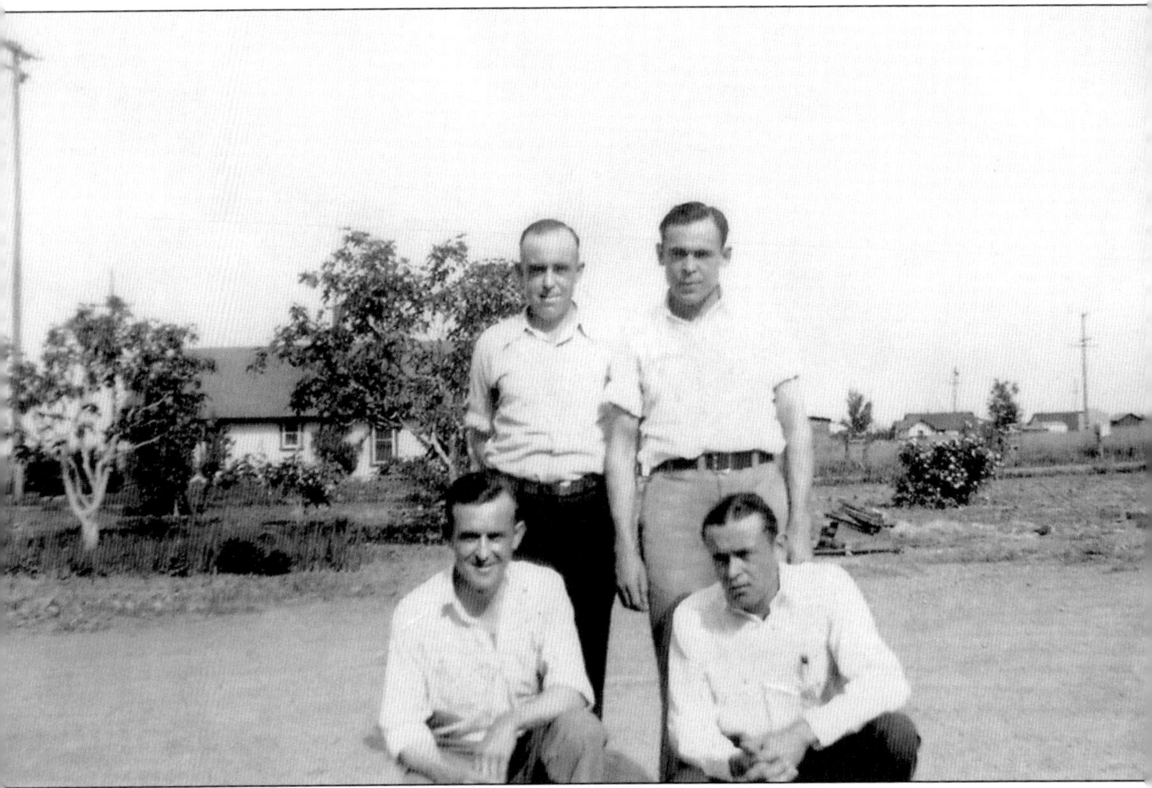

Early developers of West Pittsburg. From left to right, Albert, Lennard, Christopher, and Bernard Enes pose before the ranch house. In the background are some of the homes of the Enes Tract subdivision.

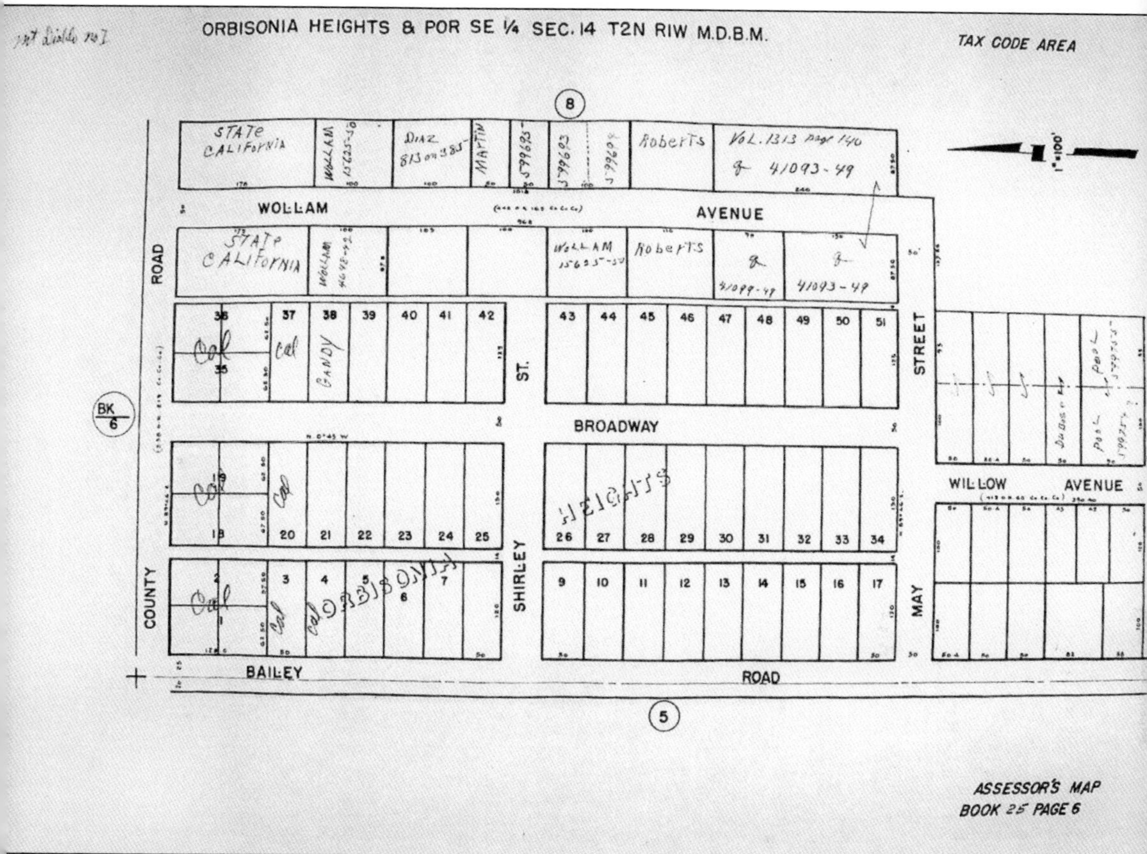

Plan of Orbisonia Heights. This early subdivision was built about the same time as the Enes Tract. At the intersection of Bailey Road and Willow Pass Road, it has seen street and sidewalk improvements in the past few years through the county's Redevelopment District.

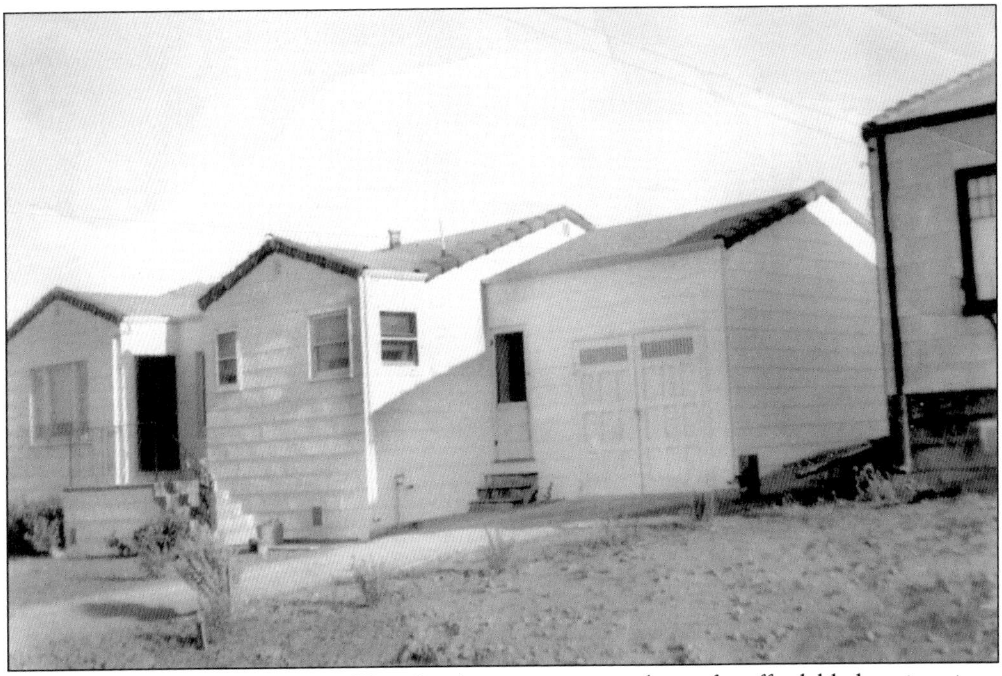

TYPICAL NEW HOMES IN 1930S. West Pittsburg was a natural area for affordable housing since factory workers for nearby plants largely populated it.

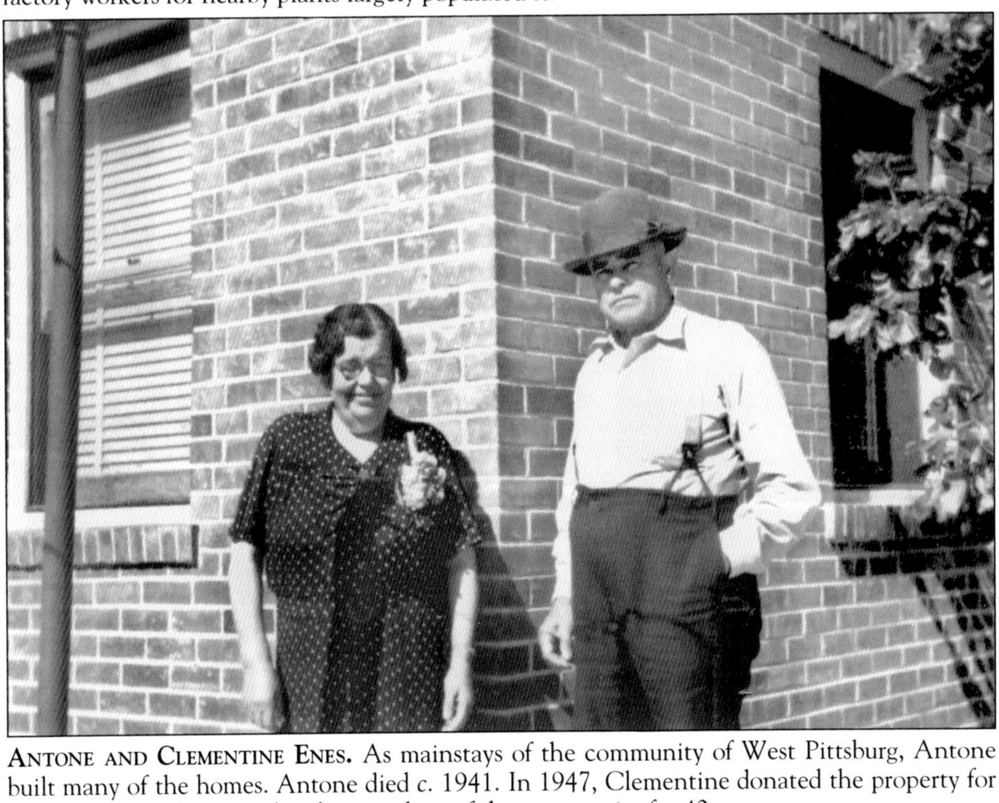

ANTONE AND CLEMENTINE ENES. As mainstays of the community of West Pittsburg, Antone built many of the homes. Antone died *c.* 1941. In 1947, Clementine donated the property for Ambrose Park, the central gathering place of the community for 40 years.

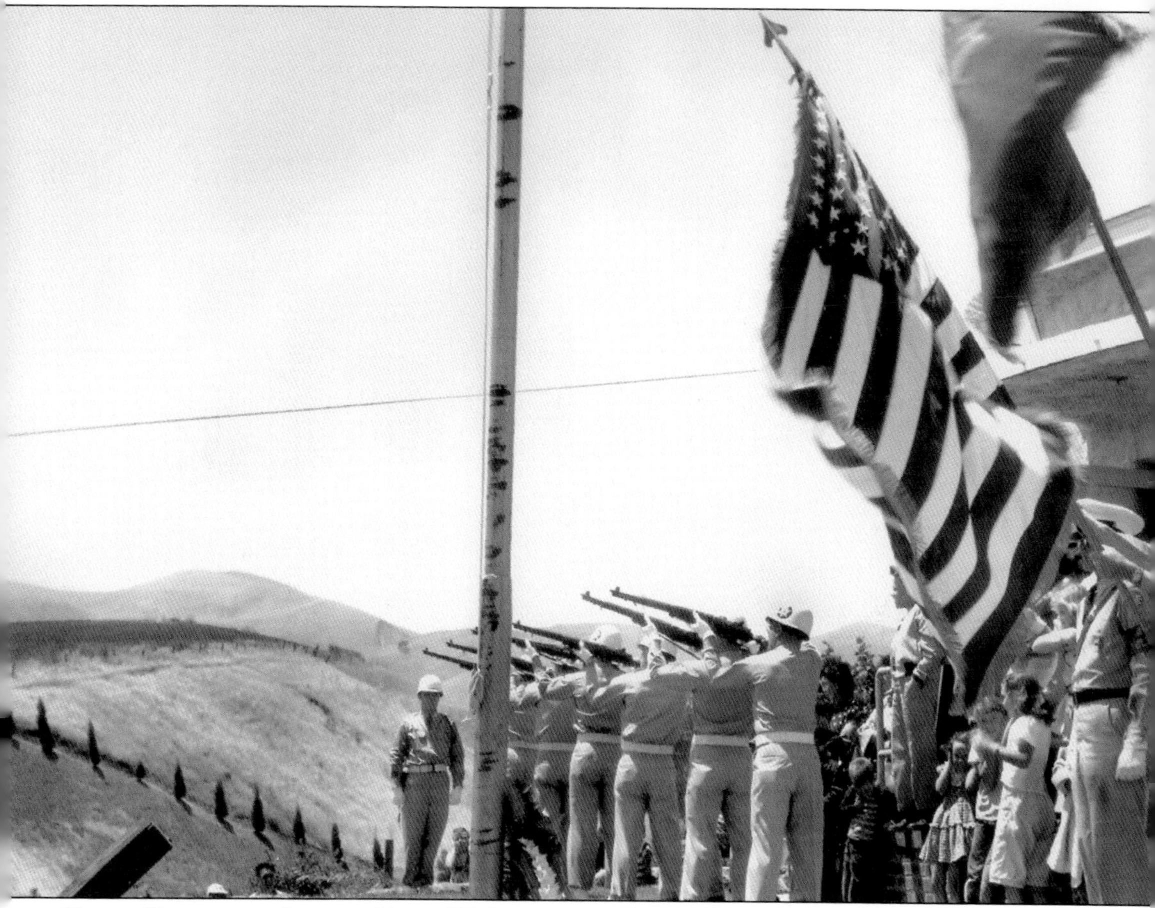

GRAND OPENING AT AMBROSE PARK. With a six-gun salute, the National Guard punctuated the opening day ceremonies at Ambrose Park. The celebration for the opening of the park marked a new era of community activity.

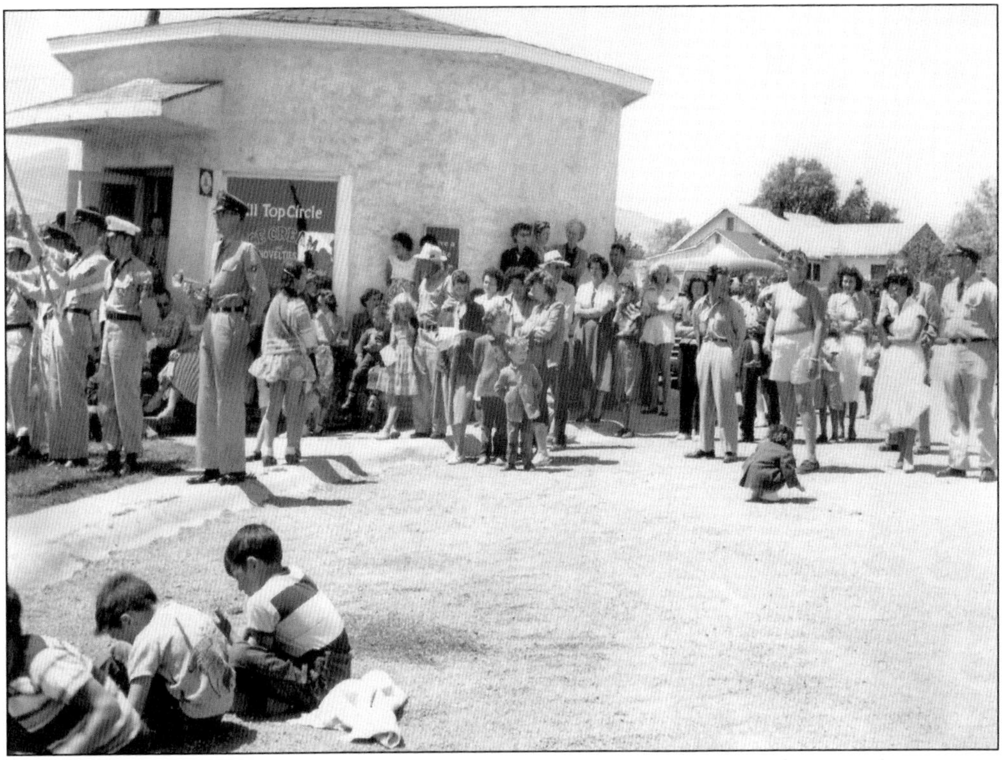

WERE YOU THERE? The Round House, called the Hill Top Circle at the opening of the park, had been Antone Enes' business office on Willow Pass Road before he died. Not big on ceremony, some of the kids were more interested in playing in the dirt.

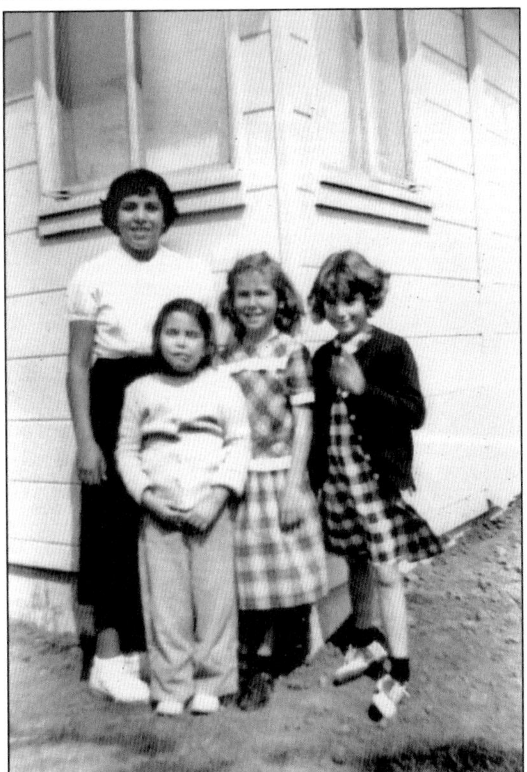

BARBARA MIDDLETON AND FRIENDS, 1951. Pictured in front of Lennard Enes' house on Hill Street are, from left to right, Barbara Middleton, Francis Middleton, Carol Enes Guadagni, and Carol Orsi.

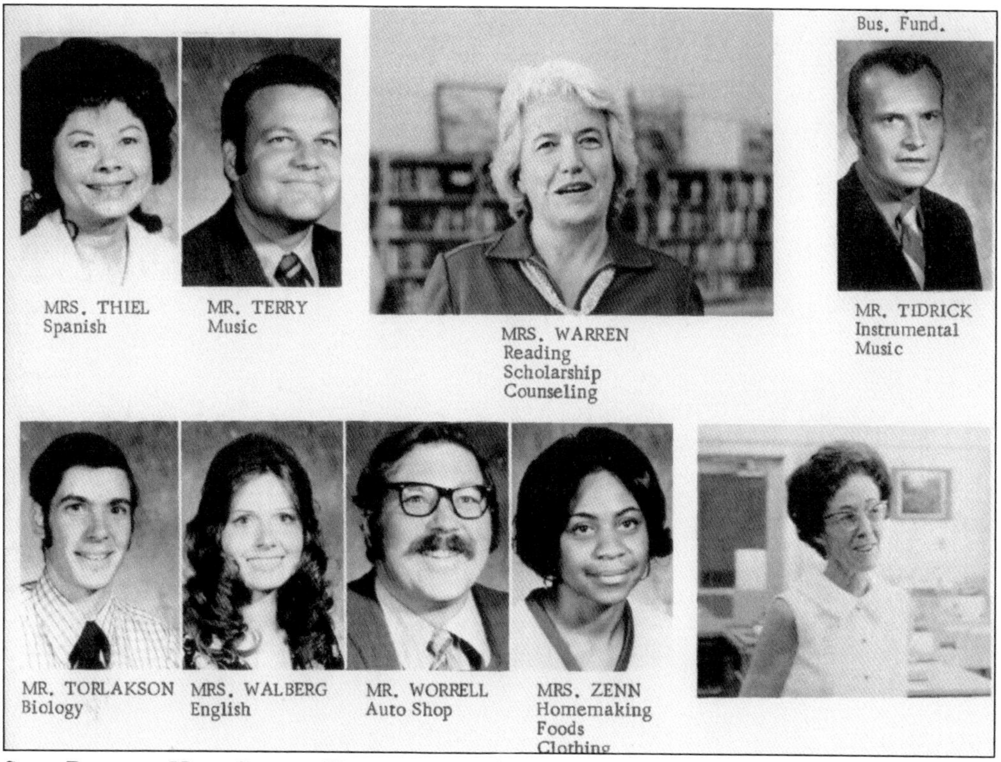

SOME PACIFICA HIGH SCHOOL TEACHERS. Pacifica High School was in many ways the heart of the community of West Pittsburg. A generation of teenagers came, learned, and went, just like in other towns in Contra Costa County. Among the teachers shown here is Mr. Torlakson, now State Senator Tom Torlakson. Having opened in 1956 after the construction of Shore Acres, the high school was closed by the school board at the end of the 1976 school year. The community was devastated by this decision and waits impatiently at this writing for the Mount Diablo School District to provide 1,000 or so high school students who live here a local education.

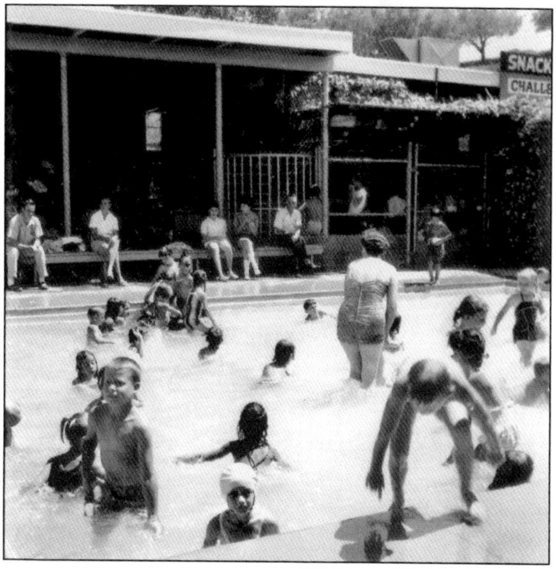

THE PLACE TO BE IN SUMMER. The whole community of West Pittsburg used the Ambrose swimming pool during the 1970s and 1980s. There were many wonderful memories built among children and parents. By 1989, the freeway had been widened and a large developer annexed to Pittsburg much of the land surrounding Ambrose Park. Cut off from those who used it, the pool has become much more expensive to maintain in relation to public usage.

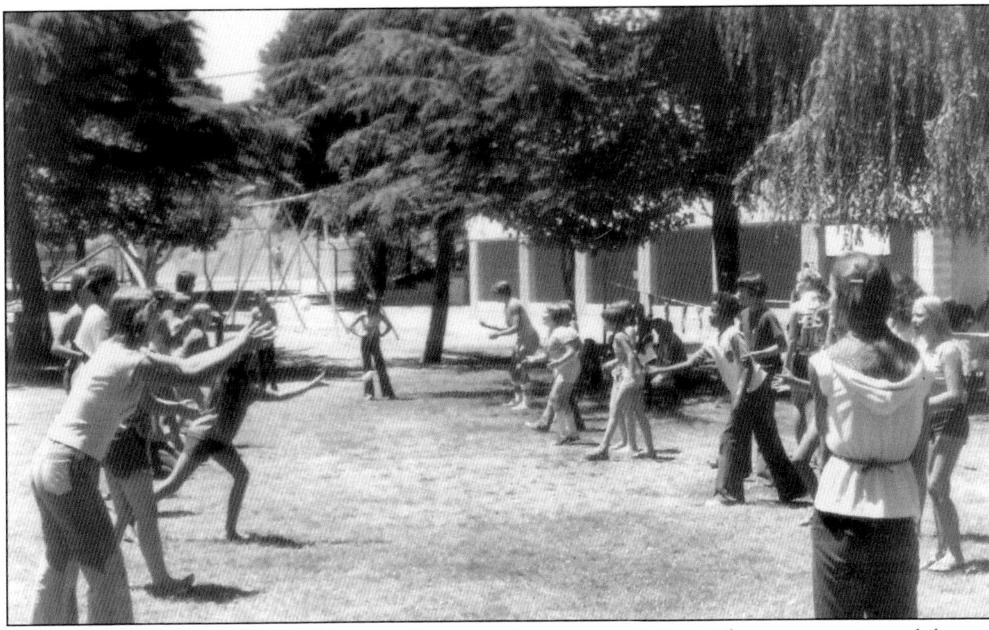

Drop at Your Own Peril: Tossing Eggs in August of 1977. The community celebrated the installation of the new Ambrose Park sign with a community-wide picnic. The park is still the site of many family picnics, and recently hosted for the 26th time the Port Chicago Reunion, held every year since the Navy evicted the town's people.

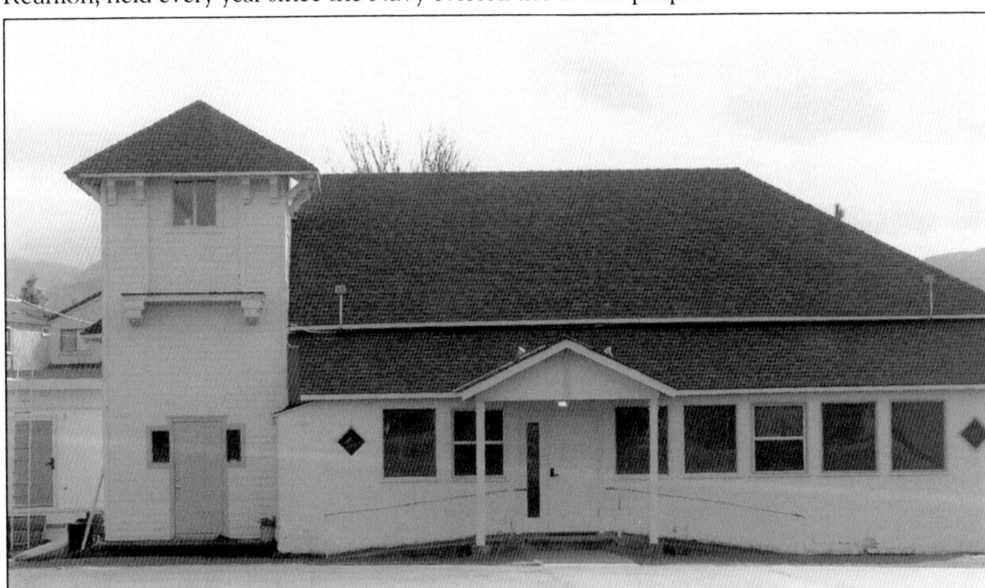

The Oldest School and Church, c. 1868–Present. This building on the western edge of Pittsburg, now the Landmark Missionary Baptist Church, was originally built about 1868 adjacent to the current Rio Vista Elementary School. It was called the Bay Point School. Around 1910 it was moved to the site of the current Ambrose Community Center on Willow Pass Road, where it became the first Ambrose School. When a new school was built in 1911 it was, for many years, used as an extra class. It was moved and used for various purposes around West Pittsburg, until it was rededicated as a church.

FOUR GENERATIONS AT AMBROSE SCHOOL. Pictured, from left to right, are Alvina Kennerly, Geraldine Kennerly, an unidentified boy, and Marilyn Levada Kennerly.

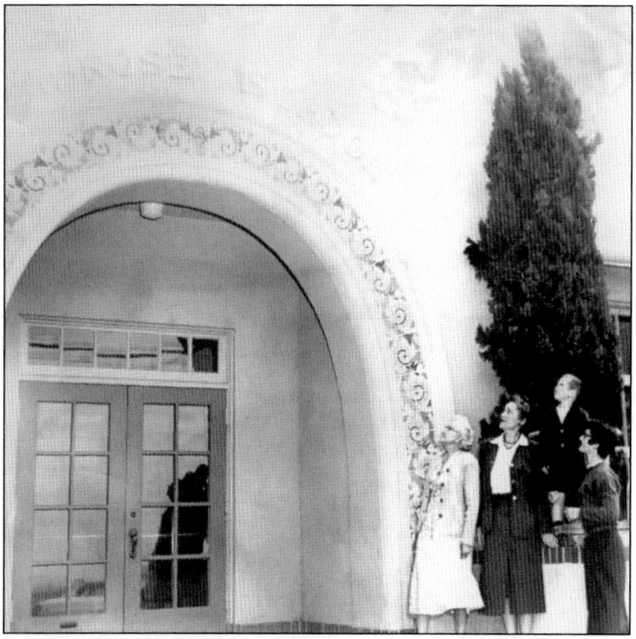

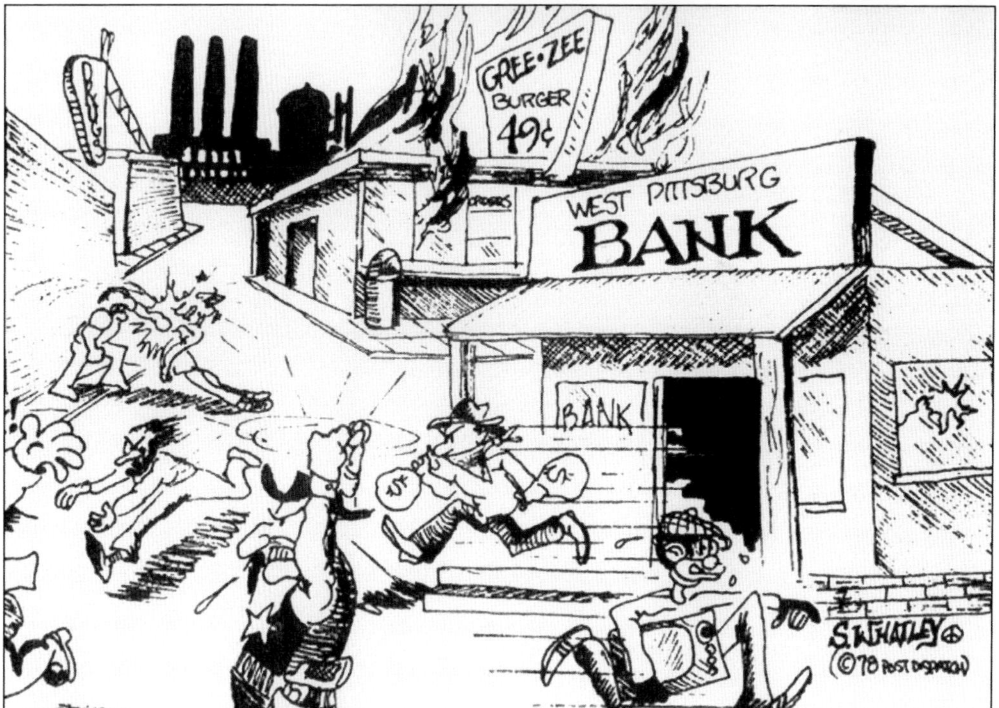

WILD WEST PITTSBURG. The 1970s were a period of explosive growth in West Pittsburg. With declining budgets, the county sheriff was hard pressed to keep the peace. Thanks to focused attention by the county newspapers, West Pittsburg became known for its crime. S. Whatley of the *Pittsburg Post Dispatch* was one of many who publicized a negative image of the community during the 1970s and 1980s.

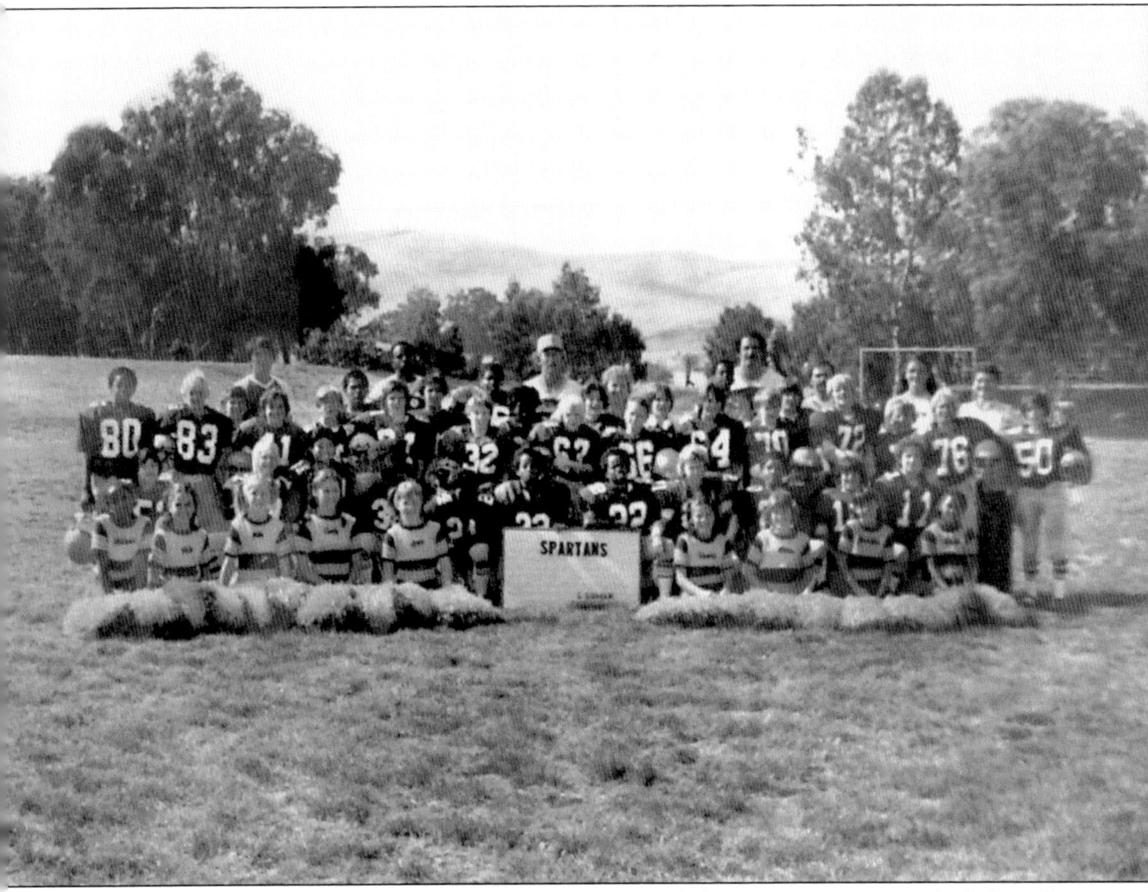

Spartans Football Team. Community leaders provided many opportunities for kids to learn and grow. Pictured here is one of the local Pop Warner teams.

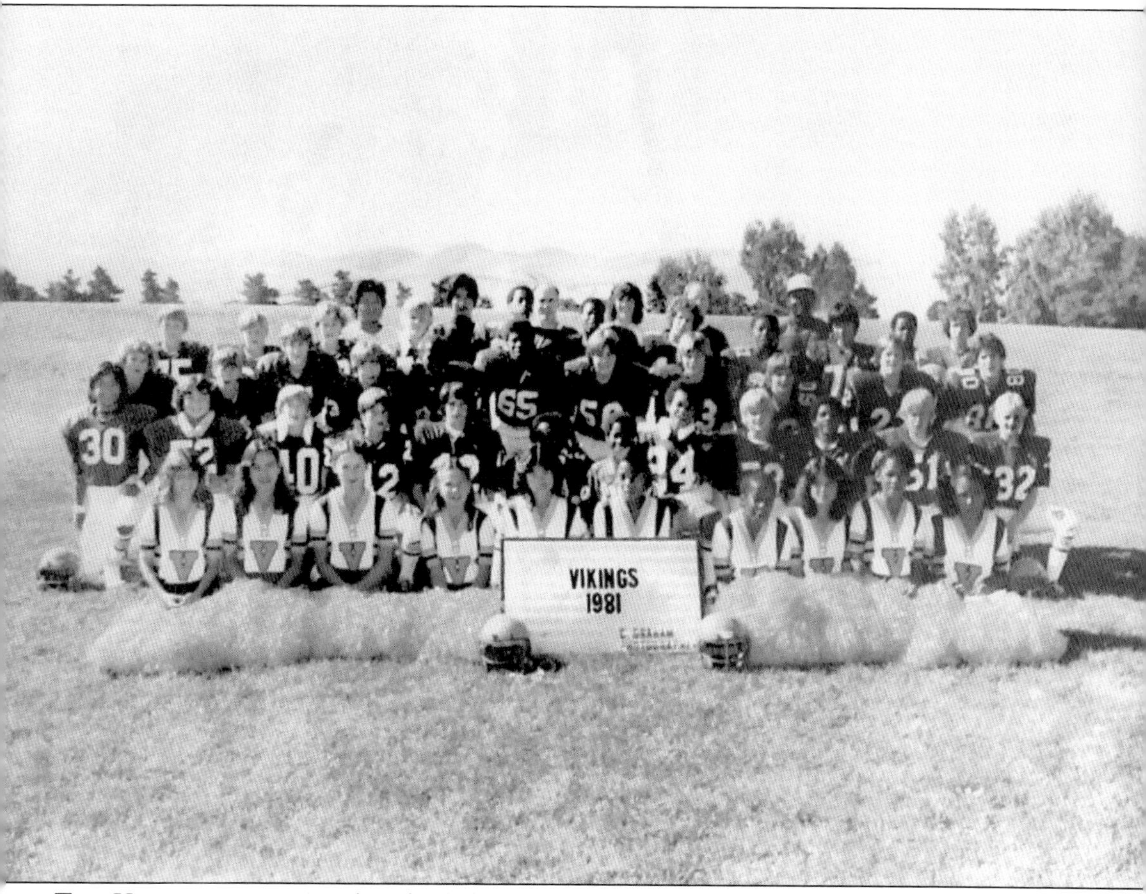

The Vikings, 1981. Another football team, coached by volunteers, involved both boys and girls.

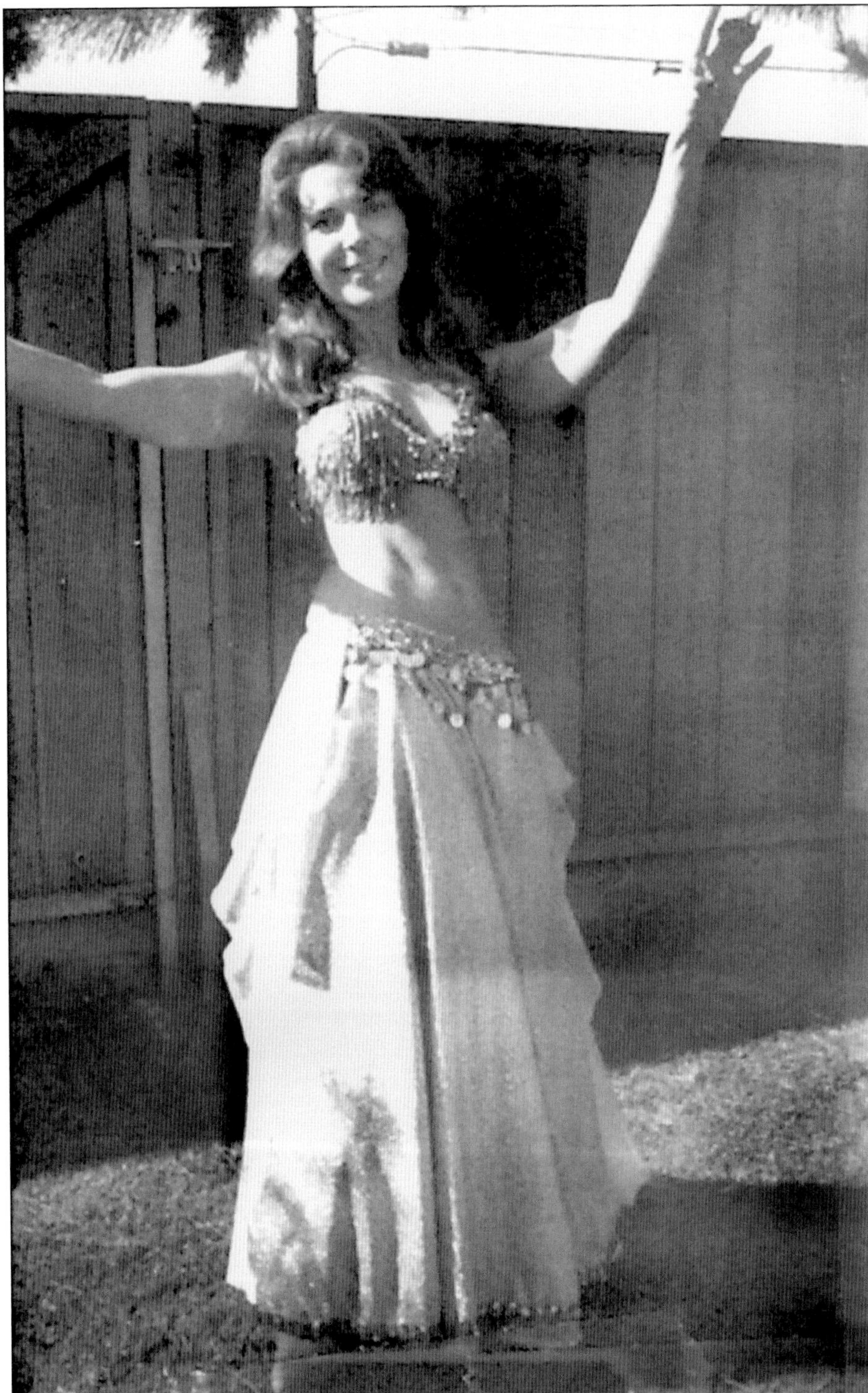

CULTURAL OPPORTUNITIES AT AMBROSE PARK AND RECREATION. Here, a pretty young girl demonstrates skills learned in one of the classes at Ambrose Park and Recreation in West Pittsburg.

Seven

NEW BAY POINT
STRUGGLES FOR COMMUNITY

What does the future hold for the community again known as Bay Point? A small portion of the Bay Point School District of the 1870s again falls under the old banner, but the site of the old town is still held by the Navy. The southern boundary has given way, bit by bit, to annexation by Pittsburg. The area is trying to define itself as a distinct entity. The expansion of Highway 4, the arrival of BART, and the growth in the foothills of new homes with beautiful views of Suisun Bay all suggest that Bay Point will grow.

With a specific geography that has always been a determining factor in its history, Bay Point's river location with the deepwater port has been its greatest asset. The tule bogs along the riverfront and the hilly sections limited population development until the last quarter century. The hills, with their water views, now become a geographic asset.

But will Bay Point survive? During the 150-year history of Township Two North Range One West, elements, events, and powers outside the control of the community have largely determined how the inhabitants lived.

All during the 19th century the Central Pacific Railroad, and land speculators from Martinez, Benicia, and Concord played determinant roles in how the land was used. From 1908, when the Smith Lumber Company created the company town of Bay Point, until the Navy condemned Port Chicago in 1969, very few entities decided the fate of the populace. From the time the railroads first rumbled through Bay Point, they have maintained overwhelming control of the wetlands within the area. They, along with the oil companies, chemical plants, and the Navy own most of the river frontage.

It was probably in the best interest of the Smith Lumber Company not to incorporate the town in 1908. W.H. Smith held almost total control. With the decline of the lumber company, Walter Van Winkle bought up much of the town. He dominated every community action in the town.

The fact that Bay Point/Port Chicago did not incorporate was central to the ability of the Navy to confiscate the town. There was no legal city structure to protect the citizens from the military interests of the federal government or the financial interests of Contra Costa County.

Today, the outside forces that determined local history continue their influence over local affairs. The newest power players are the large real estate developers and Contra Costa County. So long as Bay Point remains unincorporated, the people who live here will be subject to "the powers that be."

As the population doubled during the 1980s, the county board of supervisors and their appointees provided the only government in West Pittsburg. As crime increased, the county was slow to respond with increased police services. The overwhelming educational and social service needs in the older neighborhoods were met with rhetoric but little funding. By the mid-1990s this had begun to change. There is now a stronger county social service presence.

Will Bay Point ever have its own shopping center, a real library, or a high school? Will there ever be adequate police protection? Will local taxpayers ever have the use of the millions of dollars of property taxes paid to Contra Costa County? Will a core sense of community continue to evolve? Will Pittsburg and Concord swallow Bay Point?

Time will tell. It is up to longtime residents, as well as newcomers, to build together a community that recognizes the valuable lessons of the past and create a vision of a better future.

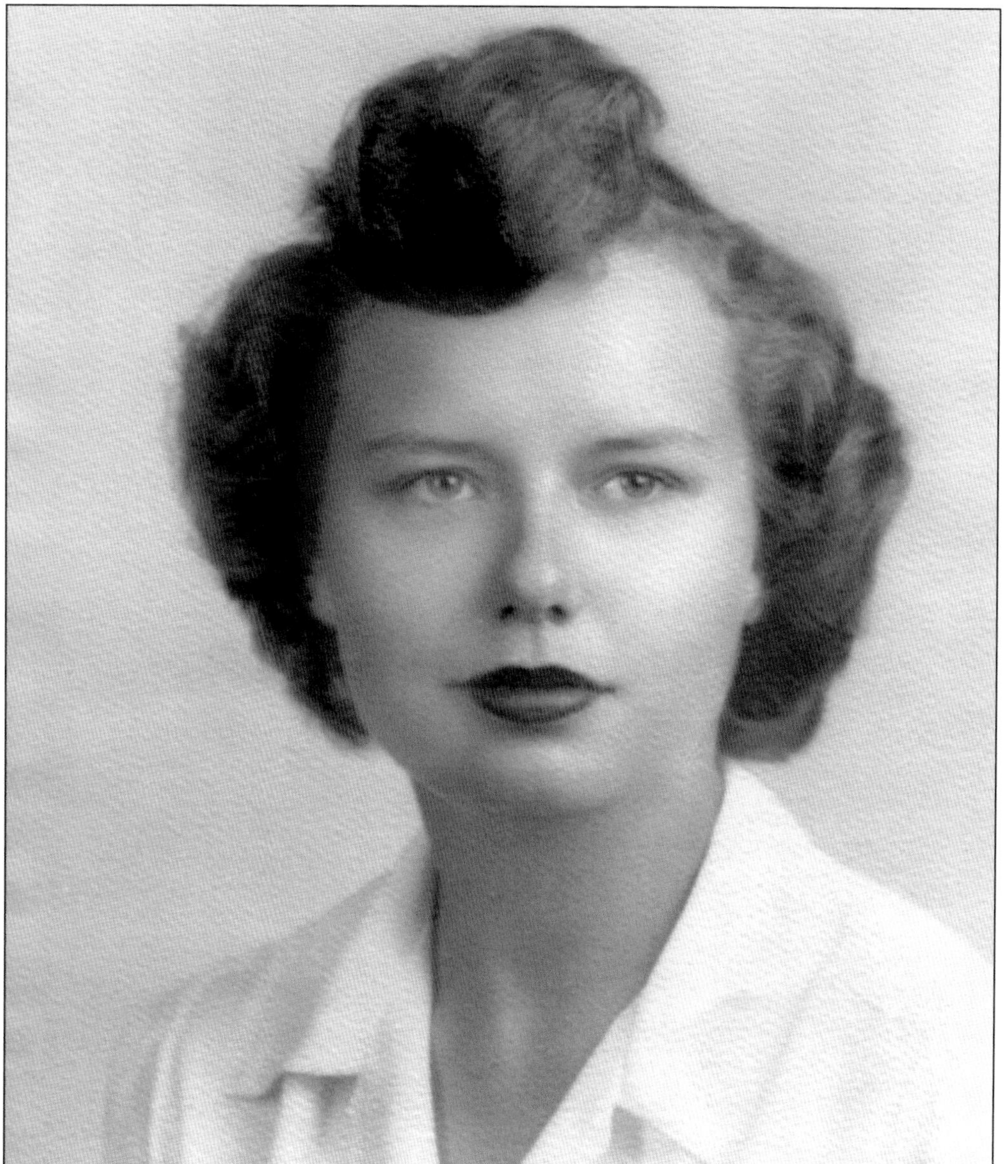

GLORIA MAGLEBY, MODERN COMMUNITY BUILDER. There have been hundreds of community leaders who over the past 155 years have kept a watchful eye over this land once and now called Bay Point. Here is one of the current spark plugs for change and improvement as she looked as a young woman working at the Naval Weapons Station during World War II. As President of the Bay Point Municipal Council, Gloria Magleby's persistence and insistence led to many new community organizations, each involving residents in organizing grassroots efforts to develop Bay Point.

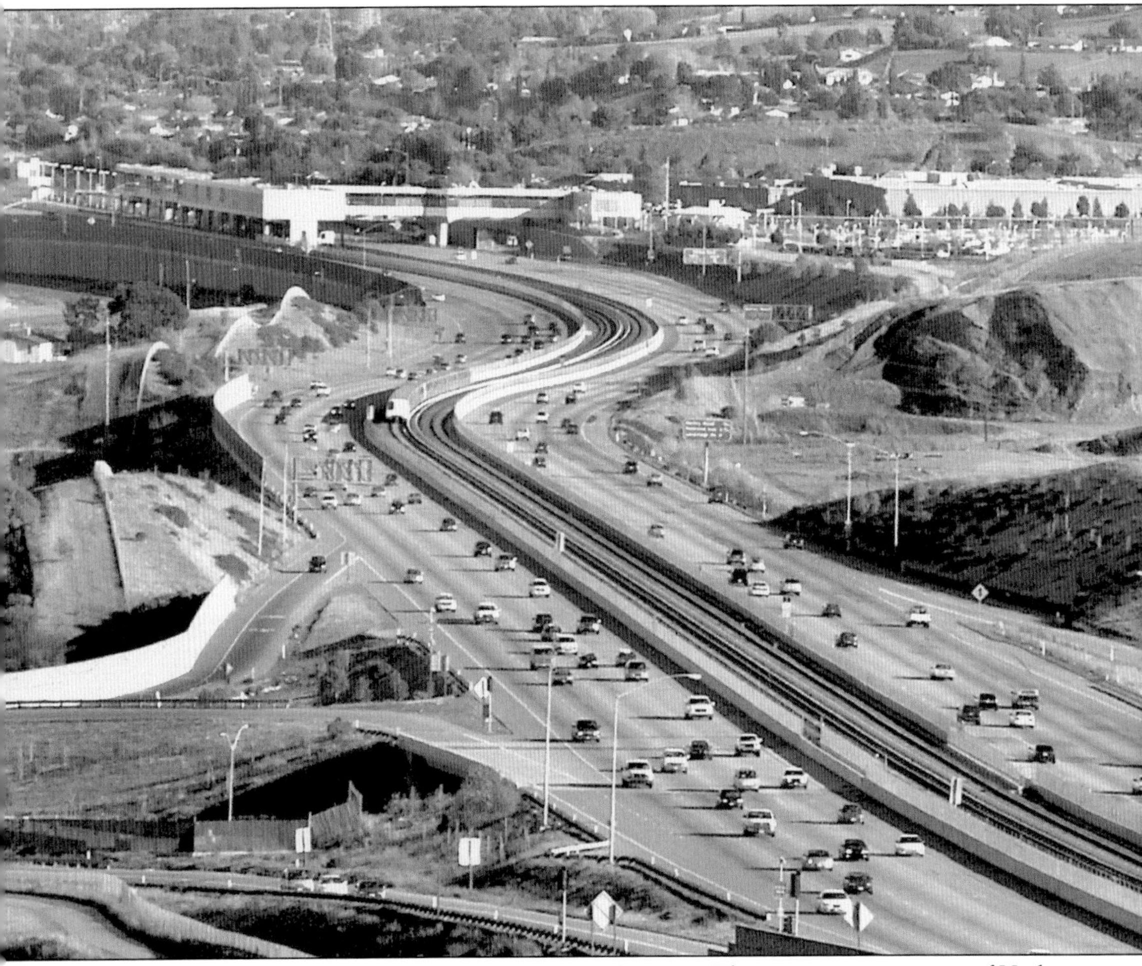

TRANSPORTATION HUB TO EAST CONTRA COSTA COUNTY. This contemporary view of Highway 4 and the Bay Point/Pittsburg BART station, from the Crespi/De Anza monument on Evora Road, shows the Central Bay Point off-ramp in the foreground.

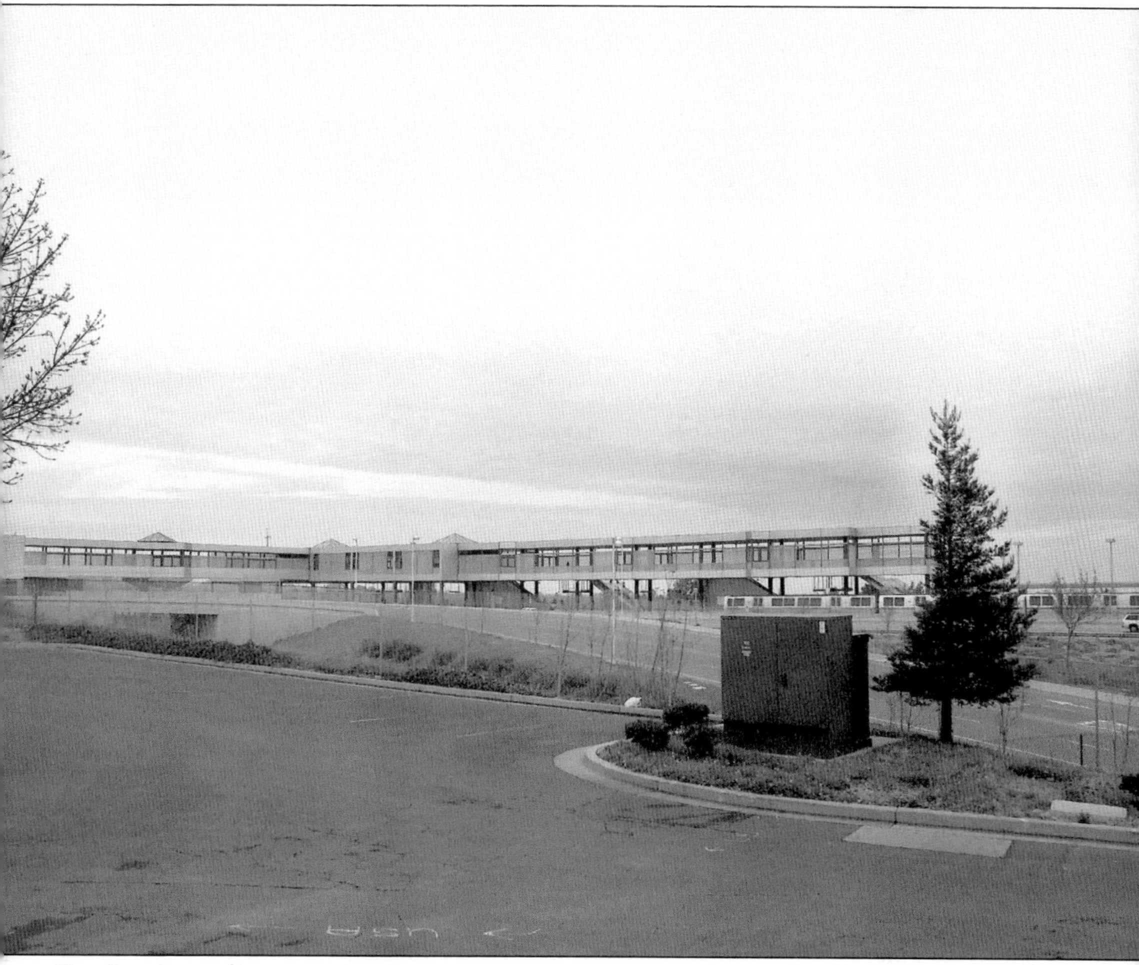

THE BAY POINT/PITTSBURG BART STATION. Straddling Highway 4, this minimalist structure provides the easternmost terminus of the Bay Area's rapid transit system. Having paid special assessments to BART for nearly 40 years, cities east of Bay Point are slated for a lesser light rail connection to BART, rather than an extension into Pittsburg and Antioch, and beyond. Commuters making rail to BART connections will most likely add to local street congestion during peak hours.

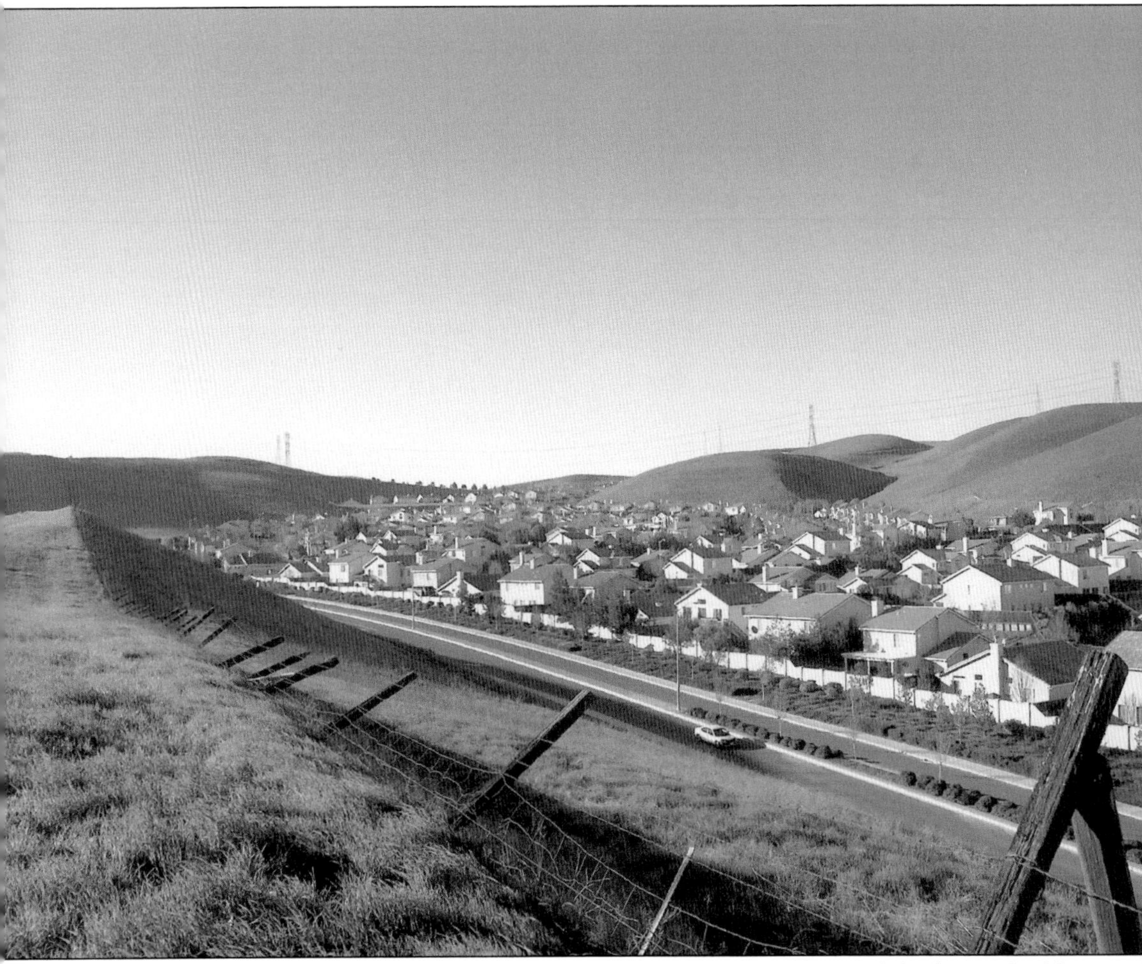

California Skyline, the Latest Hill Subdivisions. KB Homes, one of the largest builders in the United States, has been active in Bay Point for 20 years. These homes, nestled in the foothills above the old town site of Nichols, have panoramic views of Suisun Bay.

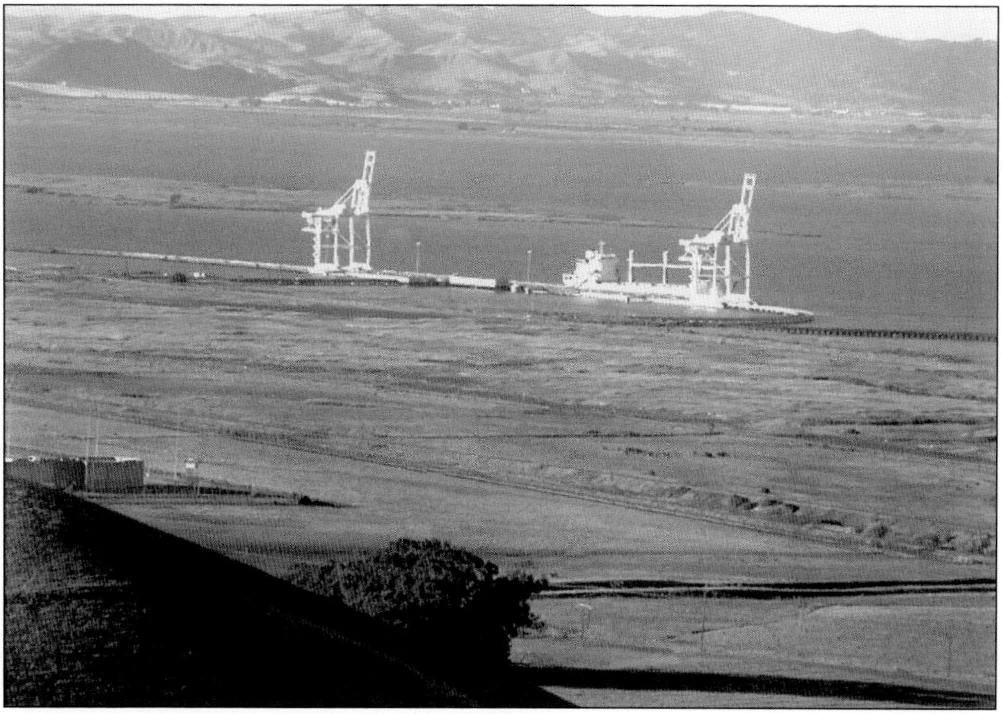

Cranes on the Border. These recently installed port facilities on the otherwise mothballed Naval Weapons Station have been planned since 1996 for the trans-shipment of spent nuclear fuel rods from around the world to storage facilities in Nevada. This secure facility continues a 60-year legacy of moving the most dangerous materials on earth into and out of Bay Point.

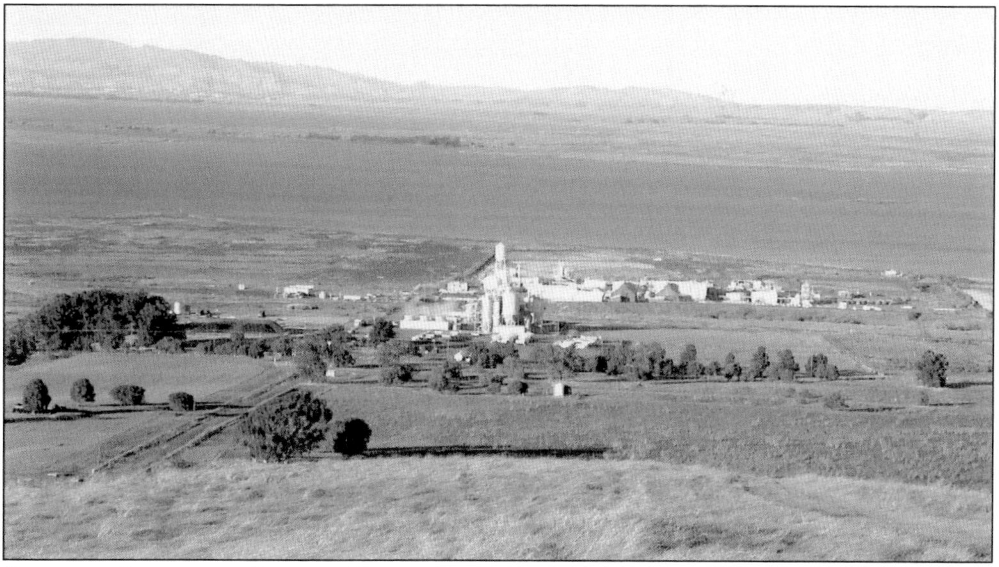

General Chemical, Oldest Active Industrial Site in Bay Point. Built in 1910, General Chemical still continues to process materials that go into chemical processes used all over the world. Built in the wetlands at the juncture of Nichols Creek and Port Chicago Highway, it also is creating a long-lasting legacy in the ground, the water, and the air of Bay Point.

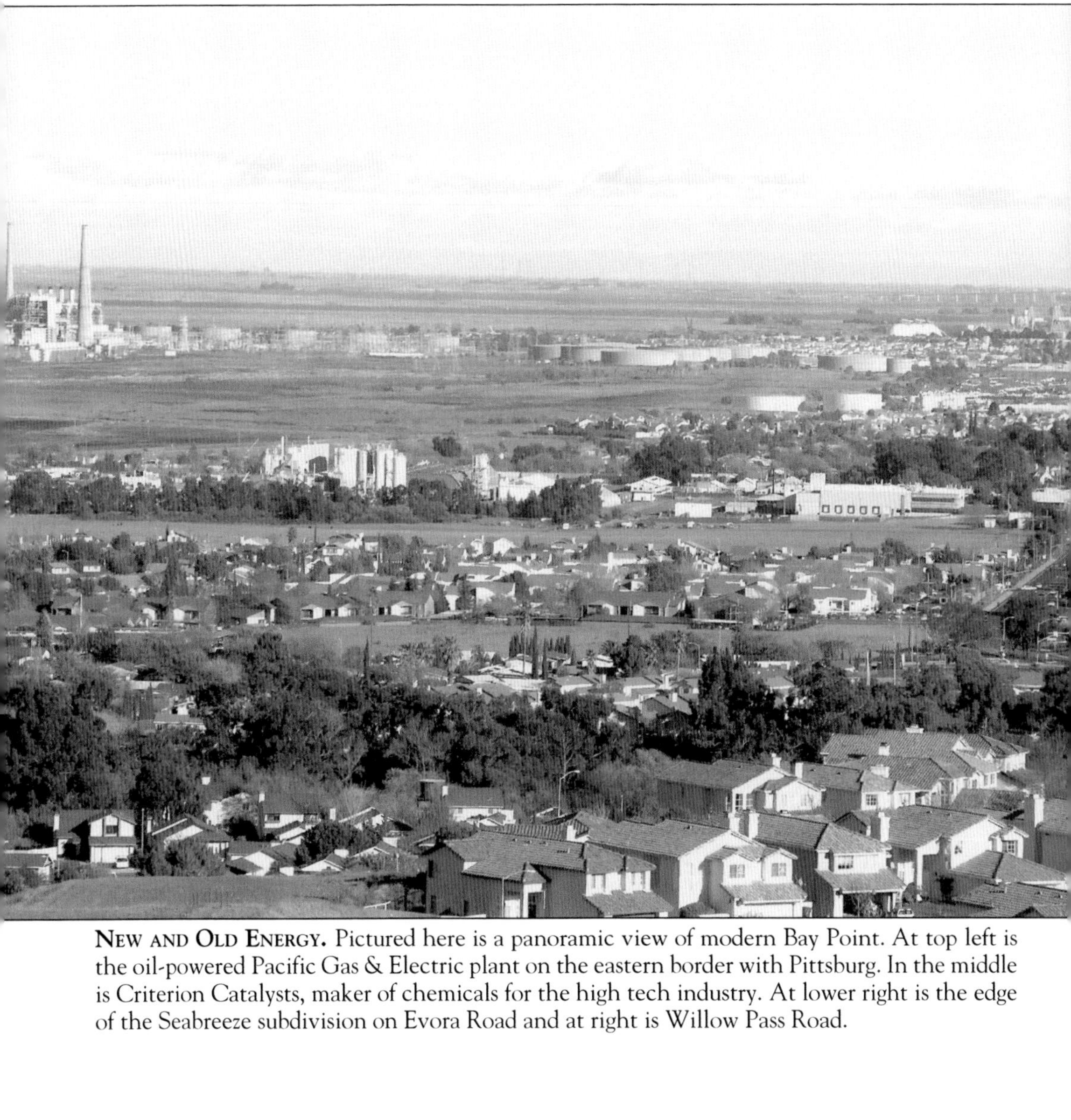

NEW AND OLD ENERGY. Pictured here is a panoramic view of modern Bay Point. At top left is the oil-powered Pacific Gas & Electric plant on the eastern border with Pittsburg. In the middle is Criterion Catalysts, maker of chemicals for the high tech industry. At lower right is the edge of the Seabreeze subdivision on Evora Road and at right is Willow Pass Road.

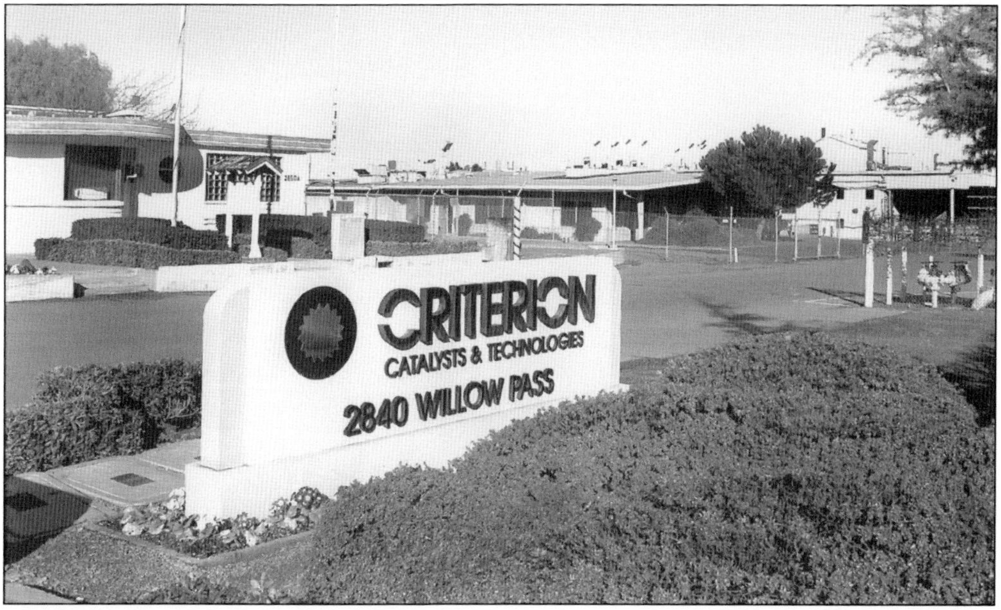

Criterion Catalysts and Technologies. This is the former Shell Chemical plant, the first major employer along Willow Pass Road. Management of this facility works hard to keep the community safe and spills to a minimum.

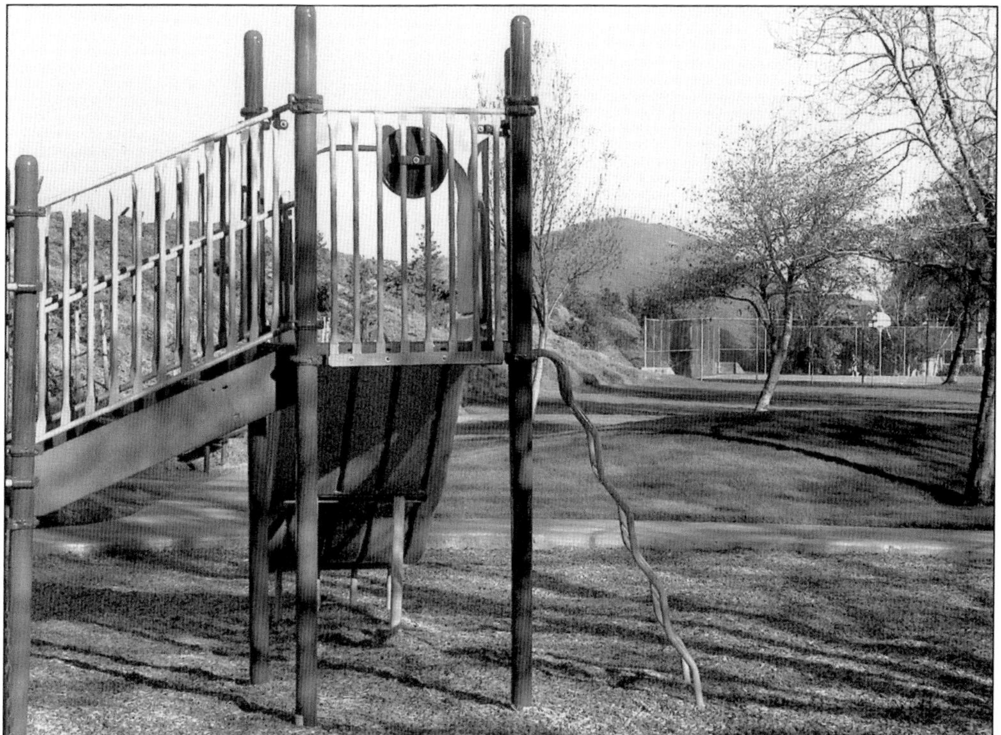

Private Playground at Mota Ranch. Situated too far from the playgrounds of Ambrose Park and Recreation, Mota Ranch kids play basketball and run in the grass on open space provided by the Mota Ranch Owners Association.

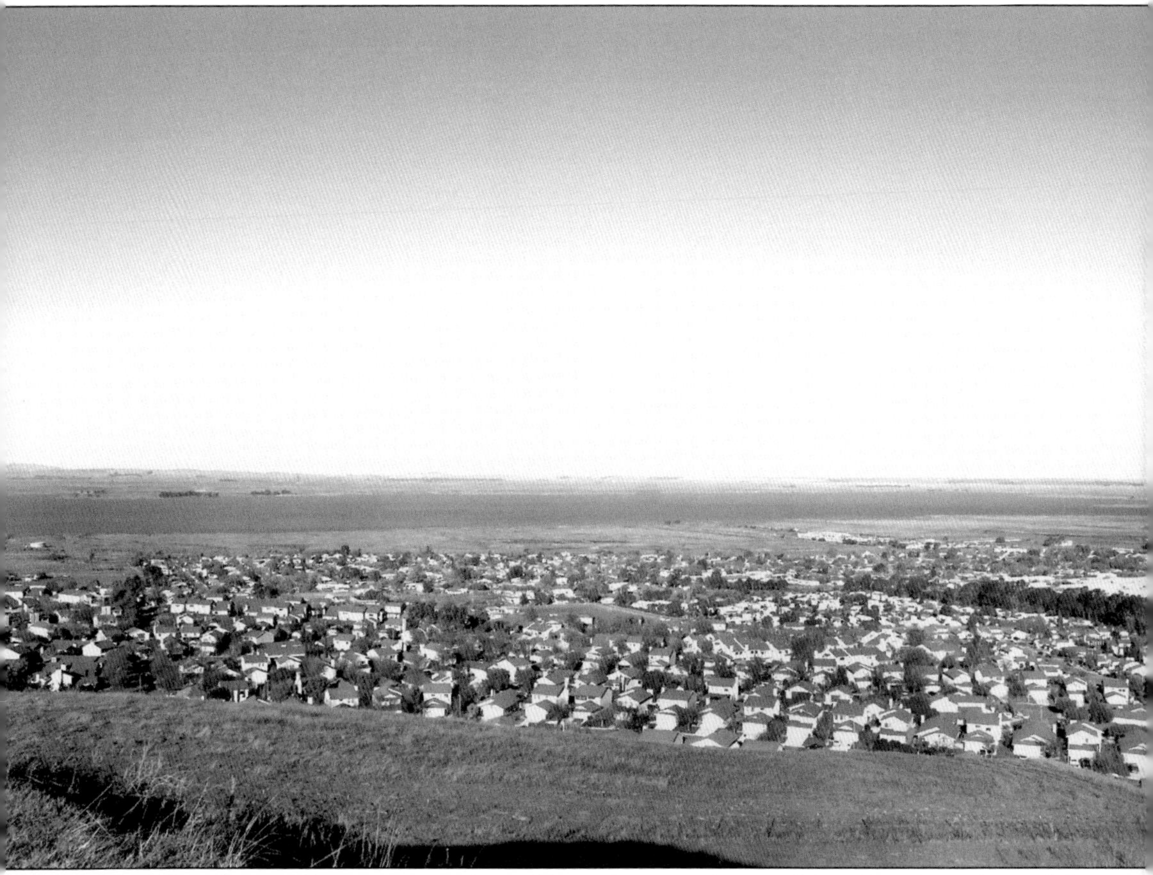

NEW BAY POINT. This panorama shows Shore Acres at the top, Mota Ranch in the middle, and California Skyline at the bottom. McAvoy Harbor is shown in the top right of the picture.

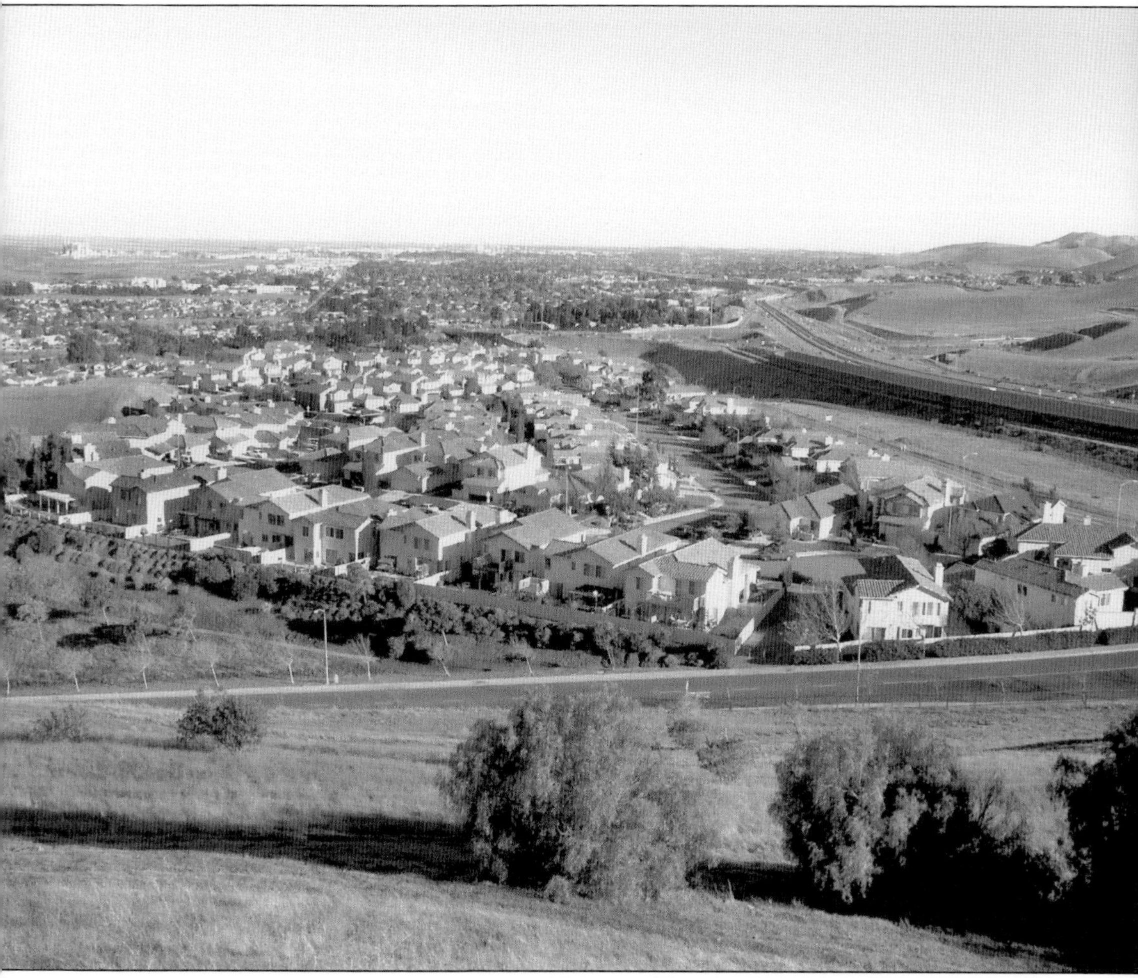

MUCH OF MODERN BAY POINT, FROM THE WESTERN HILLS. The controversial Seabreeze subdivision was many years in the planning. The West Pittsburg Alliance, and later the West Pittsburg Municipal Advisory Board, were heavily involved in public response to the builder's vision.

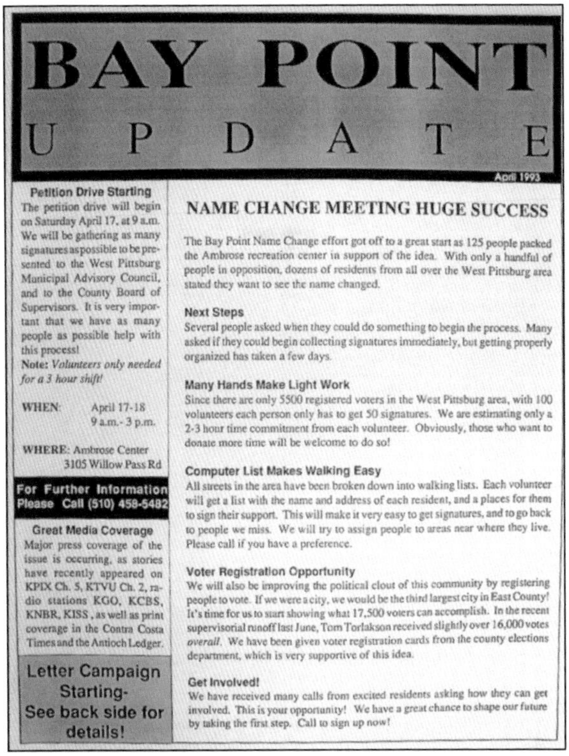

BAY POINT

UPDATE

April 1993

Petition Drive Starting

The petition drive will begin on Saturday April 17, at 9 a.m. We will be gathering as many signatures as possible to be presented to the West Pittsburg Municipal Advisory Council, and to the County Board of Supervisors. It is very important that we have as many people as possible help with this process!

Note: *Volunteers only needed for a 3 hour shift!*

WHEN: April 17-18
9 a.m.- 3 p.m.

WHERE: Ambrose Center
3105 Willow Pass Rd

For Further Information Please Call (510) 458-5482

Great Media Coverage

Major press coverage of the issue is occurring, as stories have recently appeared on KPIX Ch. 5, KTVU Ch. 2, radio stations KGO, KCBS, KNBR, KISS, as well as print coverage in the Contra Costa Times and the Antioch Ledger.

Letter Campaign Starting- See back side for details!

NAME CHANGE MEETING HUGE SUCCESS

The Bay Point Name Change effort got off to a great start as 125 people packed the Ambrose recreation center in support of the idea. With only a handful of people in opposition, dozens of residents from all over the West Pittsburg area stated they want to see the name changed.

Next Steps

Several people asked when they could do something to begin the process. Many asked if they could begin collecting signatures immediately, but getting properly organized has taken a few days.

Many Hands Make Light Work

Since there are only 5500 registered voters in the West Pittsburg area, with 100 volunteers each person only has to get 50 signatures. We are estimating only a 2-3 hour time commitment from each volunteer. Obviously, those who want to donate more time will be welcome to do so!

Computer List Makes Walking Easy

All streets in the area have been broken down into walking lists. Each volunteer will get a list with the name and address of each resident, and a places for them to sign their support. This will make it very easy to get signatures, and to go back to people we miss. We will try to assign people to areas near where they live. Please call if you have a preference.

Voter Registration Opportunity

We will also be improving the political clout of this community by registering people to vote. If we were a city, we would be the third largest city in East County! It's time for us to start showing what 17,500 voters can accomplish. In the recent supervisorial runoff last June, Tom Torlakson received slightly over 16,000 votes *overall*. We have been given voter registration cards from the county elections department, which is very supportive of this idea.

Get Involved!

We have received many calls from excited residents asking how they can get involved. This is your opportunity! We have a great chance to shape our future by taking the first step. Call to sign up now!

CHANGING THE COMMUNITY NAME TO BAY POINT. This flyer, circulated in the spring of 1994, reveals the organizational beginnings that resulted in changing the name from West Pittsburg to Bay Point. Late opposition resulted in a contentious split of opinion that lasted for a number of years.

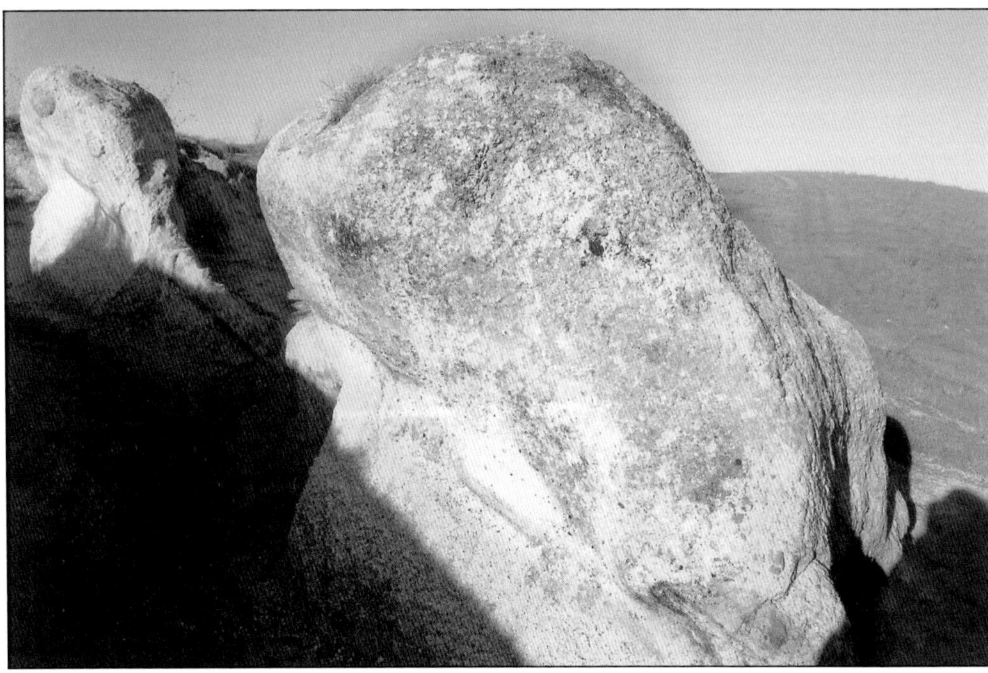

SCENIC NATURE WALK. This view of an outcropping above the California Skyline subdivision gives a sense of one of the many scenic trails around Bay Point. On close inspection, one can see carvings in the rocks that early herders made comfortable resting spots. Sheep and cattle roamed this hill, known as "Shepard's Seat," for perhaps 100 years.

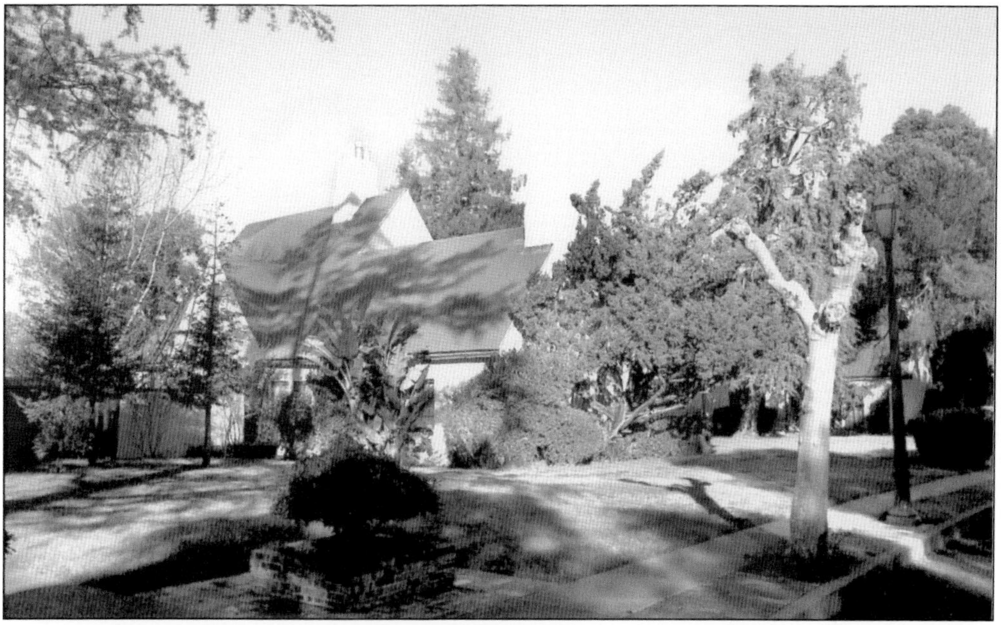

Luxury Homes. This is one of the gracious homes originally built for the managers of Shell Chemical. Located near Willow Pass Road and Bailey Road, the court provides an architectural oasis in an otherwise less scenic area.

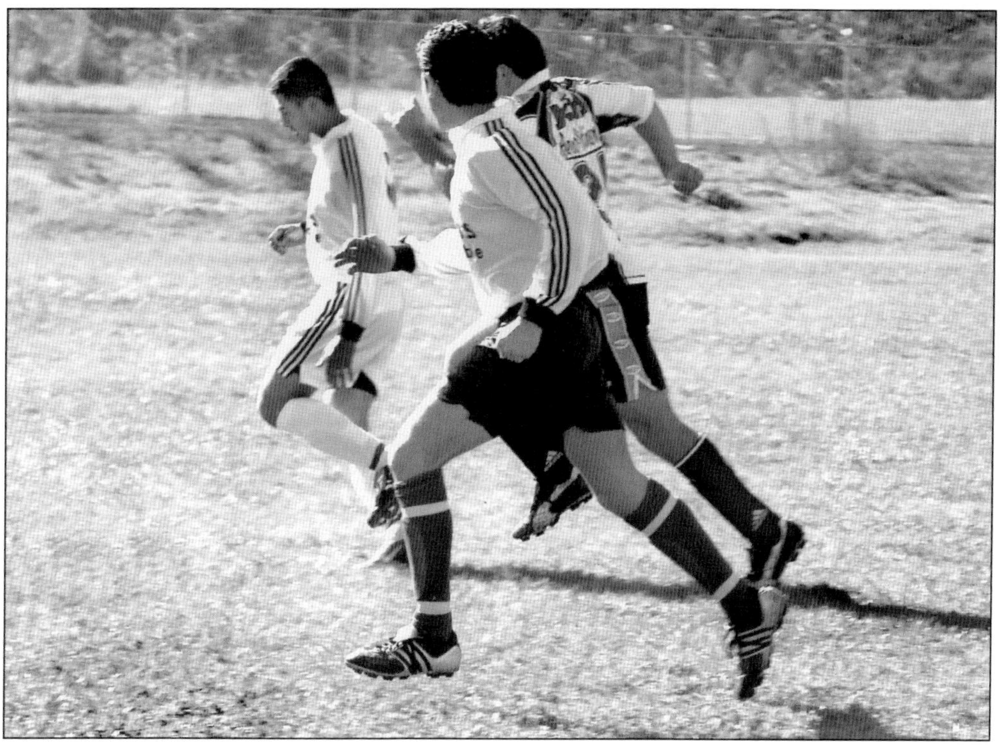

Goal! The sporting highlight of Bay Point on any given Sunday is soccer. Nearly 30 percent of the people of Bay Point are originally from Hispanic countries, where soccer is by far the most popular sport. Two of the local teams are Yahualica and Sarafin Contraras.

ACKNOWLEDGMENTS

The completion of this pictorial history of the communities between Pittsburg and Concord, California, is a testament to the growing cohesiveness of the 23,000 people in the community of Bay Point. Persons associated with most time segments in the 19th- and 20th-century communities of Clyde, Port Chicago, Nichols, West Pittsburg, and Bay Point have contributed their photos and stories to this work. Thanks go to Paul Larson, president of the Concord Historical Society, and Marti Aiello, for many years a leader in the Pittsburg Historical Society, for their assistance with photos. Thanks to James Serventi for his outstanding local history work in years past. The following directors of the nearly two-year-old Bay Point Historical Society provided a substantial core of family photographs and history and a beginning to the society's documentary archive: Gloria Magleby, Barbara Middleton, Marilyn Levada Morgan, Dan O'Hara, and Ray O'Brien. Other family archives that were graciously opened to the author came from Ronald Enes, Alma James, Nadine Gorgen, Harlan Bailey, Ella Mae Dorn, Bob Estes, Barbara Glenn, and Ward Shideler.

Doug Harris provided images from several of his documentary films on the history of East County and Bay Point. Susan Goldstein of the San Francisco History Center in the San Francisco Main Library was always willing to help in my strange historical pursuits. The Bancroft Library provided the rare map of Fr. Narcisso Duran. Steve Weir of the Contra Costa County Recorder's Office provided access to some of the great county and local maps. The John Muir Historic Site in Martinez, the National Archives, Sierra Pacific Region in San Bruno, and Criterion Catalysts in Bay Point also provided photos. Cathy Ivers provided immeasurable support and assistance with interviews, captions, and organization. And to our deceased friend Marcus O'Connell: You were a tenacious example.

This is simply a beginning of the writing of the history of the 19th-century Bay Point School District. In the latter months of preparation of this book, many people approached the author with stories, photos, and documents. Time and space allowed no more for now. For those who may have missed the deadlines, may I say, please, please contribute your photos, documents, and stories to the Bay Point Historical Society. They will be protected and made available for generations to come.

—Dean L. McLeod

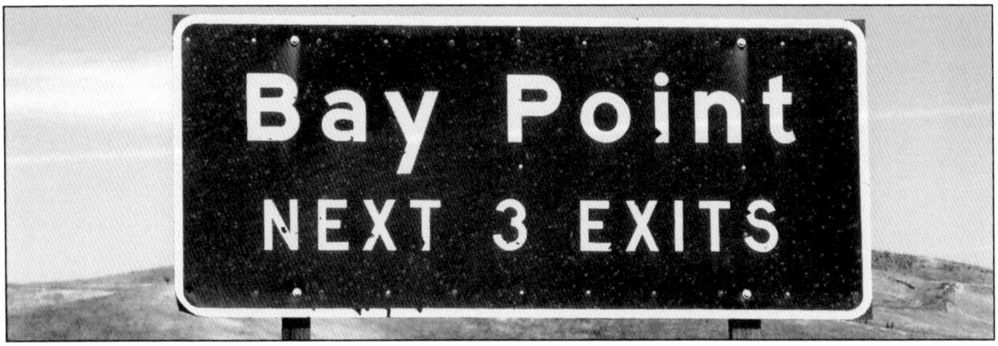

BAY POINT, NEXT 3 EXITS. The communities of Bay Point have been a destination for diverse peoples and have endured more than most the direct effects of American war policy. They have been home to heavy industry for nearly 100 years and have been subject to the massive population growth common all over Contra Costa County. Never before has there been such active grassroots efforts at community building. Try one of our exits and see who we have been and who we will become.